MW00477906

Praise for *Crossroads for Liberty*

"For more than two decades William Watkins has been exploring alternative views of our republican traditions, and, in the process, has become one of our most provocative and insightful constitutional historians. With *Crossroads for Liberty* and in an era when we are increasingly coming to realize that we live in a time of government gone amok, Watkins has produced a splendidly inspiring look at the Anti-Federalists, who were able presciently to warn us of the perils to come. Watkins not only gives us a superb exposition of their thought, but he reminds us of some of the wisdom of our First Constitution (the Articles of Confederation, which are helpfully reproduced as an appendix), and offers us some remedies for our ailing polity."

> —**Stephen B. Presser**, Raoul Berger Professor of Legal History Emeritus, Pritzker School of Law, Northwestern University; author, *The American Constitutional Order, Recapturing the Constitution, Individual Rights and the Constitution, The Original Misunderstanding: The English, the Americans and the Dialectic of Federalist Jurisprudence*, and other books

"At a time in our history when most people take it as an article of faith that the federal government must provide a solution to every major problem, from education to terrorism to economic downturn, the indispensable book *Crossroads for Liberty* advances the notion that our massive federal government is the problem, and that the solution lies in ideas that have lain dormant for over two centuries. William Watkins gives much needed consideration to the unwisely disparaged ideas of the Anti-Federalists and, particularly, the Articles of Confederation. According to Watkins, the Constitutional Convention of 1787 would have been far wiser to stick with its assigned mission of proposing amendments to the Articles, rather than creating a wholly different and far more centralized form of government that has grown into the behemoth we have today. Recognizing that we cannot turn back the clock and return to the Articles of Confederation, Watkins nevertheless believes that the Articles and their Anti-Federalist proponents have invaluable lessons to teach us, if only we open our minds to the possibility. We would be wise to listen."

> —**Alex A. Kozinski**, Judge and former Chief Judge, U.S. Court of Appeals for the Ninth Circuit; former Chief Judge, U.S. Court of Federal Claims

"In his important book, *Crossroads for Liberty*, William Watkins astutely urges us to study the Framers, but not merely the Federalists. Close attention should be paid to the Anti-Federalists and the contemporary weakening of separation of powers and checks and balances. Instead of a system of self-government, political power has shifted in ever greater degree to the President and the Supreme Court. The results should concern us all."

—**Louis Fisher**, Scholar in Residence, The Constitution Project; author of *Presidential War Power, The Law of the Executive Branch, Constitutional Conflicts Between Congress and the President*, and other books

"In the compelling book *Crossroads for Liberty* William J. Watkins, Jr. recounts the rarely examined history of lost liberty in America's infancy. In a truly eye-opening historical examination, *Crossroads* explains how the principal goal of the American Revolution in 1776—the removal of centralized power in favor of diverse and independent local and state governance, in which individual Americans could select the level and severity of the governance they wished for themselves—was abandoned in just eleven years. If you yearn, as I do, for minimal government and maximum individual liberty, you need to understand how the monster federal government came about. *Crossroads* is that well-told but sad story."

—**Andrew P. Napolitano**, Senior Judicial Analyst, Fox News Channel; Distinguished Visiting Professor of Law, Brooklyn Law School; author, *The Constitution in Exile, Constitutional Chaos, Suicide Pact, Dred Scott's Revenge*, and other books

"If there was ever a time when it behooved Americans to revisit the debates that took place between the Federalists and the Anti-Federalists in the wake of the framing of the American constitution, that time is now—as we witness a full consolidation of power in the hands of the federal government that the Federalists would no more have countenanced than the Anti-Federalists. William Watkins's important book *Crossroads for Liberty* is a timely reminder that there really was something to the fears voiced by the Anti-Federalists in the late 1780s."

—**Paul A. Rahe, Jr.**, Charles O. Lee and Louise K. Lee Chair in the Western Heritage, Hillsdale College; author, *Republics Ancient and Modern: Classical Republicanism and the American Revolution*

"Immortal though counterproductive federal programs, constantly growing government debt, seemingly endless federal usurpation of states' reserved powers, an outsized policymaking role for unelected federal judges, and unresponsive party politics are among the most notable characteristics of contemporary American political culture. To some extent, the U.S. Constitution—which was sold by the Federalists of 1787–91 as establishing a limited, decentralized, republican system—has failed to live up to its friends' promises. This arguably amounts to the failure of the American Revolution. In *Crossroads for Liberty*, William J. Watkins, Jr., recalls Anti-Federalists' warnings that things would be so, and he asks, 'Could the Articles of Confederation have been revised to meet the exigencies of the union without destroying the self-government won in the Revolution?' After concluding that the Anti-Federalists were right in insisting that they probably could have, he proposes reforms in line with Anti-Federalist thinking. This is a bracing book."

　—**Kevin R. C. Gutzman**, Professor of History, Western Connecticut State University; author, *James Madison and the Making of America*, *Virginia's American Revolution: From Dominion to Republic, 1776–1840*, and *Who Killed the Constitution? The Federal Government vs. American Liberty from World War I to Barack Obama*

"In our age, Madison's optimism for the Constitution, its careful enumeration of specific powers, and its additional boundaries etched out in the accompanying Bill of Rights, have so frequently been 'construed' to enact a central government of virtually unconstrained power. The new book, *Crossroads for Liberty*, recalling the meaningful vitality of our first Constitution, the Articles of Confederation, is a welcome antidote to our current malaise of a sprawling national government consolidating power in what has become an unlimited national leviathan, to the dismay of the Founders themselves. The Anti-Federalists were prescient in their cautionary warnings."

　—**William W. Van Alstyne**, Lee Professor Emeritus of Law, Marshall-Wythe Law School, College of William and Mary; William R. and Thomas L. Perkins Professor Emeritus of Law, Duke University; author, *The American First Amendment in the Twenty-First Century*

"With *Crossroads for Liberty*, I am delighted to have a serious treatment of the role and ideas of the Anti-Federalists. In short compass this excellent history provides some needed balance to our understanding of the Founders and the Founding. Watkins takes issue after issue that the Founders wrestled with, pointing out how our later history demonstrates the extent to which the fears of the Anti-Federalists have proven all too well-founded. *Crossroads for Liberty* is a very valuable contribution to the literature and will be of interest to both students and scholars of American constitutional history and government."

　—**Joyce Lee Malcolm**, Patrick Henry Professor of Constitutional Law and the Second Amendment, Antonin Scalia Law School, George Mason University; former Director of Research Programs, National Endowment for the Humanities; author, *Peter's War: A New England Slave Boy and the American Revolution*, *The Tragedy of Benedict Arnold*, and other books

"Given that the Anti-Federalists' predictions about the growth of national power have come true, their views of the weaknesses of the Constitution deserve to be heard. Could the amended Articles of Confederation that they favored have done a better job of protecting our liberty? Read *Crossroads for Liberty* and then decide."

—**Randy E. Barnett**, Carmack Waterhouse Professor of Legal Theory and Director, Center for the Constitution, Georgetown University Law Center; author, *Our Republican Constitution: Securing the Liberty and Sovereignty of We the People, Restoring the Lost Constitution: The Presumption of Liberty, The Structure of Liberty: Justice and the Rule of Law*, and other books

"William J. Watkins's careful exploration of the constitutional principles of the Anti-Federalists is far more than a scholarly endeavor to understand America's first governing document. *Crossroads for Liberty* is, perhaps even more importantly, a fascinating piece of counterfactual history that focuses on what might have been. How would the U.S. have developed if the Founders had agreed to continue to live under the Articles of Confederation that came out of the American Revolution? What would be the state of our liberties under this alternative regime? Would we be dealing with the administrative centralization and the hollowing out of local rule that has become increasingly characteristic of the U.S. since the Progressive Era? Watkins provides lessons for us today—and he may be correct."

—**Paul E. Gottfried**, Horace Raffensperger Professor Emeritus of Humanities, Elizabethtown College; author of *Fascism: The Career of a Concept, After Liberalism: Mass Democracy in the Managerial State*, and other books

"The U.S. Constitution is a remarkable document that is insufficiently understood by Americans today. It was the product of passionate debates by able patriots on both sides, and might well have turned out quite differently. Many college and law school students study essays by Madison, Hamilton, and Jay in defense of ratification; but the Anti-Federalist case is too often ignored. In the remarkable and much-needed book *Crossroads for Liberty*, William J. Watkins, Jr. has performed an invaluable service in carefully examining the most important Anti-Federalist insights, and we all in his debt."

—**Robert F. Turner**, Professor and Co-Founder and Associate Director, Center for National Security Law, University of Virginia School of Law; Founding President, U.S. Institute of Peace; editor, *The Jefferson-Hemings Controversy: Report of the Scholars Commission*

Crossroads *for* LIBERTY

Other Books by the Author

Reclaiming the American Revolution:
  The Kentucky and Virginia Resolutions and Their Legacy

Judicial Monarchs:
  Court Power and the Case for Restoring Popular Sovereignty
  in the United States

Patent Trolls:
  Predatory Litigation and the Smothering of Innovation

INDEPENDENT
I N S T I T U T E

INDEPENDENT INSTITUTE is a non-profit, non-partisan, public-policy research and educational organization that shapes ideas into profound and lasting impact. The mission of Independent is to boldly advance peaceful, prosperous, and free societies grounded in a commitment to human worth and dignity. Applying independent thinking to issues that matter, we create transformational ideas for today's most pressing social and economic challenges. The results of this work are published as books, our quarterly journal, *The Independent Review*, and other publications and form the basis for numerous conference and media programs. By connecting these ideas with organizations and networks, we seek to inspire action that can unleash an era of unparalleled human flourishing at home and around the globe.

100 Swan Way, Oakland, California 94621-1428, U.S.A.
Telephone: 510-632-1366 • Facsimile: 510-568-6040 • Email: info@independent.org • www.independent.org

Crossroads *for* LIBERTY

Recovering the Anti-Federalist Values of America's First Constitution

William J. Watkins, Jr.

INDEPENDENT
INSTITUTE

OAKLAND, CALIFORNIA

Independent Institute
100 Swan Way, Oakland, CA 94621-1428
Telephone: 510-632-1366
Fax: 510-568-6040
Email: **info@independent.org**
Website: **www.independent.org**

Cover design: Shanti Nelson
Cover flag photo: © Enrico Della Pietra / 123RF
Cover paper photo: © Warut Chinsai / Shutterstock
Cover stamp by Bureau of Engraving and Printing

Library of Congress Cataloging-in-Publication Data

Names: Watkins, William J., Jr., author.
Title: Crossroads for liberty : recovering the anti-federalist values of
   America's First Constitution / William J. Watkins, Jr.
Description: Oakland, CA : Independent Institute, [2016] |
   Includes bibliographical references and index.
Identifiers: LCCN 2016022395 (print) | LCCN 2016033066 (ebook) |
   ISBN 9781598132793 (hardcover) | ISBN 9781598132809 (pbk.) |
   ISBN 9781598132816 (ePub) | ISBN 9781598132823 (ePDF) |
   ISBN 9781598132830 (Mobi)
Subjects: LCSH: Constitutional history—United States. | Constitutional law
   —United States. | United States—Politics and government—1783–1789. |
   Federal government—United States—History—18th century. | United
   States. Articles of Confederation. | Federalist.
Classification: LCC KF4515 .W38 2016 (print) | LCC KF4515 (ebook) |
   DDC 342.7302/9—dc23
LC record available at https://lccn.loc.gov/2016022395

To Evelyn

He who finds a wife finds what is good and
receives favor from the LORD. (Prov. 18:22)

Contents

Acknowledgments

THIS BOOK WOULD not have been possible without the support and encouragement of David J. Theroux, President of the Independent Institute, and Roy M. Carlisle, Independent's Acquisitions Director. Their attention to detail and faith in the manuscript were instrumental in completing the work. Thanks are also due to William F. Shughart II, Independent's Research Director, who made valuable suggestions on several chapters and suffered through my English-as-a-second-language grammar abilities. A special debt of gratitude is owed to my mother, Dr. Betty P. Watkins, for her tireless copyediting work and love. Also deserving the highest encomium for their efforts are the late Gail Saari, Martin Buerger, Robert Ade, Carl Close, and Cecilia Santini.

Abbreviations

The following abbreviations are used throughout the notes and bibliography:

American Archives *Documentary History of the American Revolution*, ed., Peter Force (Washington, D.C.: Library of Congress, 1837–53) 9 vols.

Annals *The Debates and Proceedings in the Congress of the United States*, ed., Joseph Gales (Washington, D.C.: Gales and Seaton, 1834–56) 42 vols.

Creating *Creating the Bill of Rights*, eds., Helen E. Veit, *et al.* (Baltimore, Md.: The Johns Hopkins University Press, 1991).

DJA *The Diary and Autobiography of John Adams*, ed., Lyman H. Butterfield (Cambridge, Mass.: 1961) 4 vols.

Elliot's Debates *The Debates in the Several State Conventions on the Adoption of the Federal Constitution*, ed., Jonathan Elliot (Washington, D.C.: J.B. Lippincott & Co., 1888) 7 vols.

Friends *Friends of the Constitution: Writings of the "Other" Federalists 1787–1788*, eds., Colleen Sheehan & Gary L. McDowell (Indianapolis, Ind.: Liberty Fund, 1998).

JCC *Journals of the Continental Congress, 1774–1789* (Washington, D.C.: Library of Congress 1904–37) 34 vols.

JDH *The Documentary History of the Ratification of the Constitution*, eds., Merrill Jensen, *et al.* (Madison, Wisc.: 1976) 26 vols.

LDC *Letters of Delegates to Congress*, 1774–1789, ed., Paul H. Smith (Washington, D.C.: Library of Congress, 1976–93) 24 vols.

JM Notes James Madison, Notes of the Debates in the Federal Convention of 1787 (New York: W. W. Norton & Co, 1987).

TAF *The Anti-Federalists: Selected Writings & Speeches*, ed., Bruce Frohnen (Washington, D.C.: Regnery, 1999).

TFC *The Founders' Constitution*, eds., Phillip B. Kurland & Ralph Lerner (Indianapolis, Ind.: Liberty Fund, 1987) 5 vols.

TRL *The Republic of Letters: The Correspondence Between Jefferson and Madison*, ed., James Morton Smith (New York: W. W. Norton, 1995) 3 vols.

WAL *Warren-Adams letters, being chiefly a correspondence among John Adams, Samuel Adams, and James Warren 1743–1814* (Massachusetts Historical Society, 1917).

Dramatis Personae

BRUTUS. The Essays of Brutus first appeared in the *New York Journal* between October 1787 and April 1788. Brutus's essays are often attributed to Robert Yates (1738–1801), a judge and dissenting member of the Philadelphia Convention. Thomas Treadwell (1743–1831), an attorney and state senator, John Williams (1752–1806), a state senator and brigadier general in the state militia, and Melancton Smith (1744–1798), a New York merchant and opponent of Alexander Hamilton, are also among the suspected authors of the Brutus series.

CATO. The Letters of Cato first appeared in the *New York Journal* between September 1787 and January 1788. Cato's letters are often attributed to New York Governor George Clinton (1739–1812). Abraham Yates, Jr. (1724–1796), a state senator and delegate to the Confederation Congress, and John Williams are also among the suspected authors of the Cato series.

CENTINEL. The Letters of Centinel first appeared in the Philadelphia *Freeman Journal* between October 1787 and April 1788. Historians believe that Centinel's letters were written by Pennsylvania Anti-Federalist Samuel Bryan (1759–1821).

A [MARYLAND] FARMER. The Essays by a Farmer first appeared in the Baltimore *Maryland Gazette* between February and April 1788. John Francis Mercer (1759–1821), a dissenting member of Maryland's delegation to the Philadelphia Convention, is believed to be the author of the essays.

THE FEDERAL FARMER. The Letters of the Federal Farmer first appeared in the *Poughkeepsie Country Journal* between October 1787 and January 1788.

Although long associated with the Virginia statesman Richard Henry Lee, it is now believed that the Federal Farmer's letters were written by Melancton Smith or a close associate.

THE IMPARTIAL EXAMINER. Essays of the Impartial Examiner first appeared in the *Virginia Independent Chronicle* between February and June 1788. The identity of the author remains unknown.

AN OLD WHIG. The Essays of "An Old Whig" first appeared in the Philadelphia *Independent Gazetteer* between October 1787 and February 1788. The identity of the author remains unknown.

Note on the Text

Idiosyncratic and archaic spellings and punctuation from contemporary quotations have been preserved.

Introduction

THE AVERAGE AMERICAN holds a low opinion of the Articles of Confederation. Our first national constitution, they believe, was an unsalvageable disaster. Columnist Paul Greenberg sums up the prevailing understanding: "And so, year by year, the infant republic under the old, impotent Articles of Confederation grew weaker and weaker."[1] Only because of the work of the Philadelphia Convention did we survive as a nation. And what a work it was. The Constitution of 1787, we are further told, represents the high point of America's contribution to the science of government.

The Anti-Federalists, those championing the principles of decentralization embodied in the Articles, are also held in low esteem. Scholars call them "men of little faith."[2] The opponents of the Constitution, Alexander Hamilton taught us in *Federalist* No. 1, were united by an "interest . . . to resist all changes which may hazard a diminution of the power, emolument and consequence of the offices they hold under the State-establishments."[3] In other words, they were selfish, myopic men wanting to remain big fish in various small ponds. Greenberg is perplexed about how the Anti-Federalists would have risked their lives in the Revolution, "but then were unwilling to establish a new government strong enough to protect it."[4]

The prevailing wisdom tells us further that Anti-Federalists were simply complainers. John E. Semonche, a professor of history at the University of North Carolina, writes that when faced with a crisis in the continental government, the Anti-Federalists "had no ready alternative to suggest."[5] They could only criticize the proposed Constitution and urge that the people stay the course of the Articles. Their lack of ideas and losing effort in the ratification process rightly "relegate[d] their cause to the scrap heap of history."[6]

I

In imbibing the conventional wisdom, Americans are impoverished intellectually, governmentally, and historically. The Articles certainly had their problems, but this first document of union led us to victory over the superpower that was Great Britain, and it also preserved the rights of the people of the several states to govern themselves. The issue of the Revolution was whether Americans would be ruled by the centralized government in Westminster, or whether they would make their own laws in their various state and local assemblies. The Revolution was not fought to replace one puissant central government with another. Inasmuch as the two main goals of the Articles were victory over Great Britain and preservation of self-government in the states, the Articles were a success story.

Rather than men of little faith, the Anti-Federalists were men of great faith. Their faith, however, was in a concept of republicanism alien to us today. Indeed, one Anti-Federalist writer, chaffing at the "anti" prefix attached to his cause, remarked that a more accurate designation for the opponents and proponents of the Constitution would be Republicans and Anti-Republicans. "The opposers are generally men who support the rights of the body of the people, and are properly republicans," wrote New Yorker Melancton Smith as "the Federal Farmer." "The advocates are generally men not very friendly to those rights," he continued, "and properly anti-republicans."[7]

The Anti-Federalists believed that republican liberty had the best chance of survival in small units in which the people participated actively. Representatives, they reasoned, should reflect the interests of their constituents, mix with them, and be amenable to their wishes. This type of government could exist only on a small scale. Once a unit of government reached a certain size, representatives would be alien to their constituents and work with a centralized bureaucratic apparatus to impose rule from above.

Of course, even in small units, the Anti-Federalists advocated multiple checks on power. Elections should be held annually. Term limits were necessary so that no man got too comfortable wielding the reins of power. If these checks failed, the people could always nullify any offending legislation while serving on juries. Juries of the vicinage, in Anti-Federalist America, had the ultimate control over substantive law.

The Anti-Federalists also championed local militias over a standing army. The militia was a democratic institution composed of all free male citizens able to bear arms. Regular drills were community events where the people discussed political affairs and enjoyed fellowship. Unlike many professional armies, the militia was meant purely for defensive purposes and not for foreign entanglements or interventionism.

Far from having no answers to the problems facing the Confederation, the Anti-Federalists, like most citizens at the time, were willing to grant Congress additional powers over continental concerns. Unfortunately, the Articles required unanimous consent for amendments and this made change difficult. If as much energy had gone into removing the unanimity requirement for amendments as went into the Philadelphia Convention, the convention would likely have been unnecessary.

Even after the Philadelphia Convention exceeded its charge to revise the Articles and instead created a new system of government, the Anti-Federalists were quick to offer concrete suggestions when they encountered defects in the proposed Constitution. The state ratifying conventions suggested over 200 amendments and were promised that the new federal Congress would entertain these amendments early on. Congress did submit a bill of rights to the states, but it largely ignored the substantive amendments submitted by the various state conventions.

A careful examination of the amendments proposed by the ratifying conventions and the reasoning behind Anti-Federalist criticisms of the Constitution is revealing. To the surprise of moderns, these men of little faith look awfully prescient. Indeed, they were eighteenth-century Cassandras. Cassandra was the daughter of King Priam and Queen Hecuba of Troy. The god Apollo granted Cassandra prophetic powers, but later cursed her after she refused his advances. Cassandra was permitted to keep her prophetic abilities, but as punishment Apollo decreed that no one would believe her visions of the future. During the Trojan War, she continually predicted the fate of Troy, but was locked away because King Priam thought she was insane.

To our detriment, we have locked the Anti-Federalists away and dismissed them as reactionaries and cranks. An honest reassessment of their writings, however, shows that they foresaw how the national government would abuse certain constitutional provisions. Their predictions about consolidated government and government removed from the human scale have come to pass.

Our government today is approaching bankruptcy and few, if any, human activities are beyond its control. Local self-government and individual liberty have been cast aside in favor of a centralized regulation of things. If we truly desire to reform our national government, we would do well to dust off the Articles of Confederation, the Anti-Federalists' writings, and the amendments proposed by the state ratifying conventions. These principles are born of the Declaration of Independence and can guide us back to a truly republican form of government.

I

Hopeful Petitioners

IN THE WANING summer days of 1774, delegates from twelve of the thirteen British North American colonies made their way toward Philadelphia. Only the remote and sparsely populated colony of Georgia did not send emissaries. The delegates had been elected by extra-legal committees of correspondence or colonial conventions. A year earlier, Samuel Adams had called for a continental congress to meet, to draft a bill of rights, and to appoint an ambassador to the British Court. Adams's proposal received few endorsements outside of Massachusetts. Other colonial leaders feared that such a meeting would unnecessarily antagonize the mother country.

The political landscape changed markedly in March 1774 when Parliament passed the Boston Port Act, which closed Boston Harbor to all commerce. The Port Act aimed to punish Bostonians for the Tea Party that occurred in December 1773. Although the Tea Act had reduced the price of tea, the colonists vehemently objected to the measure because, if enforced, it would have set a revenue precedent and formed the foundation for other parliamentary acts undermining colonial home rule. To prevent the offloading of the tea or the seizure of the tea by customs officials, the vessels carrying the East India tea were boarded and the cargo was tossed into the frigid Atlantic.

Adams and his associates immediately called on the other colonies to stand with Boston as the British army and navy prepared to enforce the Port Act. The town's committee of correspondence suggested a "Solemn League and Covenant" whereby all colonies would suspend trade with Great Britain. Although Boston's economic distress meant economic gains for other ports and colonies, a substantial number of Americans viewed the Bostonians as kindred enduring pain for a common cause. New York's Committee of Fifty-one, for example, described Massachusetts as "suffering in the defense of the rights of America" and opined that any suggested remedy would be fruitless "unless it proceeds from the joint act and approbation of all."[1] Moreover, with tempers flaring in New England, the leaders of the other colonies saw creation of a congress as a prudent step whereby alternatives to violence could be discussed. Merchants also hoped that a general congress might deflect Boston's suggestions of a boycott of British trade.

As the delegates traveled to Philadelphia, they certainly contemplated the various local resolutions and newspaper essays offering suggestions on the goals and directions of a congress. In addition, many of the delegates were familiar with more widely circulated pieces such as Thomas Jefferson's *Summary View of the Rights of British America* and James Wilson's *Considerations on the Nature and Extent of the Legislative Authority of the British Parliament*. These two documents provide a snapshot of the forward-thinking patriot mindset as the First Continental Congress convened.

Jefferson's *Summary View* originally was written as proposed instructions to Virginia's delegates, but was published as an essay in August 1774. Jefferson urged a "humble and dutiful" address to the king protesting the "unwarrantable encroachments and usurpations" of Parliament.[2] Such an address would make clear that George III was the "central link" of the British Empire in his executive office.[3] In this capacity, Jefferson urged the king to recognize that the colonies were outside the jurisdiction of Parliament and should be governed by their own duly elected legislatures. Jefferson went so far as to describe Parliament as "a body of men foreign to our constitutions" bent on causing "further discontents and jealousies among us."[4] Hence, Jefferson entreated the king to exercise his veto power to protect the colonies from encroachments of Parliament. Of course, Jefferson did not give George III a free pass, but also complained that the king had left the colonists to the intrigues of evil ministers and parliamentarians. Further, Jefferson chastised the king for acting outside his authority in many instances, such as sending armies to America without the consent of the people.[5] Jefferson ended the essay by entreating the king to "[l]et no act be passed by any one legislature, which may infringe on the rights and liberties of another."[6]

Similarly, Wilson opened his pamphlet by questioning whether "the legislative authority of the British parliament extend[s]" to the colonies.[7] In answering this question, he averred that "no one has a right to any authority over another without his consent."[8] Wilson observed that the franchise is a powerful force whereby the electors can express their displeasure or reward faithful service. Without being held accountable by frequent elections, parliaments—though once elected—can easily become despotic. To prove his case, Wilson pointed to the Long Parliament (1640–53) which began its existence opposing the extra-constitutional government of Charles I and ended as an ignominious body distrusted by the people. Because the colonists elected no members of Parliament and laws enacted for the colonies did not operate on the MPs themselves, Wilson denied that Parliament could rightly make law for Americans. "[T]hat the colonies are not bound by the acts of the British parliament," Wilson announced, "because they have no share in the British legislature."[9] The king, however, was owed allegiance by the colonists "because they have hitherto enjoyed, and still continue to enjoy, his protection."[10] Although Wilson professed his allegiance to George III, he nonetheless reserved the right to transfer that allegiance elsewhere if the king ceased to provide security.

The First Continental Congress

The first delegates began to arrive in Philadelphia as August turned to September. Summer was still in full force and the New England delegates complained of the "extream Heat."[11] While they waited for their numbers to increase, the delegates used the time to get acquainted. Lavish dinners and other functions were held that allowed the delegates to educate themselves on the sentiments of the colonies in general. These were daily affairs and John Adams described the feasts as "incessant."[12] As they mingled, the delegates certainly learned that the Congress would be a fusion of differing interests and expectations. While almost all were alarmed by the recent parliamentary enactments, opinions were shaded by a variety of factors such as a colony's size, urbanization, claims to western lands, and slave ownership. Vast differences abounded within each colony. Patriotic fervor tended to increase as one moved toward the frontier or into large towns. Parts of some colonies had little to bind them together other than boundaries drawn on maps in London. Backcountry South Carolina, for example, was a solar system removed from urbane Charleston.

When most Americans think of the First Continental Congress, they envision a group of men preparing to declare independence. The instructions of the delegates tell a different story. For instance, Pennsylvania instructed its delegates to consult with the other colonies in obtaining a redress of grievances to establish that "Union & harmony between Great-Britain and the Colonies, which is indispensably necessary to the welfare and happiness of both."[13] The various instructions often condemned the Boston Port Act and other measures, but the delegates were charged to take a prudent and united course in protecting American rights and in securing a favorable connection with the mother country. The several colonies sent the delegates to remonstrate and cajole, not to rebel or form a new nation.

The delegates were given two choices on a meeting place: Carpenters' Hall or the Pennsylvania State House. The former had been offered by the master builders of the city and the latter by Joseph Galloway, speaker of the Pennsylvania Assembly. In an effort to show solidarity with the working people, the delegates chose Carpenters' Hall. Galloway was insulted by the rejection of the State House, and realized that the more ardent patriots—especially those from Massachusetts, Virginia, and the Carolinas—had made the decision long before a vote was taken.[14] Thus, what Caesar Rodney of Delaware called "the greatest Assembly . . . that was ever Collected in America" began its work on September 5, 1774.[15]

When the Congress convened, the first significant issue was voting. Should each colony have one vote, or should votes be weighted according to population, or wealth, or some combination thereof? All things being equal, this issue appears to be a question pitting continentalists versus localists. Patrick Henry of Virginia rose and averred that "it would be a great Injustice, if a little Colony should have the same Weight in the Councils of America, as a great one."[16] In the midst of debating this issue, an erroneous report was received that Boston had been bombarded by British artillery. This prompted Henry to push harder for voting based on population. Henry claimed that "Government is dissolved" and that distinctions between the colonies "are no more."[17]

Then, in a phrase worthy of a modern ad campaign, Henry declared that "I am not a Virginian, but an American."[18]

Although these words seem to place Henry at the head of the continentalists, one should not forget that Virginia was the most populous colony in North America. Thus, under Henry's proposal his state would exercise more power than the others. The other delegates did not buy into Henry's rhetoric. John Jay of New York doubted Henry's claims about the end of government and reminded him that the Congress had assembled to suggest changes to the current system and not to form a new constitution. Others agreed that there was simply no way to judge the importance or weight that should be accorded to each colony. Records reveal no other delegates echoing or lauding Henry's disingenuous claims about being an American. Writing home to his son, Samuel Ward of Rhode Island simply noted that "some of the larger Colonies wanted a larger Number of Voices."[19] Because the delegates did not have enough data on hand regarding the wealth or population of the different colonies, Congress had little choice but to allot each colony one vote in the proceedings. The large states acquiesced but resolved to revisit voting at a more opportune time.

With this basic issue decided, the delegates moved to other matters such as the foundation of American rights. Richard Henry Lee of Virginia argued that the colonists' rights were "built on a fourfold foundation—on Nature, on the british Constitution, on Charters, and on immemorial Usage."[20] Other delegates urged for some combination of the four. John Jay of New York stood on the law of nature coupled with the British Constitution to ascertain colonial rights. John Rutledge of South Carolina opposed recourse to the law of nature and suggested that the colonists stand firm on the British Constitution. James Duane of New York agreed that the law of nature should be avoided inasmuch as the inherent rights of Englishmen were sufficient and possibly "will make us independent."[21] Joseph Galloway of Pennsylvania explained that he had looked for the rights of Americans in the laws of nature, but discovered nothing helpful. The British Constitution, on the contrary, was the true repository of American rights. Galloway reasoned that the fundamental rule of the British Constitution was that "no Law shall be binding, but such as are made by the Consent of the Proprietors in England."[22] Because the

Americans had not consented to any law since the emigration of their ancestors, Galloway claimed that they were exempt from all acts of Parliament made since that time. He conceded that his arguments could lead "to an Independency of the Colonies," but believed that even Lord North would be forced to agree with this reasoning.[23]

Suffolk Resolves

While Congress was debating the foundations of American rights, a convention of towns was held in Dedham, Massachusetts. This meeting had been planned by Samuel Adams and the Boston committee of correspondence prior to Adams's departure for Philadelphia. Adams hoped that this Suffolk County Convention would approve the creation of an independent provincial assembly expressing allegiance to the Continental Congress rather than the British government. In conjunction with Dr. Joseph Warren, Adams had drafted a resolution to be introduced at the Suffolk Convention and planned to have these forwarded to Philadelphia after they were adopted.

Just as Adams had planned, things went smoothly in Dedham. On September 9, 1774, a series of resolutions was passed and, thanks to the hard riding of Paul Revere, reached Philadelphia in six days. On September 17, the Suffolk Resolves were presented to the Continental Congress. The Resolutions began by "cheerfully acknowledge[ing] the said George the Third to be our rightful sovereign" to whom allegiance is owed.[24] Although loyal subjects, the convention also observed that they were duty bound to defend their liberties and "to hand them down entire to future generations."[25] Recent acts of the British Parliament had infringed these liberties and thus were a nullity in the province. The Resolves especially took aim at the recent Massachusetts Government Act, which altered provisions of the colony's charter allowing for the election of many colonial officials. The Act placed this power in the hands of the British government and also directed that the royal governor would appoint judges for the courts of the province. The Resolves claimed that the changes to the charter created "unconstitutional officers" and described anyone who used the court system as an enemy cooperator. Any judge or other official accepting an appointment from the British government was urged to resign immediately.

Because of the recent actions of British forces, the Resolves urged the people to "use their utmost diligence to acquaint themselves with the art of war as soon as possible" and to drill regularly.[26] Such measures, the Resolves emphasized, were merely for defensive purposes. The people should act with restraint and refrain from rioting or any attacks on the property of others. In closing, the Suffolk Convention promised to duly submit to all recommended measures proposed by the Continental Congress "for renewing that harmony and union between Great-Britain and the colonies."[27]

To the joy of the Massachusetts delegates, Congress approved the Suffolk Resolves unanimously and recommended that the colony persevere "in the same firm and temperate conduct as expressed in the resolutions."[28] Congress also recommended that all other colonies should direct supplies to Boston so long as a need existed. John Adams declared that his comrades in the Congress expressed "generous, noble Sentiments" when considering the work of the Suffolk Convention. "This day convinced me," wrote Adams, "that America will support Massachusetts or perish with her."[29] Samuel Adams concurred with John. Pleased that the Suffolk Convention had the desired effect, he wrote home that "America will make a point of supporting Boston to the Utmost."[30]

Suspension of Commerce

Perhaps spurred on by the spirit of the Suffolk Resolves, Congress turned to the issue of a boycott of British goods. The motion was made by Richard Henry Lee of Virginia. Many delegates believed that a boycott would cripple the British economy and persuade the Crown to make reforms in colonial policy. Samuel Chase of Maryland predicted that a trade boycott "must produce a national Bankruptcy, in a very short Space of Time."[31] Thomas Lynch of South Carolina concurred with Chase's prediction and speculated that "immediate Relief" from Parliament would follow.[32] Robert Treat Paine of Massachusetts opined that without American flaxseed 500,000 Irishmen would be out of work and foment rebellion in the British Isles.[33] John Adams's diary reveals that most delegates strongly supported a suspension of commerce with Britain and that much of the debate centered on when the suspension would begin.

During the discussion of non-intercourse, Galloway rose and averred that a suspension of commerce would not result in the relief of Boston, but instead would result in the ruin of the colonies. He predicted that unemployment and poverty would follow. Sensing that non-intercourse would quickly lead to war, Galloway begged the delegates to come to terms with the mother country.[34] He proposed a plan that would have united the thirteen colonies within the British Empire. Galloway called for the creation of a continental assembly that he described as "a British and American legislature" that would "regulat[e] the administration of the general affairs of America."[35] The several colonial legislatures would choose the members of the assembly every three years. In theory, this legislature would be "an inferior and distinct branch of the British legislature" although it would handle all continental matters.[36] Each colony would "retain its present constitution, and all powers of regulating and governing its own internal police, in all cases what[so]ever."[37] In recognition of the king's authority, he was to appoint a president general to execute the laws passed by the new legislature.

James Duane of New York seconded the plan and described it as reaching "a lasting Accommodation with G. Britain."[38] Fellow New Yorker John Jay gave the plan his endorsement and advocated its adoption. Duane also urged his colleagues to submit to parliamentary laws regulating trade. Galloway picked up on this point and asserted that "Every Gentleman here thinks that Parliament ought to have the Power over Trade, because Britain protects it and us."[39] Galloway observed further that America could never be unified if each colonial legislature claimed the right of regulating trade. Such a power needed to be lodged in a central body.

The more radical members of Congress feared the Galloway plan. They distrusted any measure that bound the colonies closer to the mother country. Although the delegates all professed to be reconciliationists, a large number believed that reconciliation meant a loose relationship with Great Britain. Protests went up that the various colonial legislatures should be consulted before such a plan was debated. Others claimed that consideration of Galloway's proposal exceeded the Congress's authority. In the end, Galloway's plan went nowhere.

Economic sanctions, styled as the Association, proved to be the preferred course of conduct. Congress complained that since approximately 1763, the British ministry had embarked on "a ruinous system of colony administration . . . calculated for inslaving these colonies, and, with them, the British empire."[40] To obtain redress of grievances, the Congress resolved, beginning December 1, 1774, to cease importation of goods and wares from Great Britain, Ireland, and the West Indies. Beginning in September 1775, the colonies would cease exporting merchandise or commodities to British territories. This later date was urged by the Southern colonies that depended on exports for economic survival. The Association made an exception for the exportation of rice to Europe to assuage concerns of the South Carolina contingent that their economic fortunes would be destroyed.

The Association promised to encourage frugality and economy among the colonies and prohibited merchants from raising prices in light of the looming shortages that non-importation would cause. The Association urged that a committee be elected in every town to ensure that all colonists adhered to the terms of the economic boycott. Those who did not would have their names published in local newspapers and suffer universal odium.

Desiring to reach out to British supporters of colonial rights, the Congress also adopted an address to the People of Great Britain. Congress described Great Britain as a nation "led to greatness by the hand of Liberty" that was now "forging chains for her Friends and Children."[41] The turnabout was from one of two causes: lack of virtue or negligence "in the appointment of her rulers."[42] Hinting that the latter was the true cause, the Address warned that if America was subjugated, it would be much easier for wicked ministers and others to "enslave" the good people of the mother country.[43]

Claiming the same rights "as our fellow-subjects in Britain," the Address denied that any "power on earth has a right to take our property from us without our consent."[44] Echoing a point made by Galloway during the debates, the Address asked: "Why then are the Proprietors of the soil of America less Lords of their property than you are of yours, or why should they submit it to the disposal of your Parliament, or any other Parliament, or Council in the world, not of their election?"[45] The Address then chronicled the constitutional violations of American rights beginning with the Stamp Act and ending with statutes targeting Boston. "Place us in the same situation that we were at the close of the last war," the Address implored, "and our former harmony will be restored."[46]

The delegates approved a Declaration and Resolves in which they protested recent coercive legislation as "impolitic, unjust, and cruel, as well as unconstitutional, and most dangerous and destructive of American rights."[47] They reemphasized that Parliament lacked the power to meddle with internal colonial affairs inasmuch as the colonies "are entitled to a free and exclusive power of legislation in their several provincial legislatures."[48] In a concession to the health of the empire, the Congress declared that Americans would "cheerfully consent to the operation of such acts of the British parliament . . . restrained to the regulation of our external commerce, for the purpose of securing the commercial advantages of the whole empire to the mother country."[49]

As Congress concluded its business, many delegates felt satisfaction with the work done and hoped for good news from London. In a letter to William Lee, Richard Henry Lee expressed "great hopes that their [the proceedings'] vigor and unanimity will prove the ruin of our Ministerial Enemies and the salvation of American Liberty."[50] Fervently believing in the righteousness of the cause, Richard Henry opined "that if [the] Ministry have not their hearts hardened, as the Scripture has it, they will best consult the good of their Country and their own safety by a prudent and speedy reversal of their ill judged measures."[51]

Fearing that their adversaries' hearts might remain stone rather than flesh, the First Congress resolved that another Congress should meet on May 10, 1775. This was a prudent step inasmuch as the principles put forth in the various addresses and declarations were constitutional heresy to the British. The result of the Glorious Revolution was that Parliament claimed an uncontrollable sovereignty over the British Empire. The rejection of Parliament was, in the view of many British subjects, a rejection of the British constitution.

2

The Issue Forced

UPON RECEIVING THE petitions from the First Congress, American allies in Britain advocated prudent measures. Edmund Burke, for instance, warned that arguments used to undermine the claims of the Americans would "subvert the maxims which preserve the whole spirit of our own liberty."[1] Burke had long advocated that colonial policy should be returned to its pre-1764 standing—a time before Parliament attempted to meddle in what the colonies saw as purely internal matters. The Earl of Chatham (William Pitt) urged that all troops be withdrawn from Boston as a gesture of good faith. This proposed step toward reconciliation, however, garnered little support in Parliament. Unfortunately for the Empire, Burke and Chatham were in the minority. Most of those holding power agreed with Sir John Burgoyne that the colonists acted as "our spoilt child, which we have already spoiled with too much indulgence."[2]

On February 5, 1775, Parliament declared that Massachusetts was in a state of rebellion. The colonists, Parliament averred, "have proceeded so far to resist the authority of the Supreme Legislature, that a rebellion at this time actually exists within the said Province."[3] On March 30, 1776, King George III endorsed the New England Restraining Act. With this measure, New England was limited to trading with Great Britain and denied access to the fisheries of the North Atlantic.

Armed Conflict

In Boston, hostilities seemed imminent. The British had stationed 4,000 redcoats in a town of 16,000. Relations between the soldiers and citizens had not improved since the so-called Boston Massacre of 1770 when five citizens were killed after a mob taunted a private guarding the customs house. To make matters more dangerous, both sides were now stockpiling weapons and ammunition. Militia units drilled and the best of the citizen-soldiers were designated "minutemen" based on their training to be ready for duty in sixty seconds. Add a small spark to the Massachusetts Bay area and an explosion would surely follow.

The spark came in April when General Thomas Gage sent sixteen companies to Concord to seize munitions stored there. When patriot leaders realized that unusual troop movements were afoot, they sent Paul Revere to Lexington where Samuel Adams and John Hancock had been in hiding. Realizing that the target of the British raid was the supplies stored in nearby Concord, minutemen began assembling. When the opposing forces met in Lexington, the British regulars killed seven patriots quickly and wounded nine more. It was an easy victory for the regulars. They celebrated and then marched on to Concord.

However, at Concord, a sizeable force of patriots had gathered and persuaded the British to retreat. As the soldiers retreated over a bridge, a bottleneck developed and the stranded troops were easy targets for the militia. As the British column wound its way back to Boston, the patriots took shortcuts through the woodlands and farms and continued to harass the regulars. The Americans fought Indian style, hiding behind trees and fences to fire, and then retreating into the woods to reload. Seventy-three British troops were killed and 200 wounded. Open warfare had begun.

For the independence-minded patriots, the clash at Lexington was good news. Writing to Horatio Gates, Thomas Johnson of Maryland said that he "was not at all sorry the pent up flame has broken out."[4] Others were less sanguine. Benjamin Franklin observed that civil war had arrived and that neither he nor younger Americans "may live to see" the end of it.[5] Delegates on the journey to the Second Continental Congress reported a martial spirit in the air. For example, Richard Caswell of North Carolina described meeting hundreds of men under arms and receiving "all the Military honors due to General Officers" as he traveled northward.[6] In Philadelphia, the delegates encountered a constant "sound of Drums & Fifes" as companies drilled twice daily.[7] John Adams reported that even the pacifistic Quakers were forming companies.[8]

Second Continental Congress

The Second Continental Congress convened on May 10, 1775, in Philadelphia. Fifty of the 65 delegates attending the Second Congress had been members of the First. A Georgia parish elected Lyman Hall to serve and with his arrival all 13 colonies had representation in this continental assembly. Early in the proceedings, John Hancock presented the delegates with a letter from the Massachusetts General Congress urging creation of "a powerful army . . . to stem the rapid Progress of a tyrannical Ministry."[9] Only by throwing overwhelming force into the conflict, the letter stressed, could the redcoats be checked and American allies in England have an opportunity to punish the king's wicked advisors. After receiving the letter and documents describing the fighting at Lexington and Concord, the Congress resolved itself into the committee of the whole "to take into consideration the state of America."[10]

On May 16, Richard Henry Lee of Virginia opened the debate with proposals to raise a continental army. This caused John Rutledge of South Carolina to ask pointedly whether the Congress should aim for independence or "a Restoration of Rights & putting of Us on Our old footing."[11] John Adams rose and explained that the colonies should strive for independence from Parliament, but seek a "dependence on the Crown."[12] Concerned at the direction of the debate, John Dickinson of Pennsylvania suggested a three-pronged approach. First, the Congress should prepare for armed conflict. Second, Congress should vigorously prosecute the war lest the king's ministers conclude that the colonists lacked the fortitude to battle for liberty. Third, Congress should continue to seek reconciliation with the mother country and concede Britain's right to regulate trade.

In arguing the first two points, Dickinson quoted speeches from British statesmen expressing the general opinion that "Great Britain is contesting for her very Existence in this Dispute with America."[13] Full American independence would not come without a great fight and expense of blood and treasure. Considering the resources and manpower Great Britain was about to devote to prosecuting the war, preparations in the colonies were required. This colonial unity and firmness, Dickinson hoped, would procure relief by a change of royal advisors and measures. In his arguments for provisions for war, Dickinson said little with which even the most rabid Son of Liberty could disagree. The controversial matters arose when Dickinson turned to the idea of negotiation.

Dickinson advocated that a new petition be presented to George III that omitted claims of rights, but instead "express[ed] in the most acceptable Manner our unfeigned Devotion to His Majesty & the State from which We derive our Origin."[14] Dickinson believed that such a petition would somehow penetrate the heart of the king, but for those who doubted the efficacy of yet more parchment sent to London, Dickinson observed that nothing was lost. "Events must happen," he averred, "as if We had only prepared for War."[15] Dickinson believed that based on the bonds of kinship, the colonists ought to reach out one more time. He remarked that if American forces were victorious in a war, the triumph would be over their fathers from whom Americans inherited liberty and derived many blessings such as protection from the powers of Europe.

Dickinson questioned how Americans could have true happiness except in "a State of Dependence upon & subordination to our Parent State."[16] Dickinson explained that he meant by dependence and subordination the power of the king in making laws, enforcing laws, and in his prerogative power. Parliament also had a role to play in this system of dependence and subordination. Parliament should have the power of regulating all of the Americans' foreign trade. Dickinson denied that Parliament should have any power of taxation related to the colonies.

Hence, Dickinson suggested that Congress should send emissaries to London with the power to deal with the British and reach some agreement. Considering American success at Concord, the colonists operated from a position of strength. Negotiations would come sooner or later. Why not make all efforts to spare the people the horrors of a prolonged war by proposing terms of accommodation now? This would also show the world that the colonists had done everything possible to avoid the mass spilling of blood. Negotiations had the added benefit of giving the Association time to work and hit Britain in her pocketbook.

The New England delegates and those favoring independence scoffed at Dickinson's proposal for an address and negotiation. Writing to Moses Gill, John Adams observed that the "cancer" of the corrupt British rule "is too deeply rooted and too far spread to be cured by any thing short of cutting it out entire."[17] Rather than draft petitions, stockpiling "powder and artillery are the most efficacious, sure, and infallible conciliatory measures we can adopt."[18] The various colonies and the First Congress had sent fawning addresses to George III praising his wisdom and rule. They had expressed loyalty to the king and a willingness to defend his person with their lives. These resolves and addresses had achieved nothing and Dickinson's hopes for dependence and subordination were chimerical. This radical faction wanted to drive the British regiments quartered in Boston into the sea.

The independence-minded colonists realized, however, that they needed the reconciliationists like Dickinson. The First Congress achieved success based, in part, on its unity. British aggression at Lexington and Concord led to even more unity among the delegates and the people at large. Just the month prior to completion of Dickinson's petition, 2,200 British regulars charged American positions in the famed Battle of Bunker Hill. The regulars suffered the loss of 226 men killed and over 800 wounded. The American losses were but a fraction of this. The British obtained their objective but at enormous cost. Momentum naturally was swinging toward independence and events such as Bunker Hill, the pro-independence party knew, likely would push the reconciliationists further toward the radical camp. If they refused to petition, John Adams feared that "Discord and total Disunion would be certain."[19] For these reasons, Congress approved the so-called Olive Branch Petition drafted by Dickinson.

An Olive Branch

The petition described the difficulties between the colonists and the mother country as originating from wicked and ill-informed ministers who developed policies that were not in the interests of the king or his loyal subjects in America. These ministers had "compelled" the colonies "to arm in our own defense" and to spill blood in an effort to protect home and hearth.[20] Although the colonists disdained these ministers, they expressed great warmth for the person, family, and government of the king. If only the great king would act to extricate the colonies from the circumstances created by others, then George III would be remembered as an illustrious personage. The petition concluded by wishing the king a long and prosperous reign over all his dominions.

To modern ears, the obsequious language of the Olive Branch Petition seems out of place after hostilities had erupted. One could question how anyone in July 1775 harbored any real hope of a compromise or believed that the king would gallop to the rescue. We must remember that the events of 1774 ushered in a new era of popular participation in politics that concerned many Americans. The colonies had always been known for the spirit of equality where, in the words of historian Gordon Wood, "ordinary people were closer in wealth and property to those above them and felt freer from aristocratic patronage and control than did the common people elsewhere in the Western world."[21] But now in sundry towns, artisans and mechanics played critical roles in committees enforcing the provisions of the Association. They also assumed active leadership roles in many committees of safety that became the de facto governments in the colonies. These commoners called for expansion of the franchise and other reforms. Conservatives feared this revolution in politics and looked to the ancient institution of monarchy as a stabilizing force that could preserve a hierarchal order and prevent the uneducated rabble from making government a playhouse of folly.

Gouverneur Morris of New York expressed this fear in early 1774: "The mob begin to think and to reason. Poor reptiles! it is with them a vernal morning; they are struggling to cast off their winter's slough, they bask in the sunshine, and ere noon they will bite, depend upon it. The gentry begin to fear this. . . I see, and I see it with fear and trembling, that if the disputes with *Great Britain* continue, we shall be under the worst of all possible dominions; we shall be under the domination of a riotous mob."[22] Dickinson and his ilk knew that the Olive Branch Petition was a long-shot, but they had to try to reach a middle ground between total submission to Parliament or rebellion.

In the summer of 1775, Congress agreed on the creation of a continental army. Congress planned to raise 15,000 soldiers. To cement Virginia to the cause, John and Samuel Adams pushed George Washington as the commander of the army. Washington, clad in his old uniform worn in the Seven Years' ("French and Indian") War, proceeded to Boston where large numbers of armed New Englanders had gathered. To support the army, Congress authorized an emission of Continental currency on June 22, 1775. To prop up the currency, Congress asked each colony to levy taxes for its portion of the issue. A colony's share was determined based on its population. This was but the first of eleven issues of "Continentals." By the end of the war, Congress would have printed approximately $241,550,000 in paper money.

George III refused to accept Dickinson's petition and issued a royal proclamation making clear his position on American affairs. "[W]e have thought fit," declared the king, "by and with the advice of our Privy Council, to issue our Royal Proclamation, hereby declaring, that not only all our Officers, civil and military, are obliged to exert their utmost endeavours to suppress such rebellion, and to bring the traitors to justice, but that all our subjects of this Realm, and the dominions thereunto belonging, are bound by law to be aiding and assisting in the suppression of such rebellion."[23] This was the response many in the colonies expected. Writing to James Warren, Samuel Adams believed that his more conservative colleagues were finally understanding that "it is folly to supplicate a Tyrant."[24]

If the British position needed any more clarification, it came in December 1775 in the form of the Prohibitory Act. Parliament prohibited all trade with the colonies and declared that all ships found engaging in trade with the Americans would be taken and forfeited to the king. Historian Merrill Jensen describes this Act as "a practical declaration of independence by the British government, as formal an act of abdication as could be penned."[25]

Common Sense

When the New Year dawned and the colonists pondered the implication of the Prohibitory Act, a pamphlet appeared on the streets of Philadelphia. Within just a few weeks, more than 100,000 copies were printed. Written in plain language and meant for the common man, Thomas Paine's *Common Sense* asserted that no union with Britain should be desired. Paine began his pamphlet with an attack on the institution of monarchy—the very institution on which American conservatives were depending to rescue them from acts of Parliament and ministerial policies. Paine described the institution as one concocted by heathens and copied by the wayward children of Israel. Little did they realize that the first human king on the earth was likely "the principal ruffian of some restless gang" whose savagery "obtained him the title of chief among plunderers."[26] Hence, the idea of monarchy should repel all men capable of reason.

Paine challenged the claim that the colonies derived benefits from Britain. Observing that American products would be sought after in Europe, Paine argued that connection with Britain only involved America in unnecessary foreign wars and antagonized nations that were our natural trading partners. He also found it absurd that an island kingdom could claim to govern a continent that had differing interests from the parent country.

Paine claimed that reconciliation, after Lexington and Concord, was not a possibility. The ministry had made no good faith efforts at addressing American grievances. With bloodshed having taken place, no true union of friendship and confidence could be restored. Instead of debating reconciliation, Americans should consider forming a continental government and omit the institution of monarchy. In America, Paine declared, "law is the king."[27] The country would be an asylum for all those seeking freedom and security.

Paine's work certainly moved the people toward independence. In the words of Mel Bradford, *Common Sense* "gave to Anglo-American amity the last little push required to remove it as an impediment to independence."[28] But it would take other considerations to change the minds of the ardent reconciliationists. Despite strong words from George III, key conservative leaders still held out hope for an amicable resolution to the family quarrel. This began to change drastically in May 1776 when Congress learned that the king had hired German mercenaries. George III agreed to pay £7 for each soldier provided. While serving the king, each soldier would receive the same pay as British regulars. The king's use of foreign troops was proof (as if more was needed) that the British monarch meant to conqueror the colonies.

The hiring of mercenaries also focused the delegates on financial issues. To stand firm with the resources of Great Britain thrown at them, the colonies would need help from abroad. Great Britain's enemies might be persuaded to provide loans and military hardware to the Americans. But, before any nation considered such a step, it would need assurance that the colonies desired a full and complete separation from Great Britain. France and Spain, for example, would not risk intervention if they believed that the colonists would return to the British fold as soon as some of their demands were met. These concerns prompted Congress to consider a formal declaration of independence.

Independence

On June 7, 1776, Richard Henry Lee, acting on instructions from Virginia's convention meeting in Williamsburg, offered the following motion:

That these United Colonies are, and of right ought to be, free and independent States, that they are absolved from all allegiance to the British Crown, and that all political connection between them and the State of Great Britain is, and ought to be, totally dissolved.

That it is expedient forthwith to take the most effectual measures for forming foreign Alliances.

That a plan of confederation be prepared and transmitted to the respective Colonies for their consideration and approbation.[29]

John Adams seconded the motion. The conservative delegates were able to postpone consideration of independence until the beginning of July. However, in case independence was declared, Congress appointed a committee to have ready a declaration so no time would be lost. The members of the committee were Thomas Jefferson, John Adams, Benjamin Franklin, Roger Sherman, and Robert R. Livingston. Two days later Congress appointed a committee to prepare a plan of confederation. Each colony had one delegate assigned to this committee.

The delay in Congress had no effect on Virginians who had instructed Lee to move for independence. The issue of independence, for practical purposes, was settled in Virginia when Lord Dunmore bombarded Norfolk on New Year's Day 1776. On June 28, 1776, Virginians adopted a new constitution making clear that the union with Great Britain was severed. The Congress had yet to declare independence, but Virginia had assumed her place among the nations.

Jefferson's notes reveal that the opposition to independence in Congress was led by James Wilson, Robert R. Livingston, Edward Rutledge, and John Dickinson. They claimed that the people—especially those in the middle colonies—were not ready to break with Great Britain and that Congress should give them more time to "join in the general voice of America."[30] Some colonies had not given their delegates instructions on independence; therefore, Congress should wait until colonial assemblies met and had a chance to debate the independence issue. If Congress went forward precipitously, the conservatives averred, the secession of some colonies from the united resistance would weaken the war effort. Disunity would scare off foreign powers that might otherwise assist the colonies. The conservatives even speculated that perhaps France and Spain would come to an agreement with the British to hold the colonists in check.

The pro-independence delegates, Jefferson tells us, were led by John Adams, Richard Henry Lee, and George Wythe. They countered that "the question was not whether, by a declaration of Independence, we should make ourselves what we are not; but whether we should declare a fact which already exists."[31] The colonies had always been independent of Parliament and the people of Great Britain. Parliamentary restraints on trade and other matters had not been true law but existed "from our acquiescence only."[32] The colonies no longer owed the king any allegiance because he ceased to provide protection and was in fact "levying war on us."[33]

The supporters of independence acknowledged that some instructions to delegates were contrary to a full break with Britain, but that these instructions had been written prior to recent developments. Pointing to Maryland and Pennsylvania, Adams and his colleagues observed that the representative bodies there were out of sync with the people inasmuch as the representatives were influenced improperly by "proprietary power and connections."[34]

Turning to foreign powers, the pro-independence delegates argued that no European power would negotiate with America unless America was independent. Without a declaration of independence, American ships would not be received into foreign ports. Alliances should be sought now lest any future military setbacks deter European powers from betting on American success in the war.

The Congress took a trial vote for independence on July 1. New York's delegates abstained and protested that they had no instructions from their constituents. Delaware was divided because Caesar Rodney, a pro-independence delegate, was away from Philadelphia. South Carolina and Pennsylvania voted against independence. The supporters of Lee's motion knew that something had to be done to bring these four colonies into the fold. An afternoon of fierce politicking erupted. The South Carolinians were brought on board and delegates persuaded Pennsylvania's reconciliationist delegates to stay at home because their views were not supported by the majority of the people. Rodney arrived on July 2 and thus broke the tie within Delaware's delegation so that the majority supported independence and could thus cast the colony's vote. When the actual vote was taken shortly after Rodney's arrival, 12 colonies (with New York still abstaining) voted for Lee's motion. New York joined in the action to make it 13 when resolutions from the state's convention were received on July 15.

On July 4, Congress adopted a declaration that was the work primarily of Thomas Jefferson. Consistent with the theory of sovereignty expressed in his *Summary View*, the Declaration of Independence mostly addressed the "history of the present King of Great Britain."[35] The Declaration indirectly addressed Parliament by accusing the king of "combin[ing] with others to subject us to a jurisdiction foreign to our constitution."[36] The Declaration saw the king as the only constitutional link between the colonies and Great Britain. Because of the king's multiple abuses and refusals to respond to multiple petitions, the Congress declared him a tyrant who was "unfit to be the ruler of a free people."[37]

3

Confederation

AT FIRST BLUSH, it seems strange that John Dickinson was the chairman of the committee that produced the first draft of the Articles of Confederation. Dickinson, after all, refused to sign the Declaration of Independence. When most of his colleagues clamored for separation, he clung to hopes that the colonies could maintain some connection with the British Empire. Contrary to our modern expectations, Dickinson and the Continental Congress did not see independence as preceding confederation. Prior to the final push for independence, John Adams outlined the following sequence in a letter to Patrick Henry:

> It has ever appeared to me that the natural course and order of things was this: for every colony to institute a government, for all the colonies to confederate, and define the limits of the continental Constitution; then to declare the colonies a sovereign state, or a number of confederated sovereign states; and last of all to form treaties with foreign powers. But I fear we cannot proceed systematically, and we shall be obligated to declare ourselves independent States, before we confederate. . . . [1]

In the spring and early summer of 1776, Dickinson and the reconciliationists in Congress would not have disagreed with the need for confederation. Dickinson understood that it would take American arms to persuade the British that the colonies would not settle for the status quo. To make such an impression on a mighty empire, a coordination of American affairs was critical. As a lawyer, Dickinson would have recognized that the Congress, which was now managing a war effort, was not a strictly legal body. Its delegates had been chosen by various committees and conventions. A formal plan of confederation would give Congress legitimacy. Moreover, in the event that the British offered favorable terms for peace, perhaps the legislature of the confederation could easily be transformed into an assembly suggested by Joseph Galloway in 1775. Also, if independence was unavoidable, Dickinson and the conservatives wanted some say in the formation of the new constitution to control the democratic spirit taking hold of America.

John Dickinson's Draft

Dickinson's draft of the Articles was presented to Congress on July 12, 1776. The plan of government described the confederacy as the United States of America. In explaining the union, Dickinson's draft stated that this "League of Friendship" was formed for the security of the colonies against foreign attacks "made upon any or all of them, on Account of Religion, Sovereignty, Trade, or any other Pretence whatever."[2] (Awkwardly to our ears, Dickinson referred to the members of the proposed confederation as "colonies" rather than "states.") The third article of the draft dealt with the internal affairs of each colony and provided that laws, rights, and customs would be left to the colonial assemblies "in all matters that shall not interfere with the Articles of this Confederation."[3]

Articles IV and V restricted the colonial governments in the realm of foreign affairs. The draft prohibited the individual colonies from sending or receiving ambassadors or entering into treaties without the consent of the confederation government. Articles VI and VII set forth a privileges and immunities provision. It declared that if, for example, a citizen of North Carolina traveled to Georgia, the North Carolinian would enjoy the same rights as the Georgians possessed. The inhabitants of each colony would have the same rights of trade, navigation, and commerce in any other state.

Article VIII stated that each colony could set its own duties and imposts so long as these did not interfere with any treaty adopted by the Confederation. Articles IX–XIII dealt with military affairs and the allocation of expenses for the union. The colonies were prohibited from keeping standing armies in times of peace, but were required to keep a "well regulated and disciplined Militia."[4] When troops were raised to defend against a common enemy, each colony would appoint officers except that only Congress could appoint general officers. Absent exigent circumstances, no colony could engage in a war without the consent of the United States. All expenses for war, the common defense, or the general welfare would be paid out of a common treasury "which shall be supplied by the several Colonies in Proportion to the Number of Inhabitants of every Age, Sex and Quality, except Indians not paying Taxes."[5] A census would be conducted every three years to assure that the burdens were allocated properly among the colonies.

Dickinson's draft recognized that the various colonies might disagree with the union's valuation of losses or expenses one colony might incur for the whole. Thus, Article XII provided that each colony "shall abide by the Determinations of the United States" in these matters.[6] Articles XIV and XV appear to recognize the confederacy's control over Indian affairs and its power to establish state boundaries.

In accordance with the practice of the Continental Congress, each colony would have one vote in a unicameral legislature. The delegates to Congress would be appointed by the colonial legislatures on an annual basis. The draft mandated rotation in office by providing that delegates could serve only three years out of every six years in Congress. Each colony had the financial duty to support its own delegates. Article XVIII set forth a number of sole and exclusive powers belonging to the confederacy. For example, the confederacy could determine war and peace, coin money, settle colonial boundary disputes, establish admiralty courts, regulate Indian affairs, create a post office, borrow money, requisition supplies from the colonies, and raise military forces. Certain of these required the consent of nine colonial delegations rather than a mere majority.

Dickinson's Article XIX created a Council of State to serve as an executive body with a staff to assist Congress in the performance of its duties.

Points of Contention

Delegates had a variety of opinions about the provisions of Dickinson's draft. However, four main issues gripped the Congress: payment of common expenses, representation, western land holdings, and state power. The majority of the recorded debates focus on these questions.

In scrutinizing the funding of the confederation government, Samuel Chase of Maryland questioned the fairness of allocating expenses based on the number of all inhabitants. Chase suggested that the number of white inhabitants should be the standard. Observing that slaves were property, Chase made a crude analogy to livestock. He argued that while the Northern farmer invests his surplus profits in more cattle and horses, a Southern farmer invested his surplus in more laborers. The Dickinson provision, Chase claimed, had the effect of taxing the Southerner's investment and thus gave the Northern farmer an economic advantage.

John Adams challenged Chase's reasoning. He maintained that the number of laborers in a state, regardless of their status, was a true measure of wealth and the ability to contribute to the Confederation. "[T]hat the condition of the laboring poor in most countries, that of the fishermen particularly in the Northern states," Adams contended, "is as abject as that of slaves. It is the number of laborers which produce the surplus for taxation, and numbers therefore indiscriminately are a fair index of wealth."[7]

James Wilson of Pennsylvania agreed with Adams. If Chase's proposal was adopted, Wilson believed that the Southern states would reap a great benefit while the Northern states would bear a disproportionate tax burden. Wilson also complained that Chase's proposal would encourage the importation of slaves rather than discourage expansion of the institution. Benjamin Franklin of Pennsylvania agreed with Wilson. He asserted that slaves "weaken rather than strengthen the State, and there is therefore some difference between them and sheep; sheep will never make any insurrections."[8]

Benjamin Harrison of Virginia offered a compromise between the positions staked out by North and South. Harrison suggested that because a slave does not do as much work as a free laborer some middle ground should be reached. He suggested that for calculating expenses for the common treasury, two slaves should be counted as one free laborer.

After much debate, the Congress rejected the amendment offered by Chase. The vote, to no one's surprise, divided along sectional lines. The states voting against the amendment were New Hampshire, Massachusetts, Rhode Island, Connecticut, New York, New Jersey, and Pennsylvania. It was in their interest that slaves be counted as freemen for congressional revenue purposes. The states with large slaveholdings understood that they would have to pay less if expenses were allocated based on the number of white inhabitants. While some general denunciations of slavery were voiced, historian Merrill Jensen has observed that this part of the debate on the Articles "had little of the humanitarian about it. It was a matter of simple addition and subtraction."[9] Congress eventually abandoned Dickinson's proposal to count heads and instead divided expenses based on land values.

The issue of each state having one vote in Congress was also hotly contested. Similar to the issue of allocating expenses, a state's stance on this matter depended largely on the size of its population. Chase again waded into the debate and described representation as "the most likely to divide us of any one proposed in the draught under consideration."[10] The larger colonies demanded a vote based on their larger populations and the smaller colonies viewed an equal vote as the only way to protect their liberties. Chase urged a compromise voting scheme whereby each colony had one vote on matters of "life and liberty" but that on money issues "the voice of each colony should be proportioned to the number of it's [sic] inhabitants."[11] Roger Sherman of Connecticut also pleaded that middle ground be sought. He proposed that two votes be taken on issues concerning the confederacy: one by states and the other by population. Sherman's proposal was the only long-term solution, but would not be accepted until the Philadelphia Convention met in 1787.

Benjamin Franklin regretted that the First Continental Congress had agreed to vote by colonies. The only way the states should have an equal vote, Franklin argued, was for all states to pay an equal proportion of Confederation expenses. Franklin urged that voting should "in all cases [be] according to the number of taxables."[12]

John Witherspoon of New Jersey rejected any compromise on Dickinson's proposal for voting. Witherspoon viewed the separate states as distinct communities having an intrinsic worth that necessitated equality in Congress. "[I]f an equal vote be refused," he warned, "the smaller states will become vassals to the larger."[13] Because the Confederation's decisions would operate only on states as states, he continued, there was no reason to vote based on the number of individuals living in a particular state. Equal voting was equitable for a confederation and this proposed confederacy would last only "if it was founded on fair principles."[14]

John Adams supported Franklin's reasoning and came up with a business analogy. If A contributes 50 units, B contributes 500 units, and C contributes 1,000 units to a partnership, is it fair, Adams asked, that "they should equally dispose of the monies of the partnership?"[15] When voting on matters for the entire confederacy, Adams argued that the delegates "no longer retain our separate individuality, but become a single individual as to all questions submitted to the confederacy."[16]

James Wilson echoed Adams' comments. "As to those matters which are referred to Congress," Wilson contended, "we are not so many states; we are one large state."[17] Because states are comprised of people, Wilson rejected the argument that Congress would not act on individuals. As for the small states' fear that the large ones would govern them, Wilson said that the large states ought to equally fear the small states using their equal votes to control the confederacy.

Absent a compromise such as those suggested by Chase and Sherman, a confederacy could not be established unless the small states enjoyed some security. This security came in the form of equal voting. Although the large states vehemently protested equal voting, they decided that a confederation with states voting in this manner was preferred to no confederation at all. Hence, they acquiesced in the voting scheme offered in the Dickinson draft.

The third divisive issue was Dickinson's proposal to permit Congress to limit the bounds of those colonies claiming lands to the South Sea (the Pacific Ocean). In general, the states without vast western lands (Maryland, Pennsylvania, Delaware, New Jersey, and Rhode Island) favored such a power in Congress. They realized that states with larger holdings could defray war expenses by selling off lands. The landless states, however, would have no choice but to raise taxes to pay their share of costs incurred for the common defense. The landless states wanted Congress to control the western lands so Congress could, if it so chose, sell off the lands and use the money for the benefit of the union. Economy aside, the landless states had concerns that Virginia, already the most influential state in the union, would gain power because of her western lands. Speculators from the landless states also envied the ease with which Virginia land companies could stake out claims in areas west of the Alleghenies. The speculators believed that the Congress would be of more assistance to them than the Virginia legislature had been.

Chase, whose state had no western lands, supported locating such a power in Congress. He found it incredible that any state asserted a right to extend its borders across a continent. Harrison of Virginia responded that Virginia's large claims were based on its charter—just as Maryland's smaller boundaries were based on its charter. Harrison warned sternly that "Gentlemen shall not pare away the Colony of Virginia."[18]

Benjamin Huntington of Connecticut (a state with western claims) argued that even if the landless states could demonstrate that Virginia's claims and power posed a danger to her sister states, it does not follow that Congress can claim the right to limit a state's chartered bounds. All should unite, Huntington urged, "against mutilating charters."[19]

In the course of the debate on this issue, the delegates realized that Virginia likely would choose disunion over a confederation that stripped it of such a vast territory. To the dissatisfaction of the landless states, Dickinson's provision giving Congress the power to determine a state's boundaries was rejected. Maryland was especially unhappy about this decision and would continue to work to undo Virginia's claims.

The fourth major issue, concerning the power of the states and the locus of sovereignty, arose in February 1777 when Congress considered a report recommending that state officials detain suspected deserters from the army. An amendment to the report was offered that permitted Congress to delegate directly the power of apprehending suspected deserters to local officials without any action from the state governments. The amendment passed, but Thomas Burke of North Carolina rose and demanded that his dissent be entered in the journals of Congress. Burke was an Irish physician who received his training at Dublin University. His remarks show that he had spent some time contemplating the locus of power in the proposed Confederation.

Burke believed that the amendment set a precedent "to prostrate all the Laws and Constitutions of the states."[20] He believed that only a body close to the people should be trusted with coercion. The amendment, however, allowed the distant Congress to create a power within the sovereign states that was independent of the states and could act contrary to state authorities. This foreign power could "render Ineffectual all the Barriers Provided in the states for the Security of the Rights of the Citizens."[21] Burke then came to the central point of his arguments: "That the states alone had Power to act coercively against their Citizens, and therefore were the only Power competent to carry into execution any provision whether Continental or Municipal."[22] North Carolinians, Burke observed, were fighting a war brought on by unlawful exertions of British power. His state was fighting for the rights of self-government and would not allow Congress, or any other institution, to obtain the power to act coercively against the people.

During debates on Dickinson's draft, Burke found fault with the reservation of rights contained in Article III. Burke complained that this provision "expressed only a reservation of the power of regulating internal police, and consequently resigned every other power."[23] Burke doubted that this provision would be acceptable to the states because "it left it in the power of the future Congress or General Council to explain away every right belonging to the States and to make their own power as unlimited as they please."[24] Burke proposed an amendment "which held up the principle, that all sovereign power was in the States separately."[25] Except when the Articles specifically permitted Congress to act, state power would be supreme and controlled only by state constitutions. The Congress approved Burke's amendment. Eleven states voted in favor of the amendment, Virginia voted no, and New Hampshire was divided. Virginia typically is associated with the states' rights camp and her vote on Burke's amendment appears odd. However, we must remember that at this time Virginia still hoped to reverse the one-state-one-vote provision. Had Virginia been able to do so, it would have been very influential in the councils of the union. Thus, Virginia's delegates were not focused on limiting the power of the union.

Revisions to Dickinson's Draft

The final version of the Articles was submitted to the states for ratification in November 1777. The revised Articles retained much of Dickinson's draft, but with several significant changes. Thanks to Burke's amendment, the Articles unequivocally stated that "Each State retains its sovereignty, freedom and independence, and every power, jurisdiction, and right, which is not by this confederation expressly delegated to the United States, in Congress assembled."[26] Without this statement, Congress arguably had the authority to infringe on state law and prerogatives so long as Congress believed that such laws or prerogatives interfered with the confederation. With Burke's Article II, Congress would now have to point to a delegated power before acting. Congress could not simply cite interference with the Articles in general to support its action.

The privileges and immunities provision remained, but Congress restricted it to the "free inhabitants" of each state and made clear that it would not apply to "paupers, vagabonds, and fugitives from justice."[27] As in the Dickinson draft, each state was allotted one vote regardless of its size. The final version required that each state send two delegates to Congress, but no more than seven. The Articles, as in the original draft, mandated rotation in office and prohibited any person from serving "more than three years in any term of six years."[28] The completed Article V also made clear that freedom of speech and debate in Congress could "not be impeached or questioned in any court or place out of Congress."[29]

Congress saw the wisdom in keeping foreign affairs and matters of war under the authority of the confederacy. The Articles kept Dickinson's provisions prohibiting states from sending or receiving ambassadors. The delegates also thought the draft was correct in prohibiting states from entering into treaties without the consent of Congress. Similar to the Dickinson draft, the states were prohibited from laying imposts or duties that were contrary to treaties made by the Congress. The Articles further followed Dickinson's lead in prohibiting states from maintaining standing armies or engaging in war without the consent of Congress.

Congress departed from the draft in allocating expenses among the states. Rather than using population, the final draft decreed that expenses would be paid "by the several states in proportion to the value of all land within each state"[30] This provision was a difficult sell to the New England delegates because they believed that New England land was more valuable than Southern land. But considering the acrimony stirred over whether slaves should be counted as members of the taxable population, the use of property values was a reasonable resolution. Article VIII left it to the discretion of the state legislatures on how to raise the monies requested by Congress.

Dickinson's list of enumerated powers largely remained intact with the exception of the broad powers over the western lands. As in the earlier draft, the document required the approval of nine states before Congress could exercise critical powers such as war, borrowing or treaty-making. Article IX did establish Congress as "the last resort on appeal in all disputes and differences now subsisting or that hereafter may arise between two or more states concerning boundary, jurisdiction, or in any cause whatever."[31] Article IX also provided that in judging these disputes "no state shall be deprived of territory for the benefit of the United States."[32]

In the event that Congress recessed, it had the authority to appoint a "Committee of the States" consisting of one delegate from each state.[33] Congress could appoint a president to preside over the Committee and limited him to no more than a one-year term in any three-year period. In essence, the Committee would oversee the government while the other delegates were home attending to personal affairs. This body differed from Dickinson's Council of State inasmuch as it was not a permanent body with a staff assisting Congress. The Committee had a much more limited role.[34]

Article XII announced that the debts contracted by the Congress prior to ratification of the Articles would be "deemed and considered as a charge against the United States."[35]

Article XIII required that each state abide by Congress's determinations "on all questions which by this Confederation are submitted" to the union.[36] The Articles were declared perpetual and could not be amended absent the vote of each state legislature.

During the course of 1778–79, all the states but Maryland ratified the Articles. Maryland, still stewing over Virginia's western claims, held out until 1781. Maryland's recalcitrance, according to historian Robert W. Hoffert, "did not prevent the de facto implementation of the Articles' constitutional order. Between 1776 and 1781 the Continental Congress and the thirteen states conducted the American military, economic, and political affairs by the standard and in the forms specified by the Articles."[37]

In examining the completed document, we can discern two overriding purposes: (1) provision for common goals, and (2) securing the right of self-government in the individual states.[38] The obvious common goal was defeat of British military forces. When Congress circulated the Articles to the states for ratification, Washington was preparing to retire to Valley Forge for the winter. The French had yet to agree to provide military support to the Americans. The outcome of the war was much in doubt.

The situation was precarious, but the Articles provided Congress with the necessary tools to defeat a superpower. Under the Articles, Congress raised an army, borrowed money, contracted foreign alliances, and received funding from the several states. While the processes were not always smooth and the army continually ran short of supplies, in the end the system worked. The government operating under the Articles accomplished the great objective of independence.

Similarly, the Articles succeeded in protecting state sovereignty. The people of the states did not want to trade one officious central government in London for another situated in Philadelphia. Thomas Burke succeeded in making this clear with his proposal that led to Article II. The language in Dickinson's draft left too much debate on whether a state law or regulation interfered with the government of the Confederation. A delegate seeking to improperly augment the power of the union, under the Dickinson draft, could have used the vague language of the original Article III to usurp the power of the states. Burke's changes provided the states with protection.

Article II aside, the final document provided numerous institutional safeguards to limit Congress's power. Annual elections kept the delegates close to the state legislatures. If a delegate acted contrary to the interest of his state or ignored instructions from his state, no more than 12 months would pass before the legislators had an opportunity to terminate his appointment. Rotation in office prohibited delegates from serving more than three years in any six-year period. This forced the delegates to leave the national councils and to return home to live among the people. Just like his neighbors, a former delegate would feel the effects of Congress's enactments and could get a sense of the opinions of the people.

Absent the concurrence of nine states, Congress could not

engage in a war, nor grant letters of marque or reprisal in time of peace, nor enter into any treaties or alliances, nor coin money, nor regulate the value thereof, nor ascertain the sums and expenses necessary for the defense and welfare of the United States, or any of them, nor emit bills, nor borrow money on the credit of the united States, nor appropriate money, nor agree upon the number of vessels of war, to be built or purchased, or the number of land or sea forces to be raised, nor appoint a commander in chief of the army or navy. . . .[39]

With this provision, a super-majority was required to exercise significant powers. This limited the likelihood that Congress cavalierly would undertake action to the long-term detriment of the states.

If Congress sought to expand its powers through an amendment to the Articles, the change had to be approved by the legislatures of every state. All parties to the contract would have to be consulted and agree before additional powers were delegated.

Today, most Americans view the Articles of Confederation as a great failure. If we reevaluate this perception in light of the goals of the Confederation, we see that this perception is erroneousness. The government of the Confederation accomplished both of its main objectives: the defeat of Britain and the safeguarding of state self-government. Americans should take pride in the Articles of Confederation. In the words of historian Samuel Elliot Morrison, the Articles "were the best instrument of federal government adopted anywhere up to that time."[40]

4

Toward Philadelphia

ALTHOUGH THE UNITED STATES achieved the two major goals of the Articles of Confederation, the system of government was far from perfect. During the war years and beyond, Americans observed deficiencies in their first constitution, and other areas ripe for refinement.[1] Amendment of the Articles required the approval of all thirteen states. Because reformers failed to garner unanimous support for various amendments, serious problems could not be addressed. Wholesale change eventually would come with the Constitution of 1787 drafted by the Philadelphia Convention.

Defects Emerge

Both during the war and thereafter, the most glaring problem was funding for the union. Scholars estimate that by the end of 1780, "costs of the war had outstripped receipts from the states by nearly forty to one."[2] In March 1780, James Madison complained to Thomas Jefferson that funding concerns were endangering the revolution and he provided a list of problems: "Our army threatened with an immediate alternative of disbanding to living on free quarter; the public Treasury empty; public credit exhausted. . . ."[3] In 1781, delegate James M. Varnum lamented that the Articles "give only the Power of apportioning. Compliance in the respective states is generally slow, and in many Instances does not take Place."[4]

In light of these concerns, on February 3, 1781, Congress requested that the states give it the power to levy a five percent duty on imports.[5] The money received would be used to finance the war and retire debts. At first, it appeared that the states would adopt this proposal and give Congress an independent source of revenue. By the middle of 1782, all states except Rhode Island had approved the amendment. Rhode Island did not agree to the amendment because it wanted the money from duties for its own use. Rhode Island also claimed that it bought more foreign goods than other states and thus it would pay a disproportionate share to Congress. Finally, Rhode Island feared that such a power in Congress would undermine state sovereignty and alter the fabric of the union. Congress sent a delegation to Rhode Island in an attempt to persuade it to join the other states on this matter, but while the delegation was in route, Virginia withdrew her acceptance of the impost. With this news, the delegation turned back and admitted that the impost was dead.

In 1783, Congress again tried to persuade all thirteen states to grant it the power to levy an impost. Congress urged that such a power was "indispensably necessary to the restoration of public credit."[6] Congress proposed that the monies received would be used only to retire the national debt and that the power to levy an impost would lapse in 25 years. To address concerns about armies of congressional tax collectors swarming the states, Congress provided that the collectors of the duties would be appointed by the states but would be removable from office by Congress. This time it was not Rhode Island that scuttled the impost, but instead New York. The state received a substantial amount of revenue from duties placed on imports. New York did not want to compete with the confederacy for these funds and thus refused to augment Congress's powers.

In addition to the funding concerns, other events drew attention to the shortcomings of the Articles. First, the "defeated" British troops refused to leave key fortifications because of treaty violations. Article IV of the Treaty of Paris provided that "Creditors on either Side shall meet with no lawful Impediment to the Recovery of the full Value in Sterling Money of all bona fide Debts heretofore contracted."[7] British merchants, however, faced state legislation that effectively nullified the debts owed and they quickly complained to parliamentary authorities. Unfortunately, an embarrassed Congress was unable to persuade the states to repeal the offending debt-relief legislation.

Second, independence did not bring the prosperity expected by the commercial states of the union. Merchants envisioned new markets opening up and thus an increase in wealth. The merchants did not foresee natural trading partners such as Britain and France imposing discriminatory restrictions on American trade. The loss alone of the British West Indian trade was a major blow to the economy. With independence, American merchant vessels also lost the protection of the Royal Navy and this effectively cut off trade with the Mediterranean countries because the Barbary pirates were at liberty to plunder American ships. Hard money was scarce after the war when British merchants, recognizing the pent up demand for manufactured goods, dumped their goods on American ports. American specie was siphoned off but did not return because of Britain's protectionist measures. Without a power to regulate foreign commerce, Congress could not respond with its own restrictions to force a resolution. In light of the abysmal shape of public finance, Congress could not afford to send warships to protect American merchant vessels in the Mediterranean.

Third, in 1784, Spain had closed the Mississippi River to American commerce. Citizens in the western part of the United States depended on the river to bring their goods to market. Spain's actions threatened the livelihoods of thousands and also discouraged American expansion into the wilderness. When John Jay, the Confederation's secretary for foreign affairs, was negotiating with Spain and asked Congress for permission to give up navigation rights in the Mississippi for a period of years, this caused a great sectional rift. Southern delegates believed that Northerners were bent on limiting the growth of the South in exchange for commercial concessions from Spain. The division over this issue caused many Americans to contemplate the efficacy of dividing up the states into two or three separate federations.

Finally, when debt-ridden Massachusetts farmers revolted and closed courthouses throughout the state to prevent confiscation of their property, Congress was unable to raise money or forces to assist Massachusetts in restoring order. After receiving loans from private citizens, the state's government was able to send soldiers into the field. The rival armies met at Springfield, where the state government stored large quantities of armaments and provisions. When state forces fired their artillery into the men led by Daniel Shays, Shays' forces panicked and fled. Hence, the rebellion was quelled quickly, but this episode persuaded many that the union needed a more vigorous national government.

In March 1785, delegates of Maryland and Virginia met at George Washington's home at Mount Vernon, Virginia, to settle a dispute over the navigation of the Potomac River and conflicting commercial regulations. This conference raised broader questions about the regulation of trade between the American states. Because of the successful resolution of issues reached at Mount Vernon, Maryland proposed holding a broader convention that included Pennsylvania and Delaware. Virginia approved of Maryland's suggestion, but decided that the meeting should be even more wide ranging. The Virginia legislature then invited all thirteen states to send delegates to Annapolis, Maryland, to consider commercial matters.

The Annapolis Convention met in September 1786, but only five states sent delegates. The delegates unanimously elected John Dickinson as chairman. Disappointed with the turnout, the Annapolis Convention prepared a report in which it urged the others states to consider attending another convention that would consider much more than commerce. This Convention, scheduled to meet in Philadelphia in May 1787, should "devise such further provisions as shall appear to them necessary to render the constitution of the Foederal Government adequate to the exigencies of the Union."[8] This report was sent to the Congress and the states. Congress sat on the report for four months and finally agreed to the efficacy of a meeting "for the sole and express purpose of revising the Articles of Confederation."[9]

The Grand Convention

Delegates from the states began arriving in Philadelphia in early May 1787 and reached a quorum on May 25. With the exception of Rhode Island, all states sent delegates. The delegates unanimously elected George Washington president of the Convention and then adopted certain rules for debate. The delegates decided that voting would be by state and that each state would have one vote. To conduct business, seven states had to be present.

Because his state had initiated the calling of the convention, Virginia's Edmund Randolph rose first to speak. He presented fifteen resolutions for the Convention to consider. These resolutions, known as the Virginia Plan, formed the basis of debate. The Virginia Plan featured a national legislature with two branches. Rather than each state having equal power in the legislature, the Virginia Plan proposed that representation be linked to population or the contributions made to defray expenses of the union. Rather than an enumeration of powers, the Virginia Plan proposed that the national legislature have the power "to legislate in all cases to which the separate states are incompetent, or in which the harmony of the United States may be interrupted by the exercise of individual legislation."[10] The Virginia Plan called for a national veto power over all state legislation and proposed creation of a national executive and judiciary.

Considering that the American Revolution was fought, in large part, to lodge self-government in the individual states rather than the distant British central government, Randolph's proposal was quite radical. Opponents of the Virginia Plan argued that it was inconsistent with Congress's command to simply revise the Articles of Confederation and that it would destroy state sovereignty. To combat what some perceived as a swing in the pendulum too far to the nationalist and/or large-state side, on June 15, 1787, New Jersey's William Paterson introduced an alternative plan.

The central principles of Paterson's "New Jersey Plan" included expanding the powers of Congress to tax, regulate commerce, and compel disobedient states to comply with Congress's enactments. To ensure uniformity of national laws, the New Jersey Plan called for the creation of a national judiciary to hear appeals from state courts on federal matters. Unlike the Virginia Plan, the New Jersey Plan sought to maintain a unicameral national legislature with each state having one vote. Paterson also omitted any proposal for a veto of state legislation, and instead authorized the executive for the union to "call forth the power of the Confederated States, or so much thereof as may be necessary to enforce and compel an obedience" to the acts of Congress or treaties.[11] Supporters of Paterson's resolves were a mix of men fearful of the Virginia Plan's centralizing tendencies and also small-state men who were concerned about large-state domination of the new government. This latter group did not really oppose an energetic national government; they simply wanted their states to have a meaningful voice in national councils.

After discussion of the merits of each plan, the delegates chose to continue using the Virginia Plan as the basis for discussion. Only New Jersey, New York, and Delaware voted in favor of the using the New Jersey Plan as the framework of debate. Paterson and his colleagues had offered their alternative only after the Virginia Plan had gained much momentum. Hence, Paterson's efforts to maintain a confederation were offered too late to carry the day. The delegates already had decided that a purely federative system was insufficient to meet the exigencies of the union.

The Constitution

The Constitution crafted by the Philadelphia Convention sets forth the legislative power, which is vested in Congress, in Article I. Unlike the Confederation, the national legislature is a bicameral body with a House of Representatives and a Senate. In what is known as the Great Compromise (or sometimes the Connecticut Compromise) between the demands of large and small states, representation in the House is based on population whereas representation in the Senate reflects the equality of the states. The small states were prepared to walk out of the Convention if the large states did not agree to equal representation in at least one chamber of the national legislature. James Madison and James Wilson were willing to push the matter and bid the small state delegates adieu. However, a spirit of compromise prevailed and this issue of representation, which had plagued Americans since the Fist Continental Congress, was resolved.

The issue of slavery also required a compromise connected to that of representation. Delegates from the Northern states argued that slaves should not be counted for determining representation in the House because slaves could not participate in the political affairs of the various states. Counting slaves, they contended, would give the South an unfair advantage. Southern delegates countered that because slaves might be subject to taxation as property or by a head tax, slaves should be counted for purposes of representation. The Southerners also wanted additional representatives so they would have enough numbers to defend the institution of slavery on which their economies depended. The two sides compromised by agreeing to count each slave as three-fifths of a person. Because of the widespread objections to giving slavery constitutional standing, slaves are referred to as "other Persons" in the Constitution.

The Philadelphia Convention rejected the proposal to grant Congress a general power of legislation and instead drafted a specific list of powers. Many of the delegates feared that a general power would be too vague and subject to abuse. The Constitution's enumeration of powers contains many of the powers that appeared in the Articles of Confederation, such as borrowing money, fixing the standards of weights and measures, establishing post offices and post roads, and declaring war. The Constitution includes additional powers, such as the authority to lay and collect taxes, duties, imposts, and excises; to pass naturalization and bankruptcy laws; and to regulate commerce with foreign nations and among the states. Included in the enumeration is the Necessary and Proper Clause which permits Congress to pass all laws required for the execution of the enumerated powers.

The power to regulate commerce was much debated in the Philadelphia Convention because the Southern states, which primarily exported agricultural commodities, feared oppressive taxation on exports and the prohibition of the slave trade. Hence, Southern states demanded a two-thirds vote in Congress before a commercial regulation could become law. Northerners and Southerners reached a compromise by agreeing on clauses prohibiting Congress from interfering with the slave trade until 1808 and prohibiting Congress from taxing exports. With this protection, Southerners dropped their opposition to a commerce power that was based on a majority vote.

Article II of the Constitution places the executive power in one person serving a four-year term and subject to reelection. The Confederation had no executive body separate from Congress—Congress enacted measures and attempted to execute them as best as it could. At the Philadelphia Convention, two competing visions of the executive were offered. The more conservative delegates suggested one person with lifetime appointment or a lengthy term. Other delegates believed that this model too closely resembled the British monarchy and was reminiscent of the oppressive royal governors who ruled prior to the Revolution. As an alternative, they proposed a plural executive with a short term. The end result was a compromise between the two positions.

The delegates spent much time determining the mode of electing a president. They considered numerous methods, including election by the people, the states' chief executives, Congress, or the state legislatures. Ultimately, the Framers of the Constitution chose an electoral college in which electors are appointed for the specific purpose of choosing a president. The method of appointing electors was left up to the state legislatures. The executive's key powers under the Constitution include serving as commander in chief of the armed forces, granting pardons and reprieves, and nominating ambassadors, judges, and other officials with the advice and consent of the Senate.

Article III vests the judicial power of the United States in a Supreme Court and inferior courts created by Congress. Under the Confederation, Congress could only create courts to adjudicate maritime matters. At Philadelphia, the delegates opted for a more expansive court system. Some of the delegates, however, believed that a federal system of trial courts would be too expensive and would encroach upon the powers of the states. They contemplated the state courts serving as the trial courts of the union with appellate rights to the Supreme Court to ensure uniformity. Others believed that a federal court system was a necessity because state judges were too dependent on state executives and/or legislatures. The compromise reached gave Congress the discretion to establish lower federal courts (which it later did).

The federal judicial power extends to certain enumerated categories, the broadest of which is all cases arising under the Constitution, federal laws, or treaties made by the United States. To permit federal judges to exercise independent judgment, the Constitution provides that they serve during "good behavior" and prohibits reductions in their compensation.

Article IV is substantially similar[12] to the fourth article of the Confederation. States are required to give full faith and credit to public acts and court proceedings of other states. So, for example, if a creditor receives a judgment against a debtor in South Carolina and seeks to execute the judgment against property of the debtor in Georgia, the courts of Georgia must recognize the judgment. Article IV contains a privileges and immunities clause and permits Congress to admit new states to the union.

Article V sets forth the procedure for amending the Constitution. At base, two-thirds of the state legislatures may ask Congress to summon a constitutional convention, or two-thirds of both houses of Congress may propose amendments to the states. Under the latter method, three-fourths of the states have to agree to the amendment before it becomes part of the Constitution.

The penultimate section of the Constitution, similar to the Articles, provides that preexisting debts of the union are assumed by the new government. Laws and treaties made by the United States are declared to be "the supreme law of the land" and thus binding on state judges.[13]

Finally, Article VII declares that, to take effect, the Constitution had to be ratified by the representatives of the people of at least nine states meeting in separate state conventions. The Framers wanted the Constitution to have the widest possible sanction that could come only from the people of each state. Separate state conventions also were necessary because the people would be altering their state constitutions by transferring certain powers to the new federal government. Therefore, only the people of each state had the authority to both accept the federal constitution and implicitly alter or amend their state constitution.

In urging that the state conventions ratify the proposed Constitution, the proponents of the Constitution claimed to have created a system that mixed elements of a confederation in which each state retains full sovereignty and of a national government in which all power over the whole rests with the central government.[14] In the words of James Madison, the federal and state governments "are in fact but different agents and trustees of the people, instituted with different powers, and designated for different purposes."[15] The Constitution's friends contended that while additional powers were delegated to the government of the union, the critical change was an invigoration of powers that had been assigned to the Confederation in the Articles.[16] The new government's powers were "few and defined" and would "be exercised principally on external objects, as war, peace, negotiation, and foreign commerce."[17] Outside of these matters, the states remained free to govern their affairs as before. In the words of Peletiah Webster, "the new Constitution leaves all Thirteen States, complete republics, as it found them . . . [and] leaves all the dignities, authorities, and internal police of each State in free, full, and perfect condition; unless when national purposes make the control of them by the federal head, or authority, necessary to the general benefit."[18] As for any danger of the general government encroaching upon the states, the Framers scoffed at this and instead argued that the threat of encroachment would come from the states themselves.[19] James Wilson expressed concern in the Pennsylvania ratifying convention that "the general government will not be able to maintain the powers given it against the encroachments and combined attack of the state governments" because of the substantial residual powers of the states.[20]

Of course, a group known to history as the "Anti-Federalists" challenged the claims that the new Constitution was a mild antidote for the ills of the

Confederation. The Federal Farmer (probably Melancton Smith) complained that "we see all important powers collecting in one centre, where a few men will possess them almost at discretion."[21] The Anti-Federalists saw dangers to both the states and the people in the Convention's new plan of government. "An Old Whig" (his true identity remains unknown) speculated that the Constitution would "totally annihilate the separate governments of the several states" and leave the people at the mercy of the national government.[22] Many of the checks on the union's power found in the Articles, they observed, had been abandoned. Other purported restrictions on the general government's powers, to the Anti-Federalists, were cosmetic and thus unable to truly chain the new parliament for the union. They feared a consolidation of power in the councils of the union with the states and people struggling to maintain their dignity.

More than 225 years have passed since the Federalists and Anti-Federalists battled in newspapers, pamphlets, and the state ratifying conventions. With multiple court cases, executive actions, and congressional statutes interpreting and implementing the Constitution of 1787, we have a sufficient body of work to determine the soundness of the positions taken by both sides. Were the Anti-Federalists truly myopic "men of little faith" who hopelessly clung to the old order, or did they see with prescient eyes? Were the Federalists truly political visionaries, or did they simply recast elements of the British centralized state when making the Constitution of 1787?

In the following pages, we will take a closer look at many of the provisions of the Constitution, the arguments made by Federalists and Anti-Federalists, and examine how those provisions actually were used by the national government. We also will consider whether amendments to the Articles, rather than a new constitution, could have served the union much better.

5

The Problem of Scale

IS THERE AN upper limit to the size of territory ruled by a representative government, beyond which that government will no longer be directly representative of individuals? Was Montesquieu correct that only in a small territory can republican government subsist?[1] These were fundamental questions and were answered quite differently by the Federalists and Anti-Federalists. In fact, this issue of scale was the threshold issue of ratification. If the proposed Constitution failed this first enquiry, then there was no reason to debate its specific provisions.

Before delving into the various arguments, we should consider what the participants in the debate meant when they discussed "a republic." The celebrated Montesquieu defined republican government as "that in which the body or only a part of the people is possessed of the supreme power."[2] With this basic definition most Americans would have agreed. However, Montesquieu continued on to argue that a republic could be democratic (government by the people) or aristocratic (government by a few such as a great family). With this further characterization, most of the Framers and ratifiers of the Constitution would have disagreed.

Learned in the classics, the men of 1787 were in accord with Aristotle that rule by a few was an aristocracy and aristocracy in its deviant form was an oligarchy.

Aristotle in his works did not speak of a "republic" inasmuch as this word is derived from Latin and thus was unknown to him. He did examine a democratic polity in which the people are sovereign. Aristotle argued that although the people individually might lack specialized knowledge possessed by a few great men, the mass of the people together has more wisdom than the few specialists. "[A]s a feast to which all the guests contribute is better than a banquet furnished by a single man," Aristotle maintained, "so a multitude is a better judge of many things than any individual."[3] The deliberative body in a democracy, according to Aristotle, should be elected by the people or by the casting of lots. Such methods were in accordance with a fundamental "principle of liberty" where all citizens should "rule and be ruled in turn."[4] Democracies should embrace rotation in office and "no one should hold the same office twice."[5] The polity in view for Aristotle was small in scale along the lines of the Greek city-states with which he was most familiar.

John Adams, in his *A Defence of the Constitutions*, held that a republic is "founded on the natural authority of the people alone" and that "the property of the people should be represented in the legislature, and decide the rule of justice."[6] In *Federalist* No. 39, James Madison bestowed the republican moniker on a government "which derives all its powers directly or indirectly from the great body of the people; and is administered by persons holding offices during pleasure, for a limited period, or during good behavior."[7] Very similar to Madison, Patrick Henry, who opposed ratification, defined republican government as "[t]he delegation of power to an adequate number of representatives; and an unimpeded reversion of it back to the people at short periods."[8] Henry specified further that "[t]he governing persons are the servants of the people."[9] Thomas Jefferson averred that "action by the citizens in person, in affairs within their reach and competence, and in all others by representatives, chosen immediately, & removable by themselves, constitutes the essence of a republic; that all governments are more or less republican in proportion as this principle enters more or less into their composition."[10] Jefferson also described "the mother principle" of republican government as the government's embodiment of the will of the people and the execution of that will.[11]

The definitions of Adams, Madison, Henry, and Jefferson, although different, have two elements in common. The first is popular sovereignty. Ultimate power resides in the people. They collectively have the power to erect a government, alter it, and abolish it. Officers of government exercise delegated powers—they are the agents and the people are the principals. Second, that the will of the people be done. This occurs when the people gather in townships and exercise direct democracy. It also occurs when the people choose representatives and these representatives vote the sense of their constituents.

A Small Structure

Most Anti-Federalists agreed that popular sovereignty and rule of the majority were the two pillars of republican government. However, they were adamant that these pillars could only support a small structure. "[I]t is the opinion of the most celebrated writers on government," wrote the minority of delegates to the Pennsylvania convention, "and confirmed by uniform experience, that a very extensive territory cannot be governed on the principles of freedom, otherwise than by a confederation of republics, possessing all the powers of internal government; but united in the management of their general, and foreign concerns."[12] An "Old Whig" warned his readers that no "Republic [of so] great magnitude, ever [did], or ever can exist."[13] Turning to antiquity, the Old Whig observed that only "a few years elapsed, from the time in which ancient Rome extended her dominions beyond the bounds of Italy, until the downfall of her Republic."[14] "Cato" (probably George Clinton of New York), in arguing against the Constitution, pointed to the vast territory of the United States "together with the variety of its climates, productions, and commerce, the difference of extent, and number of inhabitants in all; the dissimilitude of interests, morals, and policies."[15] These factors and considerations persuaded him that a large republic could never form a more perfect union. At the Virginia ratifying convention, George Mason predicted that only a monarchial or despotic government could govern such an extensive country with diverse peoples and conditions. Mason believed in union, but a confederative union similar to that of the Articles.[16]

In appealing to "the most celebrated writers," the Anti-Federalists certainly had Montesquieu in mind. "It is natural to a republic," wrote Montesquieu, "to have only a small territory; otherwise it cannot long subsist."[17] He believed that in a small republic "the interest of the public is easier perceived, better understood, and more within the reach of every citizen."[18] In surveying the longevity of Sparta, Montesquieu observed that Sparta had kept its territory small and thus promoted its liberty and glory. Montesquieu recognized that small republics faced dangers from larger neighbors, but rather than growing large to compete with aggressive rivals Montesquieu advised that small republics should confederate. "This form of government," Montesquieu explained, "is a convention by which several small states agree to become members of a larger one which they intend to form. It is a kind of assemblage of societies, that constitute a new one, capable of increasing by means of new associations, till they arrive at such a degree of power, as to be able to provide for the security of the whole united body."[19] By confederating, ancient Greece had prospered; Holland and the Swiss enjoyed peace and prosperity as well.

Johannes Althusius, writing in the early 1600s, had similar concerns about size. Writing from a Reformed Protestant perspective, Althusius advocated federal republicanism rather than centralization of power in large states. He urged small states to enter into a covenant wherein the federation would handle common matters such as military defense. The smaller states and their individual units (down to the family) would govern themselves. In offering his thoughts on a republic or commonwealth, Althusius proclaimed "that a commonwealth of medium size is best and steadfast." In determining what is medium, Althusius makes reference to Rome and argues that when the Roman republic "was of medium size, it was free from many corruptions. When it grew greater in size, however, with greater might and a larger population . . . it abounded with corruptions so much that it was thrown into great calamities."[20] Althusius also praised Venice and Sparta as examples of medium-sized republics.

Representation

The issue of scale was tightly bound to the Anti-Federalist conception of representation. The Constitution's Article I, section 2, provides that "The number of representatives shall not exceed one for every thirty thousand" inhabitants. In the Virginia ratifying convention, George Mason objected to this provision: "To make representation real and actual, the number of representatives ought to be adequate; they ought to mix with the people, think as they think, feel as they feel,—ought to be perfectly amenable to them, and thoroughly acquainted with their interest and condition."[21] Similarly, "Brutus" (probably Robert Yates) observed that because the people must assent to the laws by which they are governed, their representatives must be "such[] as to possess, be disposed, and consequently be qualified to declare the sentiments of the people."[22] If the representatives lack this connection with the people, Brutus continued, "the people do not govern, but the sovereignty is in a few."[23] Because of this need for representatives to know and reflect their constituents, the Anti-Federalists believed this could best be accomplished in local assemblies. These were the true bodies, remarked the Federal Farmer (probably Melancton Smith of New York), where "the people can be substantially assembled or represented."[24]

The simple fact of the people voting, the candidates campaigning, and the winner sharing legal citizenship with his constituents did not amount to true representation. In the Anti-Federalist view, the representative should be someone who is one of the people. He should worship among his constituents, engage in commerce with them, and socialize with them. He should have similar views and inclinations as his constituents that come from a common upbringing and way of life. Virginia had a population of approximately 747,550 and was allotted ten representatives in the first Congress. This meant that each representative represented 74,755 souls. The Anti-Federalists saw no way that a representative from such a large body of people could have any real connection with them. The larger and more diverse body of the people, the more difficult it would be for the representative to share the mind of the people. "[I]t is not but impossible for forty, or thirty thousand people in this country," wrote the Federal Farmer, "one time in ten to find a man who can possess similar feelings, views, and interests with themselves."[25]

This idea of identification with the people also prompted the Anti-Federalists to support annual elections and term limits for representatives. "[B]i-ennial elections for representatives," Cato averred, "are a departure from the safe democractical principles of annual ones."[26] "Centinel" (probably Samuel Bryan) concurred and opined that two-year terms are "too long to preserve a due dependence and accountability to their constituents."[27] But even annual elections, many Anti-Federalists feared, might not ensure that the representatives keep their eyes fixed upon the people. A collegiality can develop among the office holders whereby they begin to see themselves as better or different from the people. Thus, mandatory rotation in office would, according to the Federal Farmer, "increase the numbers of those who make the laws and return to their constituents; and thereby spread information, and preserve a spirit of activity and investigation among the people."[28]

Connected with the issue of adequate representation is the attachment of the people to the government. If the people do not identify with and have confidence in their representatives, it would be difficult to secure a voluntary obedience to the government's laws. "The confidence which the people have in their rulers," Brutus explained, "in a free republic, arises from their knowing them, from their being responsible to them for their conduct, and of the power they have of displacing them. . . ."[29] If the people lack this affinity for their rulers, then force is necessary to secure obedience. The government will have to establish "an armed force to execute the laws at the point of a bayonet."[30] The Pennsylvania minority in the ratifying convention ("Pennsylvania minority") echoed Brutus's sentiments. Inasmuch as the Congress "will not possess the confidence of the people" and thus Congress cannot voluntarily "induce them to support" the government's measures, Congress will resort to arms "to compel obedience to good laws" or illiberal ones.[31] The Pennsylvania minority opined that the Federalists' realization of this fact resulted in delegating to Congress the power to call out the militia to execute the laws of the union.

Factions and *The Federalist*

The classic Federalist response to the scale arguments raised by the Anti-Federalists is Madison's *Federalist* No. 10. Madison rejected the idea that a proper representative must mirror his constituents. Instead, he focused on the dangers of faction in popular government and how representation in a large country can quell factional machinations. Madison defined faction as "a number of citizens, whether amounting to a majority or minority of the whole, who are united and actuated by some common impulse of passion, or of interest, adverse to the rights of other citizens, or to the permanent and aggregate interests of the community."[32] In highlighting the danger of faction, Madison called to mind pernicious quarrels in the states such as those between debtors and creditors. Debtors clamored for paper money, which would lead to inflation. By paying a creditor with inflated currency, the debtor essentially reduced the burden of the debt. Fiat money legislation was recognized by numerous Americans as emblematic of the injustice that pervaded many state assemblies.

After defining faction and establishing that the mischief of factions is inimical to ordered liberty, Madison moved to the remedy. Madison conceded that no republican government could remove the cause of faction. There would always be haves and have-nots demanding special treatment. At the Philadelphia Convention, Madison had proclaimed that "[a]ll civilized Societies would be divided into different Sects, Factions, & interests, as they happen to consist of rich & poor, debtors & creditors, the landed, the manufacturing, the commercial interests."[33] Thus, Madison concentrated on lessening the effects of faction. If a faction garners less than a majority, Madison observed that "relief is supplied by the republican principle, which enables the majority to defeat the sinister views by regular vote."[34] But if the majority of the people seek to strip the minority of some fundamental right, then the franchise by itself is insufficient protection.

Madison believed that a republican government on a large scale would be "most favorable to the election of proper guardians of the public weal."[35] A large republic, Madison argued, will "refine and enlarge the public views, by passing them through the medium of a chosen body of citizens, whose wisdom may best discern the true interest of their country."[36] When representatives are chosen in large districts, "it will be more difficult for unworthy candidates to practice with success the vicious arts by which [local] elections are too often carried."[37] Representation on a small scale, Madison averred, does reflect the people's will (whether that will be liberal or illiberal). A larger republic will tend to promote the more intelligent and reflective leaders to office who will resist the intemperate demands of the mob—even a mob made up on the majority of the citizens.

Not only does a large republic elevate better men to office who will resist the demands of the mob, but it makes it more difficult for factions to form. "Extend the sphere, and you take a greater variety of parties and interests; you make it less probable that a majority of the whole will have a common motive to invade the rights of other citizens; or if such a common motive exists, it will be more difficult for all who feel it to discover their own strength, and to act in unison with each other."[38] In other words, a diversity of interests makes it more difficult for factious citizens to find commonality with others in promoting a nefarious agenda.

While Madison's arguments might have sounded tenable to his readers in 1787, experience causes us to question the soundness of the tenth *Federalist*. Looking at the current state of the union, one can easily doubt whether large congressional districts (approximately 700,000 persons per representative) yield a legislature of whiz-kids. The country's debt crisis is a prime example. At this writing, America has a national debt of over $18 trillion. Opinion polls indicate that the debt is typically among the top three issues most troublesome to Americans. The best and brightest elected in this continental republic, however, are unable to balance the budget and pay down the debts of the union. This is not some complicated question of astrophysics; it is instead an issue with which millions of ordinary Americans grapple when they reduce expenses (or get a second job) to keep the checkbook in the black and work toward paying off mortgages and student loans. Establishment of public credit was one of the driving forces in forming the Constitution of 1787. Today, despite vast resources, our credit is a disaster.

Critics might counter that Congress knows how to balance the budget; the fault is with the people who demand that the government provide them with health care, old-age benefits, and a host of other entitlements. It certainly is true that many Americans cling to the nanny state even as we push on to national bankruptcy. But *Federalist* No. 10 promised a crop of leaders who would not pander to the passions of the multitude and instead would seek "the true interest of their country." An $18 trillion debt, with each citizen's share approaching $60,000, cannot be in our interests. The embarrassment that is the federal budget should dispel the myth that a large republic yields representatives who care more about the public good than catering to various factions.

What about Madison's assertion that the diversity of a large republic will make it more difficult for factions to form? Since the beginning of the Republic, groups of people with similar interests have been reaching across state lines and working with fellow travelers to implement an agenda benefiting themselves. In the 1790s, Americans divided into rival camps over the French Revolution. The Jeffersonian Republicans sought to build up the ties of commerce with France and to support the establishment of a new French republic. They viewed the French Revolution as a continuation of the American Revolution and hoped that American political principles would spread throughout Europe. The Hamiltonians, on the other hand, sought to steer commerce back toward Great Britain and desired to withdraw all American support for the French. The Hamiltonians saw the French Revolution as a threat to order and good government. They believed that the worst excesses of the French Jacobins, such as the Terror, would be mimicked by the Jeffersonians in America. The rivalry between the two parties caused much strife that promised a constitutional crisis that was averted by the election of 1800 when the people soundly rejected Hamilton's Federalist Party.

Another example of factionalism is the controversy over the protective tariff. This issue almost led to war in the 1830s as manufacturers and farmers pursued self-interest. After the War of 1812, Congress passed a protective tariff to aid the manufactories that had opened when British trade was cut off by an embargo. Over the years, the tariff rates increased and placed some foreign-made items out of reach. Southerners, who purchased large quantities of foreign manufactured goods, advocated free trade and contended that the tariff was sacrificing the South's interests to the North's. While all consumers paid a higher price for goods, Southerners pointed out that a portion of the tariff money went into the pocket of Northerners and thus allowed them to recoup the amount of the duty. Once Congress raised the tax to 50 percent of the value of imported goods in the Tariff of Abominations, South Carolina nullified this measure and almost went to war with President Andrew Jackson.

These two examples show that long before modern communications, various interests easily reached across state lines to work together for common goals. The Jeffersonian Republicans from multiple states worked together to support France and to eventually defeat the Federalist Party at the ballot box. Although the Federalist Party lost the elections of 1800, in the years prior to this they too coordinated efforts to throw support to Britain and to enact anti-French legislation. Likewise, men from across the South joined to denounce high tariff rates and to oppose protectionism. The North was similarly united against free trade and succeeded in propping up Northern industries by imposing stiff tariff schedules.

Undoubtedly, each side in these controversies saw their opponents as a faction in the Madisonian sense. To Southerners, for example, the pro-tariff forces comprised a body of citizens (and a numerical majority) "united and actuated by some common impulse of passion, or of interest, adverse to the rights of other citizens, or to the permanent and aggregate interests of the community."[39] Southerners saw the right of free exchange of goods as essential to their lives and believed that the Northerners meant them economic harm. To

Northerners, the Southerners were a minority faction placing their economic well-being over that of the greater community. Northerners claimed that having homegrown manufactories would make America less dependent on foreign countries and thus more secure. To them, the Southern faction was avaricious and short-sighted.

In short, Madison's claims in *Federalist* No. 10 are questionable. By extending the sphere of centralized government influence, little evidence exists that we are rewarded with highly intelligent representatives who resist policies that are not in the long-term interests of the country. The problems surrounding the federal budget and national debt are examples of the failure of Madison's extended-sphere arguments.

Similarly, history teaches that long before modern communications, factions formed and operated in our continental republic. No matter how large a country is, like-minded individuals will seek each other out and form political alliances. Francophiles, farmers, Anglophiles, and manufacturers, in the examples discussed above, had no difficulty in communicating and working together for common ends. Today, modern technology makes it even easier for concerted action in this diverse land.

In light of the failure to deliver on *Federalist* No. 10's promise that a large republic can control the effects of faction and reduce formation of factions, perhaps Americans should reexamine the question of scale. Maybe Montesquieu was correct that only in a small territory can republican government persist. If we give the Anti-Federalist view of representation any credit, we cannot seriously argue today that one representative adequately represents a 700,000-citizen district. The matter is even more absurd when we look at the Senate, which has been popularly elected since ratification of the Seventeenth Amendment in 1913. California, to cite the worst example, has over 37 million residents and has two senators. Even diehard Federalists must cringe at such an extended sphere for a mere two senators.

One must be careful not to assume that the answer to the scale problem is simply to vest more power in the state capitols. Even in 1787, many Anti-Federalists believed that some states had grown too large for republican government. "The extent of many states in the Union", wrote Cato, "is at this time almost too great for the superintendence of a republican form of government."[40] Cato believed that the large states "must one day or other, revolve into more vigorous ones, or by separation be reduced into smaller, and more useful, as well as moderate ones."[41]

Thomas Jefferson also believed that republicanism required that power should be devolved to smaller bodies of government. Jefferson urged that Virginia's counties should be divided "into Wards of such size as that every citizen can attend, when called on, and act in person."[42] Jefferson praised the townships of New England and described them as "vital" to their republicanism and "the wisest invention ever devised by the wit of man for the perfect exercise of self-government, and for its preservation."[43] While Jefferson recognized that legitimate national, state, and county concerns could arise that would not be the province of the wards, he believed that in these small bodies pumped the heart of republican government. In the wards, the people truly could participate and address the "numerous and interesting concerns of the neighborhood."[44]

Today, almost every issue is debated on a national level and the people routinely look to Washington, D.C. for answers. If Americans were to rethink the issue of scale, Jefferson's call for a division and subdivision of governmental duties should be heeded. In something akin to the wards can we discover the republicanism touted by the Anti-Federalists.

A devolution of power to local bodies increases the chance that a representative will mix with the people, and be acquainted with their interests and conditions. In these bodies, the people actually can be represented by one of their own. Such a change would give representative government a chance— something it does not have when a comparative handful of individuals "represent" over 300 million souls.

6

Consolidation

WHAT WAS THE new government created by the Constitution? Or better yet, what was its destiny? The Federalists and Anti-Federalists vehemently disagreed on the answers to these questions. The buzzword in the debates was "consolidation." When Americans of the 1780s heard the word consolidation they sensed danger. They associated consolidated governments with that of George III and the monarchies of Europe. The War of Independence was a war for self-government; consolidation meant a relinquishment of that right.

When speaking of consolidation, Americans meant the accretion of power collected at one point or in one entity. This concentration of power in the new national government, according to New York's Robert Yates and John Lansing, was the chief reason they refused to support the work of their colleagues at the Philadelphia Convention. "We therefore gave the principles of the Constitution, which has received the sanction of a majority of the Convention, our decided and unreserved dissent; but we must candidly confess that we should have been equally opposed to any system, however modified, which had in object the consolidation of the United States into one government."[1]

When objecting to consolidation various Anti-Federalists saw it arising from different sources. For some it was the abandonment of a strictly confederative government. For others, it was the types of powers granted to the new general government.

Patrick Henry, speaking in the Virginia ratifying convention, immediately questioned the discarding of the confederative structure. "Who authorized them to speak the language of, *We, the people*, instead of *We, the states*? States are the characteristic and soul of a confederation. If the states be not the agents of this compact," Henry reasoned, "it must be one great, consolidated, national government, of the people of all the states."[2] Luther Martin of Maryland also lamented the change in governmental structure by which Americans were losing "*truly federal principles*, the bases of which were the *thirteen state governments preserved in full force and energy.*"[3] The Pennsylvania minority echoed those sentiments and complained that "the new government will not be a confederacy of states, as it ought, but one consolidated government, founded upon the destruction of the several governments of the states."[4]

Federal or National?

To modern ears, it sounds as if Martin and others desired to limit artificially "truly federal principles" to a confederation. However, their insistence was not myopic. From antediluvian times until the late 1700s, a federal government was a government of a confederation. Through a confederate structure, city-states and other entities entered into a relationship for mutual protection or other generally beneficial reasons. The members of a federation maintained their full independence while cooperating under the defined circumstances set out by articles of confederation, a league, or treaty.[5]

As historian Forrest McDonald has observed, in the late 1700s, the idea of compacts or agreements for the purpose of forming a government was limited to three circumstances.[6] The first is where a ruler contracts with his people to provide them safety in return for allegiance. The prince secures the lives, liberty, and property of those falling under his dominion and the people recognize and submit to him as their sovereign. Such compacts are closely associated with the writings of John Locke during the Glorious Revolution of 1688 when the British people "contracted" with William and Mary after James II abdicated the throne. The second is an agreement of the people of a single political society to form a representative government. This type of compact was found in each state wherein the people claimed sovereignty and adopted republican constitutions. At stated intervals, the people exercised the franchise and thus participated in choosing fellow citizens to govern within the bounds of the constitution. The final example is the creation of a league of fully independent states. The Articles of Confederation, of course, was the most familiar to Americans as epitomizing this type of government. Each state stands as a fully independent entity, but contracts with other similar entities to promote common ends.

Hence, Patrick Henry and other Anti-Federalists found confusing the mixed federal and national features of the Constitution. It did not fit into the accepted categories of political science. Such a creature could only be some sort of consolidated government. "Is this a monarchy," questioned Henry, "like England—a compact between prince and people, with checks on the former to secure the liberty of the latter? Is this a confederacy, like Holland— an association of a number of independent states, each of which retains its individual sovereignty? It is not a democracy, wherein the people retain all their rights securely. Had these principles been adhered to, we should not have been brought to this alarming transition, from a confederacy to a consolidated government."[7]

James Madison and other Federalists denied that the new government must necessarily be consolidated because it abandoned a pure confederative structure. In the preface to his *Notes of the Debates in the Federal Convention*, Madison asserted that the delegates to the Philadelphia Convention were "anxious for a system that would avoid the inefficacy of a mere confederacy without passing into the opposite extreme of a consolidated government."[8]

According to Madison, the proposed document was "neither a national or federal constitution; but a composition of both."[9] In examining the hybrid creation in *Federalist* No. 39, Madison began by the mode of ratification. Be- cause the people of each state would gather in separate conventions to debate and ratify the Constitution, Madison believed that this was a federal feature of the government. No great national act of ratification was conceived, but rather the sovereigns of each state—the people—would determine whether their distinct political society would unite with others that chose to ratify.

Madison next turned to the Congress. The Senate, in which each state had an equal vote and its members were chosen by state legislatures, was another federal feature of the Constitution. The Senate's structure was indicative of the dignity and sovereignty remaining in each state. The House, on the other hand, was a national aspect of the Constitution. The House's power came "from the people of America, and the people will be represented in the same proportion, and on the same principle, as they are in the Legislature of a particular State."[10]

Madison saw the Electoral College as itself a mixture of federal and national principles. Electors were to be appointed by the state legislature and the number of electors for a state depended on its number of representatives and senators. The president of the Senate counted the electoral votes and the candidate receiving the largest number of votes would assume executive office. But if no person secured a majority of votes, the election was thrown into the House of Representatives where voting was by state with each state having one vote. Thus, Madison had difficulty in describing the election of president as a purely national or federal act.

The operation of the new government, according to Madison, was also a mixture of federal and national qualities. Inasmuch as Congress's laws would operate directly upon individuals rather than states, Madison agreed that this was a national feature and far different from federative principles. But because not all power was lodged in Congress owing to its delegated powers, Madison refused to describe the government as national. "In this relation, then the proposed Government cannot be deemed a *national* one; since its jurisdiction extends to certain enumerated objects only, and leaves to the several States a residuary and inviolable sovereignty over all other objects."[11]

Finally, Madison examined the method by which constitutional amendments could be adopted and again found a mix of federal and national principles. "In requiring more than a majority, and particularly, in computing the proportion by *States*, not by citizens, it departs from the *national*, and advances towards the *federal* character: In rendering the concurrence of less than the whole number of States sufficient, it loses again the *federal*, and partakes of the *national* character."[12]

Imperium in Imperio

Madison's advocacy of this new type of government also raised Anti-Federalist concerns about the concurrent jurisdiction of the general and state governments. Both would operate on individuals. In some cases, both would have similar powers. The power of taxation is the prime example. The general and state governments could both tax the people to fund their respective governmental functions. Concurrent jurisdiction set forth in the Constitution sounded very much like an *imperium in imperio*, i.e., sovereignty within sovereignty. In eighteenth-century political thought, only one governmental sovereign over a single jurisdiction was possible.[13] Divided sovereignty was a "solecism in politics."

In 1778, the Worcester, Massachusetts, Committee of Correspondence cogently set forth prevailing theory: "The supposition of two different powers in a State assuming the right of controlling the people, whose doings are liable to interfere with each other, forms that great political solecism imperium in imperio, a head within a head, and the State in which a monster of this nature exists, will soon be brought under that fatal denomination of a kingdom divided against itself, which cannot stand."[14] Samuel Adams similarly expressed this concern in the context of his fear that Roman Catholic rulers would be forced to be obeisant toward the Pope and thus would introduce "into the states under whose protection they enjoy life, liberty, and property, that solecism in politics, imperium in imperio, leading directly to the worst anarchy and confusion, civil discord, war, and bloodshed."[15]

The Anti-Federalist Centinel agreed with the Worcester Committee of Correspondence. "It is a solecism in politics for two co-ordinate sovereignties to exist together," Centinel wrote in 1787, "you must separate the sphere of their jurisdiction, or after running the race of dominion for some time, one would necessarily triumph over the other."[16] Based on the broad powers granted to Congress, Centinel predicted that the federal government with its "decisive superiority in the outset" ultimately would prevail.[17]

The Anti-Federalist Brutus worried that the *imperium in imperio* of the Constitution would lead to the destruction of the state governments. If the raising of revenue for state governments interfered with national officials filling national coffers, he predicted that state law would be suspended. "If this be true, and if the states can raise money only by permission of the general government," Brutus concluded, "it follows that the state governments will be dependent on the will of the general government for their existence."[18] Observing that the Constitution made the acts of the national government the supreme law of the land, he reasoned that in any area wherein the two sovereigns allegedly possessed concurrent jurisdiction, the national government would have its way. Thus, Brutus saw divided sovereignty as a chimera able to exist in the imaginations of the Federalists but not in actual practice.

Thomas Tredwell, in the New York ratifying convention, made a similar point. "The idea of two distinct sovereigns in the same country, separately possessed of sovereign and supreme power, in the same matters at the same time, is a supreme absurdity, as that two distinct separate circles can be bounded exactly by the same circumference."[19] Eventually, Tredwell predicted, the state governments would be reduced to dependent status and look "on the bounty of Congress for their support, and consequently their existence."[20] Madison and the Federalists, confident that the atom of sovereignty could be split, rejected prognostications about the demise of the states. They pointed to the careful enumeration of powers in the Constitution and assured the Anti-Federalists that divisions between the states and the nation were clear for all to see and thus would be honored.

Confederative government and divided sovereignty aside, a number of Anti-Federalists also feared consolidation from the nature of the powers granted to the national government. The Federal Farmer saw "all important powers collecting in one centre, where a few men will possess them almost at discretion."[21] Expansive powers would be a mechanism for an ultimate victory in any conflict with the states or individuals: "Should the general government think it politic, as some administration (if not all) probably will, to look for a support in a system of influence, the government will take every occasion to multiply laws, and officers to execute them, considering these as so many necessary props for their own support."[22] The Federal Farmer conceded that the written plan of the Philadelphia Convention proposed a partial consolidation of the states, but he prognosticated that over time a total consolidation would be the natural result.

Whether the consolidation resulted from abandonment of a confederate government or the types of powers granted to the national government, the result meant that the people had no intermediary body. Anti-Federalists saw great value in state governments interposing between the people and the national government. Even when the government at the center is empowered to choose an ultimate end, the Anti-Federalists saw worth in state governments being allowed to choose the means. The diversity of the United States, they believed, required this flexibility for reasonable continental objectives to be achieved with equity and efficiency.

They understood that in some cases state intermediaries could thwart plans to make the United States a great power. This, however, did not concern the Anti-Federalists. "If we admit this consolidated government," warned Henry, "it will be because we like a great, splendid one. Some way or other we must be a great and mighty empire; we must have an army, and a navy, and a number of things. When the American spirit was in its youth, the language of America was different: liberty, sir, was then the primary object."[23] Henry questioned why the Federalists desired to mimic the consolidated governments of Europe. In those countries the people did not enjoy the freedom that Americans did. "Shall we imitate the example of those nations who have gone from a simple to a splendid government? Are those nations more worthy of our imitation?"[24] Thus, Henry articulated an alternative and forgotten view of American exceptionalism. The United States, in Henry's view, could be different from the European nations by maintaining a confederated government where the people were left to manage their own affairs and to govern themselves in communities. The proposed national government, he believed, eventually would make the United States just like the other powers of the world with nettlesome national officials managing and taxing all aspects of life.

Today, the American system of divided governmental sovereignty is considered a great contribution to political science. We are told that the Framers successfully split the atom of sovereignty. But we should not blindly assume that the plan proposed by the Philadelphia Convention solved the issues presented by an *imperium in imperio* and created a new form of government. If the Anti-Federalists could browse copies of the current United States Code and Code of Federal Regulations, they would lament that their predictions of consolidation have come to pass. The national government directs or regulates myriad local activities from education to poor relief. The enumerated powers of the Constitution serve as little or no limitation on the reach of national officials. As will be discussed in the following chapters, the national government uses its spending power to coerce the states to administer programs and to regulate per Washington's instructions.

Moreover, many state budgets depend on federal tax dollars. Tennessee, for instance, has seen federal funds account for approximately 40 percent of state government spending.[25] This addiction to federal subvention clouds an assertion that the states, in any meaningful sense, are co-sovereigns with the national government. The state governments depend heavily on the national government's money for their existence.

Rather than praising divided sovereignty as the signal contribution of the Framers, perhaps we should question whether it really is a successful experiment. Our national government is no different from the modern consolidated governments of Europe. To paraphrase Patrick Henry, we are a great, splendid superpower. Little is left to remind us of the confederation that Henry defended or even the mixed federal and national constitution promised by Madison.

Power has accrued at the center. As will be seen in subsequent chapters examining specific provisions of the Constitution and how they have been used and interpreted, it is hard to argue that we do not live under a consolidated national government.

7

Taxing and Spending
for the General Welfare

ONE OF THE provisions most likely to lead to consolidation, according to the Anti-Federalists, was the introductory language to Article I, section 8. Prior to setting forth the delegated powers, the Constitution declares that "Congress shall have Power To lay and collect Taxes, Duties, Imposts and Excises, to pay the Debts and provide for the common Defence and general Welfare of the United States."[1] Anti-Federalist criticism focused primarily on the granting of a new power to the national government (taxation), and fear that the "general welfare" language would be construed so broadly as to render the enumeration of powers meaningless.

The most common complaint of Anti-Federalist writers regarding the taxing power was the Philadelphia Convention's decision to make no distinction between internal and external taxes. According to the Federal Farmer, external taxes "are import duties, which are laid on imported goods," and these duties typically are "collected in a few seaport towns, and of a few individuals."[2] Only a few officials are needed to collect these taxes, he continued, "and they can be carried no higher than trade will bear, or smuggling [will] permit."[3] Internal taxes, on the other hand, encompass such things as "poll and land taxes, excises, duties on all written instruments" and "may fix themselves on every person and species of property in the community."[4] A poll tax is one imposed on all voters at the time of casting ballots. Such broad taxes also require more federal involvement for their enforcement and collection.

The distinction between internal and external taxation was integral to the events leading to the American Revolution. The infamous Stamp Act of 1765 was the first direct, internal tax levied on the North American colonies by Parliament. The act required that almost every form of paper used in the colonies be affixed with an official stamp. The colonists regarded the Stamp Act with odium and believed that, if accepted, it would create a harmful precedent. In passing various resolutions and in attacking the persons and properties of the stamp-tax collectors, the colonists sought to register their protests that such internal taxes should be levied only by colonial legislatures. Parliament, the colonists insisted, did not have knowledge of local circumstances and the MPs would not feel the bite of the tax inasmuch as Americans did not have representation in Parliament.

By bringing up the distinction between internal and external taxes, the Federal Farmer hoped to remind his readers of the Revolution's assumption that internal taxes were the province of state assemblies and not the central government. "When I recollect how lately congress, conventions, legislatures, and people contended in the cause of liberty, and carefully weighed the importance of taxation," the Farmer observed, "I can scarcely believe we are serious in proposing to vest the powers of laying and collecting internal taxes in a government so imperfectly organized for such purposes."[5]

"An Old Whig" agreed with the Federal Farmer: "The true line of distinction which should have been drawn in describing the powers of Congress, and those of the several states, should have been that between internal and external taxation."[6] Massachusetts's Anti-Federalists argued that the Constitution should be amended so that "Congress do not lay direct taxes, but when the moneys arising from the impost and excise shall be insufficient for the public exigencies."[7] Hence, the Massachusetts Anti-Federalists assumed a more moderate position. They would not prohibit the general government from ever levying direct taxes on the people, but sought to limit the power to times of crises.

In Virginia, Patrick Henry suggested that Congress should be allowed to tax the people directly only if the states were non-compliant with requisitions. To do otherwise, Henry believed, would be to risk the proliferation of federal tax agents sweeping across the land and oppressing the people.[8] Similar to Henry, John Lansing in the New York convention defended the system of requisitions as a check on the central government's power. Lansing argued that the problems with requisitions under the Confederation could have been solved had Congress been granted the power to legislate directly on individuals if the states, after a specified time period, failed to meet the particular quota or amount requisitioned.[9] Thus, the concept of requisitions was not so infirm that it should be abandoned for a plenary taxing authority placed at a distance from the people.

The Federalists countered that a full taxing power should be vested in the general government. Alexander Hamilton in *Federalist* No. 15 averred that the requisitions passed by the Confederation Congress, though in theory "are laws, constitutionally binding on the members of the Union, yet in practice they are mere recommendations which the States observe or disregard at their option."[10] Hamilton further complained that the failure of some states to pay their allotted amount "furnished the pretext of example and the temptation of interest to the complying, or to the least delinquent States."[11] The requisition system, Hamilton concluded, was "a system of imbecility in the Union, and of inequality and injustice among the members."[12]

After scoffing at the idea that requisitions should play any part in the new Constitution, Hamilton tackled the distinctions about internal and external taxes. To differentiate between the two types of taxes, he argued, "would violate the maxim of good sense and sound policy, which dictates that every POWER ought to be in proportion to its OBJECT."[13] If the federal government needed an independent source of revenue, then the Constitution should ensure that it possessed all necessary means for raising revenue. Americans could not be sure that external taxes would be sufficient to meet the needs of the national government if emergencies or other unforeseen circumstances arose. Considering that the known debts and interest from the war years were enormous, restrictions on the taxing power should be disfavored.

While Hamilton argued for a plenary power to tax, he predicted that most revenue would be raised through external taxes. "In America," Hamilton lectured, "it is evident that we must a long time depend for the means of revenue chiefly on . . . duties" from imported goods.[14] Whereas a rich nation such as Great Britain could tax the people directly to raise revenue, Hamilton assured his readers that American farmers and mechanics simply did not have the resources to pay such assessments and thus they should not expect that the new government would depart from a scheme of duties. Madison concurred with Hamilton on this point and wrote that the taxing power largely would be connected with foreign commerce.[15] The Federalists all agreed that for the foreseeable future the new government would place tariffs on goods shipped into the country to raise revenue in the ordinary course of business.

Of course, these promises about reliance on duties were short-lived. During Washington's first administration, Congress enacted an excise tax on whiskey. Federalists in the ratification debates had promised that such a tax would be used only in case of great national emergencies. This excise caused great hardship in frontier regions of the United States where cash was scarce and whiskey was used as an item of barter. Riots erupted and eventually the Whiskey Rebellion was underway. Federal tax collectors were tarred and feathered and skirmishes took place between armed bands and federal troops. The resistance was well organized in Pennsylvania and caused Washington to nationalize 13,000 militiamen to quell the uprising. Hamilton personally accompanied the army into the countryside and the rebels dispersed quickly. Although the tax remained on the books, noncompliance was the rule. The tax never yielded much more than the costs of its enforcement.[16]

Prior to 1913 and the passage of the Sixteenth Amendment, tariffs accounted for over half of federal revenue with excises coming in a distant second. Except for several real estate tax levies and an income tax enacted during the Civil War, Congress had leaned primarily on external taxes throughout the 1800s. In the late 1890s and early 1900s, voices rose against this type of financing and argued that tariffs raised the price of essential items for the poor. They also pointed out that the federal treasury was left to the vicissitudes of international trade and consumer consumption patterns. Ideas about free trade were gaining ground and high tariffs, many argued, deprived Americans of the benefits of comparative advantage. Class warfare played a role inasmuch as progressives contended that the great wealth of American industrial barons should be taxed and redistributed to the poor. These forces led to the Sixteenth Amendment, which permits Congress to lay taxes on any and all sources of income.

Income taxes are now the primary source of federal revenue. They fund a system of entitlement programs that make up well over half of our $3.67 trillion budget. The power granted to Congress by the Sixteenth Amendment dwarfs the power to enact internal taxes that so worried the Anti-Federalists. Our blind acceptance of such taxation and national administration of a welfare state demonstrates that we have lost the healthy fear of centralized power that animated the American revolutionaries and the opponents of the Constitution. Would that we debate the propriety of internal versus external taxes rather than debating how much (not whether) the federal budget will increase each year.

Furthermore, the taxing power now is used by Congress to promote certain social welfare legislation that it favors. The individual mandate to purchase health insurance found in the Patient Protection and Affordable Care Act ("PPACA") is the best example. In *National Federation of Independent Business v. Sebelius* (2012),[17] the Supreme Court had to determine whether the individual mandate was a tax or a penalty—a distinction critical to the outcome of the case. A tax is an enforced contribution to provide for the support of the government, whereas a penalty is imposed as punishment for an unlawful act. A penalty must be supported by an enumerated power permitting broad regulatory action, but a tax need not be tied to any other delegated power.

In finding the individual mandate to be a tax, the *Sebelius* majority was not swayed by Congress's decision to describe the so-called tax as a "penalty" or President Obama's adamant denials that he was raising taxes with the individual mandate. Nor did the statutory language make an impression upon the Court. The PPACA commands that every "applicable individual shall . . . ensure that the individual . . . is covered under minimum essential coverage."[18] Right after this mandate, the statute states that if a person fails to comply with this requirement, "there is hereby imposed . . . a penalty."[19]

The Court held that the Act "makes going without insurance just another thing the Government taxes, like buying gasoline or earning income."[20] Accordingly, through the tax code, the national government can use its coercive power to force individuals to buy health insurance. Defending the PPACA as an exercise of the taxing power clearly was a second-string argument used by the government's lawyers, but the Court's opinion instructs Congress on how to craft future police-power legislation so as to pass muster as a humdrum tax.

General Welfare

The Anti-Federalist distrust of the broad taxing power was exacerbated by the general welfare language. According to Centinel, "whatever taxes, duties, and excises that they may deem requisite for the general welfare, may be imposed on the citizens of these states, levied by the officers of Congress, distributed through every district of America."[21] Apart from taxation, Anti-Federalists saw the General Welfare Clause as conferring a plenary power on the national government. Virginia's Richard Henry Lee feared that those two words permitted Congress "[t]o judge of what may be for the general welfare" and to pass laws "with every possible object of human legislation."[22]

Brutus observed that "[t]o provide for the general welfare, is an abstract proposition, which mankind differ in the explanation of, as much as they do on any political or moral proposition that can be proposed."[23] Because of the elasticity of the concept of general welfare, Brutus envisioned competing political parties both appealing to this clause and contending that their pet project advanced the general welfare of the country. The clause, Brutus believed, would be a source of power and controversy for years to come.

James Madison, writing in *Federalist* No. 41, rejected the notion that the general welfare clause "amounts to an unlimited commission to exercise every power which may be alleged to be necessary for the common defense or general welfare."[24] The Anti-Federalists' objection might have weight, Madison noted, but for the careful enumeration of powers that followed this introductory language. Madison continued:

> For what purpose could the enumeration of particular powers be inserted, if these and all others were meant to be included in the preceding general power? Nothing is more natural nor common than first to use a general phrase, and then to explain and qualify it by a recital of particulars. But the idea of an enumeration of particulars which neither explain nor qualify the general meaning, and can have no other effect than to confound and mislead, is an absurdity, which, as we are reduced to the dilemma of charging either on the authors of the objection or on the authors of the Constitution, we must take the liberty of supposing, had not its origin with the latter.[25]

If general welfare was the standard, then why bother to give Congress the power to regulate commerce, establish post offices, and to raise an army and navy? Surely those matters are for the general welfare and no specific enumeration would be required. Thus, Madison strongly argued that the text did not support Anti-Federalist fears about a plenary grant of power.

Noah Webster, writing as "a Citizen of America," concurred with Madison. Webster saw the general welfare language as immaterial because "no powers are vested in Congress but what are included under the general expressions."[26] He praised the Philadelphia Convention for its careful efforts "to draw the line between federal and provincial powers" in the enumeration found in Article I.[27]

Once the Constitution had been ratified, it did not take the Federalists long to retreat from Madison's and Webster's explanation of the meaning of the General Welfare Clause. On December 5, 1791, Secretary of the Treasury Alexander Hamilton presented to Congress a Report of Manufactures. In this report, Hamilton urged that measures should render the United States independent of foreign nations for military and other essential items. Hamilton contended that the security and wealth of a nation are linked materially to a robust manufacturing sector. Hamilton suggested protective tariffs, government monetary support of certain industries, government grants to inventors, internal improvements, and the payment of the travel expenses of skilled foreigners who emigrated to the United States.

Hamilton anticipated that his opponents would raise constitutional issues about the authority for many of his proposals. In the Report on Manufactures, Hamilton asserted that the General Welfare Clause provided the authority to raise and spend money for purposes not specifically enumerated in the Constitution. "The phrase [general welfare] is as comprehensive as any that could have been used," Hamilton lectured, "because it was not fit that the constitutional authority of the Union to appropriate its revenues should have been restricted within the narrower limits than the 'general welfare,' and because this [phrase] necessarily embraces a vast variety of particulars, which are susceptible neither of specification nor of definition."[28] So long as goals are in the interest of the nation, Congress may spend money as it sees fit.

Madison was aghast at this interpretation. In his 1800 Report to the General Assembly of Virginia, Madison examined his state's protest against the Alien and Sedition Acts of 1798. The Acts caused great controversy inasmuch as the Federalist-controlled Congress criminalized speech critical of the national government and gave President Adams expansive power to remove foreigners from the United States if suspicion existed that they posed a danger to the country. In the Report, Madison addressed directly Hamilton's interpretation of the General Welfare Clause. Madison pointed out that the Articles of Confederation also contained a general welfare provision and the "similarity in the use of these phrases in the two great federal charters, might well be considered, as rendering their meaning less liable to be misconstrued."[29] The general welfare language of the Articles of Confederation had never been understood to grant powers beyond the enumeration set forth in the Articles, and thus neither should this same language be construed in the Constitution of 1787. Madison described the assertions of Hamilton's Report on Manufactures as "extraordinary" and chided Congress for failing to rebuke Hamilton for such an untenable interpretation of the General Welfare Clause.[30] A government bound only by ideas of the general welfare, Madison continued, would be of an unlimited jurisdiction. Before Congress spends money, it must first point to an enumerated power. If no such enumerated power exists, then no expenditure should take place.

The debate on the scope of the General Welfare Clause continued until 1936 when the Supreme Court decided to resolve the issue. In *United States v. Butler* (1936),[31] the Court considered provisions of the Agricultural Adjustment Act of 1933. In that statute, Congress sought to maintain a balance between agricultural production and consumption to stabilize prices for farmers. In defending the statute, the government claimed that the General Welfare Clause authorized Congress to spend money for "anything conducive to national welfare."[32] Because Congress believed that the raising of prices for farmers would be conducive to the good of the whole, it should be allowed to appropriate money and to spend to achieve that ultimate goal. The Court accepted this argument and held that the spending of money "is not limited by the direct grants of legislative power found in the Constitution."[33] Nonetheless, the Court struck down the Agricultural Adjustment Act of 1933 because certain tax components of the law violated the Tenth Amendment. The Court could not countenance taxing farmers who refused to plant fewer acres and transferring this money to farmers who agreed to reduce acreage and crops under cultivation. The control of agricultural production, the Court ruled, is beyond Congress's broad powers. The AAA of 1935 corrected that "defect" and was sustained.

In 1987, the Court further opined on the power of Congress to spend for the general welfare. In *South Dakota v. Dole* (1987),[34] the Court considered a challenge to the constitutionality of conditioning a state's receipt of federal highway funds on adoption of a minimum drinking age of 21. If a state declined to adopt the higher drinking age, it would lose five percent of funds it otherwise would receive from Congress. The Court affirmed the Hamiltonian position announced in *Butler* and set forth the "limits" of the General Welfare Clause. First, the Court noted that the spending must be for general public purposes and that Congress is the best judge of whether spending meets this requirement. Second, a statute tying some state action to the receipt of funds must be unambiguous so states may "exercise their choice knowingly, cognizant of the consequences of participation."[35] Third, the conditions set must be related to a federal interest in the particular national project. Finally, Congress may not impose a condition if it violates some other constitutional provision.

Encouragement or Coercion?

With raising the drinking age from 18 to 21, the Court held that the spending at issue was designed to promote the general welfare because Congress found that lower drinking ages gave young people an incentive to mix alcohol with automobile driving. Young people traveled across state lines in search of jurisdictions with lower drinking ages. A dangerous situation thus arose on the nation's roads that permitted Congress to act. The statute imposing the conditions clearly set forth the "rules" so that appellant South Dakota could make a knowing and intelligent decision. Such encouragement of state action, the Court ruled, was well within Washington's spending power.

Yet at what point does "encouragement" become "coercion" and hinder the power of sovereign states to make decisions and implement the will of their people? When does the Hamiltonian spending power reduce a sovereign state to a quasi-department of the general government? This issue was argued by twenty-six states when they challenged Congress's expansion of the Medicaid program in the PPACA. When originally implemented in 1965, Medicaid was a federal–state partnership whereby medical care was provided to the neediest of Americans. Federal dollars are used to pay for 50 to 83 percent of the total program costs in each state.[36] As of 2012, federal Medicaid funds accounted for 7 percent of all federal spending and 40 percent of federal funds granted to the states. Medicaid spending accounts for, on average, 20 percent of state budgets.[37]

The PPACA attempted to expand Medicaid eligibility and required states to offer Medicaid benefits to all persons under age 65 with incomes up to 138 percent of the federal poverty level.[38] If the states did not expand eligibility as demanded by Washington, they would lose all Medicaid funding. If, for example, the state of Florida had refused to expand the program and lost all federal aid, the costs of Medicaid alone would have consumed approximately two-thirds of that state's tax revenues.[39] Considering that Florida's residents feel a national tax-bite of approximately $110 billion per year, the state knew that it could not raise its own taxes to cover the additional cost of the expanded Medicaid program. It would also greatly vex Floridians to see none of their $110 billion in taxes going to Florida's needy, but rather to the poor residing in other states.

Faced with this situation, can any state really decline to expand Medicaid in accordance with the PPACA? Are the states truly independent and autonomous in the realm of poor relief—an area clearly within their reserved powers? Or are they in reality taking direct commands from a more powerful sovereign? No one can seriously argue that the states are not acting under duress. The national government holds a proverbial gun on the states and instructs them. A state's "agreement" to expand Medicaid under these circumstances is as knowing and voluntary as a victim's agreement to give a bandit all the victim's cash while the bandit brandishes a weapon.

In *Sebelius*, the Supreme Court agreed that the national government had gone a bridge too far with the Medicaid expansion. It held that when the states first agreed to take the federal money for Medicaid, they could not have foreseen such a dramatic change in the conditions of accepting the grant. "Though Congress's power to legislate under the spending power is broad," the Court lectured, "it does not include surprising participating States with post-acceptance or retroactive conditions."[40] The threat to withdraw Medicaid funds absent state expansion of the program, the Court concluded, was not a financial inducement, but an unconstitutional "gun to the head."[41]

While it is comforting to see some limitation placed on federal spending power, *Sebelius* still leaves the national government with expansive authority to spend money unrelated to the Constitution's delegated powers. So long as Congress threatens to only pull a percentage of funding (as in *Dole*) and does not dramatically change the scope of the program mandated, it can still bribe and coerce the states into serving the federal government. *Sebelius* simply prohibits the most flagrant abuse of the states' status as sovereigns.

In sum, as we contemplate the size of our budget and the stick wielded by the national government with its taxing power, Patrick Henry's protestations about fully abandoning the requisition system have some appeal. The Articles' provisions on requisitions were flawed, but they did give the states a potent check on the Confederation Congress. In hindsight, perhaps the Anti-Federalists were right that Congress should first make requisitions of the states before resorting to internal taxes in case of state noncompliance. Under such a system, the states would have the discretion to levy their own taxes, but the national government could assume this authority only if the states failed to provide revenue in a timely manner. A check would be in place, but the general government would not be completely handcuffed.

The taxing power aside, as feared by the Anti-Federalists, the discretion to spend for matters outside of Congress's delegated powers consolidates authority at the center and removes protection promised by the Framers' careful enumeration of powers. The spending power is an effective tool in Congress's hands—perhaps the most powerful in its arsenal. Congress can encourage/coerce the states to take actions that would otherwise be outside of its delegated powers. This power impairs state sovereignty and cripples the federal components of our mixed system of government. Such a result surely is not for the general welfare of the union.

8

The Regulation of Commerce

THE CONFEDERATION CONGRESS lacked a power to regulate commerce. Both the Federalists and Anti-Federalists described this as a defect in the Articles. In his third letter on the proposed Constitution, Centinel observed that the lamp of experience showed all Americans that the absence of power "in the regulation of commerce and maritime affairs" was to our detriment.[1] "The Impartial Examiner" (his true identity remains unknown) noted that "[i]t seems to be agreed on all sides that in the present system of the union Congress are not invested with sufficient powers for *regulating commerce*."[2] The Pennsylvania minority readily agreed that Congress "should be enabled in the amplest manner to regulate commerce."[3] Alexander Hamilton in *Federalist* No. 22 joined the chorus and opined that "[t]he want of a power to regulate commerce is by all parties" agreed to be a cause that rendered the Articles "altogether unfit for the administration of the affairs of the Union."[4]

Under the Constitution, Congress has the power to "regulate commerce with foreign nations, and among the several states, and with the Indian tribes."[5] But what does "commerce" mean? Did the Constitution grant the national government a power to regulate all economic or gainful activity? Or did the Framers and ratifiers have something else in mind? Dictionaries at the time defined commerce as "[i]ntercourse, exchange of one thing for another, interchange of anything; trade; traffick."[6] While this dictionary definition is helpful, to fully understand what Americans meant by "commerce" we must briefly examine the arguments for the commerce power and the specific defects sought to be remedied.

Foreign Commerce

The first component of the Commerce Clause is regulation with foreign nations. At the conclusion of the Revolution, many Americans expected greater prosperity because they would no longer be under the power of Parliament. They resented Great Britain's mercantilist trade policy that ensured the mother country enjoyed a positive balance of trade in its relationship with the colonies. Historians estimate that from the 1740s on, Americans imported approximately £500,000 more than they were exporting to Great Britain. Twenty-five percent of all British exports were purchased by Americans. This flow of funds to the mother country contributed to Great Britain's national prosperity.

Parliament's Navigation Acts provided that only ships with predominantly British crews could carry goods to or from a colony. This enabled the British to enjoy full profit of the carrying trade. If, for example, a foreign merchant sought to ship items to America, the merchant's ship would have to be offloaded in a British port and the goods transferred to a British ship. The British also prohibited shipment of some American commodities—even if loaded into British vessels—to foreign ports. Britain did not want its colonies clothing or feeding potential enemies. Hence, the colonists could not export such items as rice, cotton, wool, or naval stores to foreign countries.

The North American colonists did not manufacture many goods, but when they did, they often faced restrictions meant to protect British industries. For instance, the Hat Act of 1732 forbade the shipping of beaver hats out of the colonies. This measure protected British hat makers from competition from their North American kinsmen. The Iron Act of 1750 prohibited the colonists from erecting forges and furnaces that produced steel. With this legislation, Parliament sought to restrict the growth of finished goods made in the colonies and to encourage the supply of raw materials to British manufacturers. The end result of these mercantilist regulations meant that British manufacturers and merchants dictated the prices of goods bought and sold by the Americans.

Although independence effectively voided measures such as the Hat Act and Iron Act, the colonies did not enjoy free trade with the world. Natural trading partners such as Britain and France imposed discriminatory restrictions on American trade. As part of the empire, the colonies had enjoyed a lucrative trade with the British West Indies. With the colonies outside of the

British fold, Parliament excluded American vessels from the West Indies. Parliament also allowed only American vessels to transport American goods to Britain. Subjects in Canada, for example, could not contract with American ship owners for the transportation of their raw materials to the mother country.

In arguing for a commerce power in the North Carolina ratifying convention, William R. Davie asserted that the union "should be empowered to compel foreign nations into commercial regulations that were either founded on the principles of justice or reciprocal advantages."[7] He lamented that the Confederation Congress was unable to achieve any results and that our commerce is "equally unprotected abroad by arms and negotiation."[8] Charles Pinckney of South Carolina described the want of a commerce power as leading to the destruction of American trade "occasioned by the restrictions of other nations, whose policy it was not in the power of the general government to counteract."[9]

James Bowdoin in the Massachusetts convention observed that "[o]ther nations prohibit our vessels from entering their ports, or lay heavy duties on our exports carried thither; and we have no retaliating or regulating power over their vessels and exports, to prevent it."[10] "A vessel from Roseway or Halifax [Canada]," Thomas Dawes, Jr., told the Massachusetts convention, "finds as hearty a welcome with its fish and whalebone at the southern ports, as though it was built, navigated, and freighted from Salem or Boston."[11] This would continue to be the case, Dawes predicted, "until we have laws comprehending and embracing alike all the states in the Union."[12]

In *Federalist* No. 22, Hamilton complained that the lack of a commerce power "has already operated as bar to formation of beneficial treaties with foreign powers."[13] He did not fault foreign countries for declining to negotiate with the Confederation Congress inasmuch as the states seemed determined to chart their own commercial courses rather than to combine and seek mutual advantages. With America in such a disunited posture, Hamilton said that foreigners "found from experience that they might enjoy every advantage they desired in our markets, without granting us any return, but such as their momentary convenience might suggest."[14]

North Carolinian Hugh Williamson agreed that the disunited posture of various state commercial regulations made America an easy target for foreign merchants. If a state sought to force concessions from a foreign power through its commercial laws, "[a] neighboring State immediately alters her laws and defeats" the purpose of the coercive measure and thus simply throws "the trade into a different channel. Instead of supporting or assisting, we are uniformly taking advantage of one another."[15]

Clearly, all sides agreed that Congress should have the power to regulate foreign commerce for the benefit of deep-water shipping and foreign trade. This brand of commerce, as noted by the Federalist "Phildemos," was necessary "to vend the surplus of our produce to foreign nations."[16] Independence, to a certain extent, brought more onerous British trade restrictions than had existed within the Empire and thus impaired this vending. To regain access to the West Indies and to promote the carrying trade, Congress needed the authority to strike at the British with an American Navigation Act. So long as the states controlled imposts and access to their ports, the actions of one recalcitrant member of the union could defeat national policy. Twelve states might agree to place a hefty tax on British manufactured goods, but if, say, New York declined to adopt the tax, then British goods would flow into the country via New York City and that state's ports would enjoy a booming business. Cognizant of the ability to pit the states against one another, foreign powers had no incentive to grant privileges to American commerce.

Interstate Commerce

The second part of the commerce clause deals with commerce among the several states. Madison described the purpose of this power in *Federalist* No. 42:

A very material object of this power was the relief of the States which import and export through other States, from the improper contributions levied on them by the latter. Were these at liberty to regulate trade between State and State, it must be foreseen that ways would be found out, to load articles of import and export, during the passage through their jurisdiction, with duties which would fall on the makers of the latter, and on the consumers of the former.[17]

In the Connecticut ratifying convention, Oliver Ellsworth agreed with Madison and pointed the finger at New York. Ellsworth began by averring that "[o]ur being tributaries to our sister states is in consequence of the want of a federal system."[18] The government of New York, he continued, "raises 60 or £80,000 a year by impost. Connecticut consumes about one-third of the goods upon which this impost is laid, and consequently pays one-third of this sum to New York."[19] If Connecticut sought to import goods through other states, the same result would be likely: "If we import by the medium of Massachusetts, she has an impost, and to her we pay a tribute."[20]

New Yorker Alexander Hamilton did not deny Ellsworth's complaint:

> The opportunities, which some States would have of rendering the others tributary to them, by commercial regulations, would be impatiently submitted to by the tributary States. The relative situation of New-York, Connecticut and New-Jersey, would afford an example of this kind. New-York, from the necessities of revenue, must lay duties on her importations. A great part of these duties must be paid by inhabitants of the two other States in the capacity of consumers of what we import. New-York would neither be willing nor able to forgo this advantage.[21]

Hamilton also advocated an interstate commerce power to promote a great free trade zone within the union: "An unrestrained intercourse between the States themselves will advance the trade of each, by an interchange of their respective productions, not only for the supply of reciprocal wants at home, but for exportation to foreign markets." With state jealousies quieted and goods flowing freely across America, Hamilton predicted that "[t]he veins of commerce in every part will be replenished, and will acquire additional motion and vigour from a free circulation of the commodities of every part."[22]

Trade and the exchange of goods clearly were in mind when referring to "interstate commerce." The Framers did not want some states serving as "tributaries" of others. Such state duties discouraged the flow of goods and could have far-reaching consequences. A Connecticut manufacturer, forced to import needed parts or items through New York City, might see business damaged because of exorbitant charges incurred at its sister state's port. Those costs would have to be passed on to consumers, or if the market could not bear higher costs, a native manufacturer might be forced to close its doors. Free trade among the states, almost all agreed, would promote the division of labor and efficient use of American capital.

Of course, as the term "interstate commerce" implies, the Framers had in mind trade between persons of one state and another. Purely internal selling or exchange—intrastate trade—was excluded. The great Virginia legal scholar St. George Tucker observed matter-of-factly that by delegating to Congress the power to regulate commerce "among" the states, the Constitution left "the regulation of internal commerce of each state, to the states, respectively."[23] Federalist Tench Coxe discerned that because an article was not injected into interstate commerce until it was involved in the sale or exchange with a citizen of another state, Congress lacked the authority to pass inspection laws pursuant to the commerce power, even though the growing or production of quality items was "a matter of the utmost importance to commerce of the several states, and the honor of *the whole.*"[24]

The third component of the Commerce Clause focuses on the Indians. The Indians are referenced specifically because of a provision of the Articles whereby Congress was charged with "regulating the trade, and managing all affairs with Indians, not members of any of the states, providing that the legislative right of any state within its own limits be not infringed or violated."[25] Determining the status of Indian tribes living in the United States proved to be confusing. Were the tribes foreign nations, loose associations of individuals, or domestic dependent nations under the guardianship of the national or state governments? To determine whether an Indian residing within the borders of a state was a "member" of a state only complicated the matter. Add to the mix the prohibition against infringing upon state legislative prerogatives, and Congress's power to regulate trade with the Indians under the Articles was useless. Hence, Indians were specifically included in the Commerce Clause of the Constitution.

Debate on Federal Commerce Authority

While there was much unanimity in the need for a commerce power, many Anti-Federalists were uncomfortable with the grant of the power without certain restrictions. In the Philadelphia Convention, George Mason championed a proposal for a two-thirds vote in the national legislature before commercial regulations could be passed. Without this security, the Southern states would be delivered "bound hand & foot to the Eastern States, and enable them to exclaim, in the words of Cromwell on a certain occasion—'the lord hath delivered them into our hands.'"[26] The Convention rejected this proposal. During the ratification debates, Mason cited the rejection of the two-thirds requirement as one of the principal reasons the Constitution should be refused. "[T]he five Southern States," Mason predicted, "whose produce and circumstances are totally different from that of the eight Northern and Eastern States, may be ruined, for such rigid and premature regulations may be made as will enable the merchants of the Northern and Eastern States not only to demand an exorbitant freight, but to monopolize the purchase of the commodities at their own price, for many years. . . ."[27]

Richard Henry Lee shared Mason's fear that the Northern states would enact commerce regulations to oppress the South. "In this congressional legislature a bare majority of votes, can enact commercial laws, so that the representatives of the seven northern states, as they will have a majority, can by law create the most oppressive monopoly upon the five southern states, whose circumstances and production are essentially different from theirs. . . ."[28] Many Anti-Federalists suggested that the two-thirds requirement rejected in Philadelphia should be resurrected in the form of a constitutional amendment. For example, the North Carolina convention proposed an amendment stating that "no navigation law, or law regulating commerce, shall be passed without the consent of two thirds of the members present in both houses."[29]

The strife from sectional differences over commerce did come to pass, but did so in the form of a protective tariff rather than a navigation act. The agricultural states of the South sold their crops on the world market and then purchased manufactured goods from Europe. The higher the tariff, the fewer manufactured goods could be purchased by Southerners. Congress enacted protective tariffs as early as 1789, but the rates did not become oppressive to Southerners until after the War of 1812. During the war years when trade with Britain was halted because of an embargo, multiple factories were founded in the North. After the war, Congress sought to protect these new manufacturers by passing a tariff averaging 25 percent of the value of imported goods.

Many Southerners complained, but a nationalistic spirit derived from the war years caused prominent Southern statesmen such as John C. Calhoun to support the tariff.

Over the next few years tariff rates increased and the prices of agricultural commodities fell. Cotton, for example, brought 30 cents per pound in 1818 and just a dime per pound by the late 1830s. In 1824, Congress increased the tariff to an average of 33 ½ percent the value of imported goods. Just four years later, the protectionists in Congress jacked up the rates to an average of 50 percent of the value of imported goods. The combination of low commodity prices and high tariffs caused widespread hardship throughout the South.

Calhoun came down from the nationalistic high spawned by the War of 1812 and joined other Southerners in embracing nullification of the Tariff of 1828—known as the Tariff of Abominations. South Carolina declared this tariff null and void within the jurisdiction of the state. South Carolina argued that tariffs other than for the purpose of raising revenue exceeded Congress's delegated powers. The nullification controversy almost led to war between South Carolina and President Andrew Jackson. Both sides mobilized forces. Jackson sought to maintain the primacy of the union, and South Carolina sought to maintain the principle that the people of the several states were the final arbiters of the constitutionality of legislation. Fortunately, a compromise was reached on the tariff that lowered rates, and this caused South Carolina to rescind its Ordinance of Nullification.

Modern Abuses

The Commerce Clause is today a main source of national power. George-town Professor Randy Barnett further describes the Commerce Clause as "the enumerated power that has most often been used by Congress to restrict the liberties of the people."[30] Congress uses the commerce power to pass laws dealing with such diverse matters as civil rights, possession of child pornography, and the use of marijuana. Prior to 1937, for the most part, the Commerce Clause was exercised to regulate the exchange or trading of goods between people in different states. Franklin Delano Roosevelt's "New Deal" legislative program changed this. A key part of the New Deal program was the National Labor Relations Act of 1935. Passed pursuant to the Commerce Clause, the law encouraged collective bargaining and prohibited employers from discouraging union activity in their hiring practices. In *NLRB v. Jones & Laughlin Steel Corp.*,[31] a steel manufacturer challenged the Act as a usurpation of the states' reserved power to regulate labor relations. The company argued that the manufacturing of steel was a local activity beyond the reach of Congress. The manufacturing process preceded and is separate from the interstate selling and shipment of steel; therefore, federal regulation of employment relations cannot be a valid exercise of the commerce power. Employment conditions are independent from intercourse for the purpose of trade, which is commerce.

The Supreme Court rejected this argument and held that workforce unionization, though an intrastate activity, bore such a close relationship to interstate commerce that congressional regulation was proper. "Although activities may be intrastate in character when separately considered," wrote the Court's majority, "if they have such a close and substantial relation to interstate commerce that their control is essential or appropriate to protect that commerce from burdens and obstructions, Congress cannot be denied the power to exercise that control."[32] Because labor unrest contains the possibility of obstructing the flow of steel products across state lines, the Court deemed the regulated activity to fall within Congress's reach.

The commerce power further expanded when the Court upheld provisions of the Agricultural Adjustment Act of 1938 that permitted the federal government to set quotas on the amount of wheat grown. Farmers were allotted a certain amount of acreage for the raising of wheat. If they planted more than their allotment, they could be assessed a monetary penalty. Through this program, Congress sought to control the price of wheat from year to year. Roscoe C. Filburn brought suit to challenge the Act. For the 1941 crop, the government allotted Filburn 11.1 acres of wheat. Filburn instead planted 23 acres and the regulators demanded that he pay a $117.11 fine.

In his lawsuit, Filburn argued that the wheat beyond his allotted 11.1 acres was for home consumption. He objected to marketing quotas that embraced not just what he sold to others, but what he used to feed livestock and to provide for his family. Filburn urged the Supreme Court to find that such activity was purely local and thus beyond the reach of the interstate commerce power. The Court rejected Filburn's arguments and noted that a local activity may be regulated "if it exerts a substantial economic effect on interstate commerce."[33]

While the Court conceded that Filburn's few acres might not seem to have a substantial effect on the national market, the Court stated that the matter must be looked at in the aggregate. "That [Filburn's] own contribution to the demand for wheat may be trivial by itself is not enough to remove him from the scope of federal regulation where, as here, his contribution, taken together with that of many others similarly situated, is far from trivial."[34] Because wheat produced for home consumption by Filburn and other farmers could affect the market inasmuch as demand would drop, the government could dictate the quantity of wheat grown by Filburn.

Wickard v. Filburn represents a substantial departure from the original understanding of the Commerce Clause. Aside from the evidence discussed in the beginning of this chapter, Federalists repeatedly stressed that local activities such as agriculture and manufacturing would not be subject to national intervention. In *Federalist* No. 17, Hamilton observed that commerce, finance, foreign affairs, and war were the chief ends of the national government. Items such as "[t]he administration of private justice between citizens of the same State, *the supervision of agriculture*, and other concerns of a similar nature" were the province of the states and "can never be desirable cares of general jurisdiction."[35] Oh, but desirable they were and continue to be.

Over the years, the Court has built on the foundation of *Wickard v. Filburn*. A prime example is *Gonzales v. Raich*.[36] The question presented in *Raich* was whether Congress may prohibit the medicinal use of cannabis under the federal Controlled Substances Act—even if the cannabis at issue is grown using only soil, water, nutrients, tools, and supplies made or originating in a single state, never crosses state lines, and never is sold in the stream of commerce.

The *Raich* case arose out of California, which passed a Compassionate Use Act in 1996. Under the law a patient or his primary caregiver may possess or cultivate cannabis solely for the personal medicinal use of the patient as recommended by a physician. Pursuant to state law, Angel Raich and Diane Monson used cannabis for medicinal purposes. Raich suffered from an inoperable brain tumor, seizures, paralysis, chronic pain, life-threatening weight loss, and many other ailments. Monson was afflicted with chronic back pain and muscle spasms caused by a degenerative disease of the spine. Their physicians concluded that Raich's and Monson's pain could not be relieved with ordinary medication and thus prescribed marijuana.

Despite Raich's and Monson's compliance with California law, in 2002 federal drug enforcement agents besieged Monson's home. A three-hour stand-off ensued that resulted in the agents confiscating and destroying all six of her cannabis plants. The federal Controlled Substances Act trumped the state Compassionate Use Act.

Denying the constitutionality of the federal law as applied to them, Raich and Monson headed to the courts and eventually reached the Supreme Court. Not surprisingly, the High Court's opinion in *Raich* relied heavily on *Wickard*. Like the growing of wheat for personal consumption, Justice John Paul Stevens noted for the *Raich* majority that "the diversion of homegrown marijuana tends to frustrate the federal interest in eliminating commercial transactions in the interstate market in their entirety."[37] "[P]roduction of the commodity meant for home consumption, be it wheat or marijuana, has a substantial effect on supply and demand in the national market for that commodity."[38] The fact that some purely *intra*state activity is ensnared by the Controlled Substances Act was "of no moment" to Justice Stevens. Raich's and Monson's activities fell within the commerce power.

The most troubling aspect of the *Raich* decision is the expansive definition of "economic activity" used by Justice Stevens. In prior decisions that somewhat limited Congress's power under the Commerce Clause, the Court noted that the cumulative effects analysis of *Wickard* is applied only if the activity Congress seeks to reach is "economic." The *Raich* majority defined "economic" as "the production, distribution, and consumption of commodities."[39] According to the *Raich* decision, the growing of plants for use at home is economic activity because it involves the production and consumption of a "commodity." Under this reasoning, the growing of a single tomato plant in a container on one's balcony is economic activity and thus may be regulated by Congress. Congress could even prohibit a child from painting a picture to hang on the wall in the child's room because this involves the production of a commodity. Moreover, if all children created their own art, then this could substantially affect the interstate market for art.

Justice Clarence Thomas, in his dissenting opinion, correctly summed up the result of *Raich*: "If Congress can regulate this under the Commerce Clause, then it can regulate virtually anything—and the Federal Government is no longer one of limited and enumerated powers."[40]

The reasoning of *Wickard* and *Raich*, coupled with the post–New Deal uses of the commerce power, effectively obliterates the idea of a limited national government with few and defined powers. In 1787, the ideas and goals behind the commerce power were not vague, but the Court's and Congress's claim that commerce equals productive activity confers a limitless power. With Congress now claiming the power to regulate all economic activity rather than just commerce, Mason's and Lee's advocacy of the two-thirds requirement for Commerce-Clause legislation is appealing. If the Commerce Clause is now transformed into a broad police power, then surely a supermajority should be required before Congress acts. Lee and Mason worried about the Northern states oppressing the Southern states with navigation laws. Today, it is the ruling class oppressing the people of all fifty states.

9

The Necessary and Proper Clause

THE LIST OF Congress's delegated powers found in Section 8 of Article I concludes with the Necessary and Proper Clause. The Constitution grants Congress the power "[t]o make all laws which shall be necessary and proper for carrying into execution the foregoing powers, and all other powers vested by this constitution in the government of the United States, or any department or officer thereof."¹ The Federalists and Anti-Federalists disagreed on the import of this so-called Sweeping Clause. The former contended that the clause granted nothing that did not already exist, while the latter feared that this addition nullified the enumerated powers.

"Under such a clause as this," asked "An Old Whig," "can any thing be said to be reserved and kept back from Congress? Can it be said that the Congress have no power but what is *expressed*?"² This clause reminded "An Old Whig" of the Declaratory Act of 1766 in which Parliament claimed the power to pass legislation governing the colonies in all cases whatsoever. This hated act of Parliament, "An Old Whig" opined, "was not more extensive" than the Necessary and Proper Clause.³

The Federal Farmer concurred with "An Old Whig's" analysis. He believed that with the Necessary and Proper Clause tacked on to the enumerated powers, "it is almost impossible to have a just conception of [Congress's] powers, or of the extent and number of the laws which may be deemed necessary and proper to carry them into effect."⁴

Centinel believed that not only could Congress claim powers not granted but that it could also threaten the state governments. "Whatever law congress may deem necessary and proper for carrying into execution any of the powers vested in them, may be enacted," wrote Centinel, "and by virtue of this clause they may control and abrogate any and every of the laws of the state governments, on the allegation that they interfere with the execution of their powers. . . ."⁵ Brutus similarly feared that such a comprehensive power might "be exercised in such a manner as entirely to abolish the state legislatures."⁶

In the Pennsylvania ratifying convention, James Wilson dismissed the objections raised by the Anti-Federalists. According to Wilson, the Necessary and Proper Clause "is saying no more than that the powers we have already particularly given shall be effectually carried into execution."⁷ Alexander Hamilton, in *Federalist* No. 33, similarly described the effect of the clause. "And it is *expressly* to execute these powers that the sweeping clause, as it has been affectedly called, authorizes the national legislature to pass all *necessary* and *proper* laws," explained Hamilton. "If there is any thing exceptionable, it must be sought for in the specific powers upon which this general declaration is predicated."⁸ Seen in this light, Hamilton continued, the Necessary and Proper Clause "may be chargeable with tautology or redundancy, is at least perfectly harmless."⁹

James Madison also addressed the clause in *Federalist* No. 44. Madison began by observing that it would have been difficult if not impossible for the Philadelphia Convention to have enumerated all powers necessary and proper to the executing of the enumerated powers. Had the Convention attempted such a thing, the result would have been a digest of laws rather than a constitution. Moreover, the members of the Grand Convention were not clairvoyant and thus could not foresee changes bringing about new applications of the delegated powers.

Similar to Hamilton, Madison also claimed that the Necessary and Proper Clause was a redundancy:

> Had the Constitution been silent on this head, there can be no doubt that all the particular powers requisite as means of executing the general powers would have resulted to the government, by unavoidable implication. No axiom is more clearly established in law, or in reason, than that wherever the end is required, the means are authorized; wherever a general power to do a thing is given, every particular power necessary for doing it is included.¹⁰

The National Bank

The power of the Necessary and Proper Clause was tested early during Washington's first term as president. In 1791, Secretary of the Treasury Alexander Hamilton recommended that Congress establish a national bank. Hamilton described the bank as "an institution of primary importance to the prosperous administration of [national] finances, and would be of the greatest utility in the operations connected with the support of public credit."[11] Hamilton informed Congress that the "most enlightened commercial nations" had established national banks and that the United States should follow suit.[12] The trade and industry of England, Holland, and other countries had been aided greatly by national banks. If the United States desired to put its finances on a solid footing like those nations, Hamilton urged, a bank would be a key ingredient.

In outlining the main advantages of a national bank, Hamilton cited the "active augmentation" of gold and silver.[13] When simply used as instruments of exchange, gold and silver, according to Hamilton, are "dead stock."[14] But if specie is deposited in a bank, paper bank notes circulate in their place and give the precious metals "an active and productive quality."[15] Through fractional reserve banking, Hamilton continued, "banks in good credit can circulate a far greater sum than the actual quantum of their capital in gold and silver."[16] The capital of a country is increased and permits the loaning of money to merchants and manufacturers in excess of bank reserves. "[B]y contributing to enlarge the mass of industrious and commercial enterprise, banks become nurseries of national wealth."[17]

Hamilton also cited the ability of a national bank to assist the government in responding to emergencies. In case of war or threatened invasion, large amounts of capital have already been collected in one place and thus can be used effectively to support the government. The government can obtain loans and quickly pay and supply troops needed to meet the threat.

Hamilton also claimed that "[t]he facilitating of the payment of taxes" would be another benefit of a national bank.[18] A person short of money could procure loans from the bank to answer the call of the tax collector. In addition, a taxpayer would not be burdened with the "trouble, delay, expense, and risk" of transferring gold and silver.[19] Bank notes would make the process easier and quicker for all parties involved.

Hamilton's bank ignited a fervent debate in the House of Representatives. Southerners charged that the bank would benefit the mercantile interest centered in the North while doing nothing for the yeoman farmers. They also questioned its constitutionality. Even if a national bank would be conducive to the financial health of the union, whence, they asked, did the power to charter this corporation come?

To answer this question, the bank's proponents advanced remarkably broad theories of constitutional interpretation on the floor of Congress. Fisher Ames of Massachusetts opined that "Congress may do what is necessary to the end for which the constitution was adopted."[20] And just what were the ends? According to Theodore Sedgwick, who also represented Massachusetts, "the public good and general welfare" were the ultimate ends.[21] Elbridge Gerry concurred with his neighbors from Massachusetts and pointed Congress to the Constitution's preamble. Providing for the common defense and general welfare, he observed, were the great objects of the Constitution and should guide interpretation of the enumerated powers. John Lawrence of New York argued that since there was nothing expressly included in the Constitution forbidding a bank "we ought not to deduce a prohibition by construction."[22] He continued: "A full uncontrollable power to regulate the fiscal concerns of this Union, is a primary consideration in this Government; and, from hence, it clearly follows, that it must possess the power to make every possible arrangement conducive to that great power."[23]

Congressman James Madison was shocked as he listened to the arguments of his colleagues. The construction put forward would destroy the system of enumerated powers crafted in Philadelphia. He reminded Congress that if no power pertaining to creation of a national bank was enumerated, then the only means of justifying it would be the Necessary and Proper Clause. But to use this clause, the proposed legislation had to be "direct and incidental" to some specific power.[24] Remote implications should not be relied upon or else Congress may "reach every object of legislation."[25] Madison also reminded Congress that the Philadelphia Convention had considered listing the power to charter corporations in the enumerated powers, but decided against giving such a power to the federal government. This decision, coupled with Federalist promises that the national government would be limited, counseled against creation of Hamilton's bank.

Despite Madison's advocacy, Congress passed the bank bill and sent it to President Washington for his signature. Washington, however, was uncomfortable with the legislation and asked Attorney General Edmund Randolph and Secretary of State Thomas Jefferson for their opinions on the bill. Both Randolph and Jefferson believed that the bill was unconstitutional. In his opinion, Jefferson began with the Tenth Amendment: "The powers not delegated to the United States by the Constitution, nor prohibited by it to the States, are reserved to the States respectively, or to the people."[26] Jefferson described this as the foundation of constitutional interpretation. "To take a single step around the powers of Congress," he warned, "is to take possession of a boundless field of power, no longer susceptible of any definition."[27]

Jefferson examined the enumerated powers and concluded that all of them could be performed without the creation of a bank. Jefferson acknowledged that the bank might make the collection of taxes more convenient, but he denied that convenience and necessity were synonyms. Necessary, in Jefferson's view, restrained the national government "to those means, without which the grant of power would be nugatory."[28]

To modern ears, Jefferson's view of the Necessary and Proper Clause might seem rigid. We must understand his stance in the context of the debate. The nationalists in Congress propounded a vision of the Constitution and the Necessary and Proper Clause that would have permitted any measure tangentially connected with the broad goals of the union. These nationalists paid little attention to the idea of restrictions on enumerations of power. Instead, they contended that so long as the bank or anything else was not specifically prohibited, then Congress should presume that it had the requisite power. Aghast at the nationalist interpretation, Jefferson sought to craft a bright-line test to guide use of the Necessary and Proper Clause. He hoped that his interpretation would persuade Washington to champion the careful enumeration of powers so often touted by Federalists in the ratification debates.

The opinions of Randolph and Jefferson certainly concerned Washington. As he mulled the matter, he asked Hamilton to also provide an opinion on the constitutionality of the bank. After studying Randolph's and Jefferson's opinions, Hamilton complied and averred that the analysis of his colleagues in the cabinet "would be fatal to the just and indispensable authority of the United States."[29] A means was necessary, according to Hamilton, so long as it was useful or helpful to the exercise of a delegated power. Pointing to recent federal legislation erecting lighthouses and buoys for the furtherance of commerce, Hamilton observed that while these navigational aids were helpful to ships participating in the carrying trade, they were not strictly necessary. But few people complained that these lighthouses and buoys were authorized in contravention to the Constitution. "If the end be clearly comprehended within any of the specified powers, and if the measure have an obvious relation to that end, and is not forbidden by any particular provision of the constitution," Hamilton reasoned, "it may safely be deemed to come within the compass of the national authority."[30]

Impressed with Hamilton's arguments, Washington signed the bank bill into law.

McCulloch v. Maryland

The Supreme Court joined the debate on the Bank of the United States almost thirty years later when it heard the case of *McCulloch v. Maryland* (1819).[31] Actually, this case concerned the Second Bank of the United States. The charter of the original bank expired in 1811. A charter for the Second Bank of the United States was issued in 1816—with the approval of President James Madison. Madison believed that the public had accepted a national bank as constitutional and thus he abandoned his earlier opposition.

The Second Bank was unpopular with Jeffersonians and quickly gained a reputation as a corrupt institution. Historians agree that the Second Bank was plagued by mismanagement. James W. McCulloch was the cashier for the Maryland branch of the bank and faced a state fine for circulating a bank note without the stamp required by Maryland law. While much of the case dealt with a state's power to tax a branch of the bank, opponents of the Second Bank also raised questions about the constitutionality of its existence.

Chief Justice John Marshall rightly began his analysis of the case by asking whether "Congress [has] power to incorporate a bank."[32] He readily admitted that no enumerated power existed allowing the chartering of a corporation, and then turned to whether the creation of a bank was incidental to some enumerated power. Like Hamilton had done before him, Marshall took note of the powers to raise taxes, borrow money, regulate commerce, and raise military forces. The government must "be allowed to select the means" to carry out its delegated power so long as the means are "convenient, or useful, or essential."[33] Marshall further implied that the means had to bear a reasonable fit or relationship to the ultimate end proposed. "Let the end be legitimate, let it be within the scope of the constitution, and all means which are appropriate, which are plainly adapted to that end, which are not prohibited, but consist with the letter and spirit of the constitution, are constitutional."[34] Based on these principles, the Court upheld the chartering of the Second Bank of the United States.

Modern Usage

Debate about the scope of the Necessary and Proper Clause continues in the twenty-first century. Sadly, modern uses and arguments stretch the clause beyond even what Hamilton and Marshall envisioned. In *United States v. Comstock* (2010),[35] the Supreme Court considered the constitutionality of a statute permitting the civil commitment of a person convicted of a sex crime beyond the period of his incarceration. For example, if a district court sentenced a defendant to ten years imprisonment—the statutory maximum—for possession of child pornography, 18 U.S.C. § 4248 permits continued confinement if the defendant is deemed dangerous.

The Supreme Court framed the issue as follows: "The question presented is whether the Necessary and Proper Clause . . . grants Congress authority to enact the statute before us."[36] Surprisingly, the Court did not frame the issue in terms of whether § 4248 carried into effect an enumerated power granted in the Constitution. When one delves into the opinion, it is no surprise why the Court framed the question in the manner that it did. The opinion is almost bereft of any concern with the enumerated powers of Congress. Indeed, nowhere in the five-factor test employed by the Court to judge the constitutionality of this detention statute can be found a reference to powers delegated to the national government. In upholding the statute, the Court reasoned that because Congress can enact criminal laws pursuant to enumerated powers, and the building and operation of prisons is an incident of this power, it follows that

Congress can detain a dangerous federal prisoner for as long as he is deemed a threat to society.

That reasoning is faulty. While Congress may have the power to enact criminal laws and to incarcerate individuals convicted of violating those laws, it does not follow that Congress may enact statutes to keep individuals in custody after their prison terms. The power to construct and operate prisons is not an independent grant of power under the Constitution. The operation of a penal system is permitted because it carries into execution one of Congress's other enumerated powers. Section 4248, however, does not aid in the punishment of individuals found guilty of breaking federal laws. Instead, it allows detention of prisoners who have completed their sentences. Under the Court's reasoning, so long as the statute is related to an ancillary power that in turn is related to an enumerated power, Congress can rely on the Necessary and Proper Clause. This is nothing but the house-that-Jack-built argument criticized by Jefferson and others.

The Anti-Federalists feared that the Necessary and Proper Clause would whisk away the idea of enumerated powers and offer the national government an unlimited reservoir of power. The approach to the detention statute in *Comstock* does just that. While reasonable persons might reach different conclusions about the necessity and propriety of a national bank, at least Hamilton could point to enumerated powers when making his proposals. The *Comstock* majority relieves Congress of this basic requirement. "An Old Whig's" comparison of the Necessary and Proper Clause to the Declaratory Act looks less like hyperbole and more like prophecy.

10

Voter Qualifications

UNDER THE ARTICLES, delegates to the Confederation Congress were "annually appointed in such a manner as the legislature of each state shall direct."[1] The states reserved the power to recall delegates and to appoint new delegates in their place. The Articles required that the states send at least two delegates, but prohibited a state delegation from exceeding seven members. The Constitution of 1787 retained state legislative appointment of senators, but decreed that members of the House "be chosen every second year by the people of the several states."[2] For House elections, the Framers left the matter of voter qualification to the states: "the electors in each state shall have the qualifications requisite for the electors of the most numerous branch of the State Legislature."[3] Thus, the Voter Qualifications Clause allowed states to require that a voter hold a certain amount of property or be current on tax payments, but those requirements had to apply equally to voters for a state's lower house and to voters for the federal House. As a matter of fact, House members were the only officials elected popularly as of 1787.

At the Philadelphia Convention, Gouverneur Morris of Pennsylvania objected to leaving the qualifications of electors to the states. He wanted to set forth national requirements for electors such as a freehold requirement. Connecticut's Oliver Ellsworth expressed comfort with the states retaining full authority over voter qualifications and observed that "suffrage was a tender point and strongly guarded by most of the State Constitutions."[4] He contended that "[t]he States are the best Judges of the circumstances & temper of their own people."[5] Other delegates pointed out the difficulty in defining a freeholder and some inveighed against property requirements. In the end,

Morris's proposal was defeated soundly and garnered the vote of only one state delegation: Delaware.

Times, Places, and Manner Clause

The Constitution also left the states with the power to set "[t]he times places and manner of holding elections for Senators and Representatives."[6] However, it allowed Congress "at any time by law [to] make or alter such regulations, except as to the place of choosing Senators."[7] At the Philadelphia Convention, Madison argued that this congressional oversight was necessary for two reasons. First, he worried that if a state legislature had a favorite policy or candidate, it "would take care so as to mold their regulations as to favor the candidates they wished to succeed."[8] Such gamesmanship would be unscrupulous and should be banned from federal elections. Second, Madison feared that the states might "fail or refuse altogether" to hold elections for the House.[9] If the states did so, they could destroy the national government.

Hamilton picked up on this theme in *Federalist* No. 59 when he wrote that the Times, Places, and Manner Clause "rests upon the evidence of this plain proposition, that every government ought to contain in itself the means of its own preservation."[10]

Hamilton assured Americans that Congress would only use the Times, Places, and Manner Clause "whenever extraordinary circumstances might render that interposition necessary to its safety."[11] Madison, in the Virginia ratifying convention, further predicted that so long as the states regularly held elections for federal offices, "congressional control will very probably never be exercised."[12]

The Anti-Federalists distrusted the power granted to Congress in the Times, Places, and Manner Clause. They were concerned that Congress could use that power to make it onerous for the ordinary people to vote. Congress might make the place of voting difficult to attend by establishing it far away from population centers. Or, Congress might set the time for voting during the harvest when it would be almost impossible to leave ripe fields and travel to polling places. "Congress may establish a place, or places," wrote Cato, "at either the extremes, center, or outer parts of the states: at a time and season too, when it may be very inconvenient to attend; and by these means destroy the rights of election."[13] Brutus shared Cato's concern. "The proposed Congress may make the whole state one district, and direct, that the capital . . . shall be the place for holding the election."[14]

Centinel saw the Times, Places, and Manner Clause in a more sinister light. He believed that the clause was necessary to give the national government legitimacy after it had overridden the several states. "[W]hen the state legislatures drop out of sight," he averred, "from the necessary operation of this government, then Congress are to provide for the election and appointment of representatives and senators."[15]

Some of the Constitution's opponents expressed concern that Congress would use the Times, Places, and Manner Clause to alter state voting requirements in an effort to perpetuate themselves in office. Federalists such as John Steele of North Carolina soon reassured Anti-Federalists that "[t]he power over the manner of elections does not include that of saying who shall vote."[16] Rufus King in Massachusetts and Edmund Randolph in Virginia made similar representations to their respective conventions.[17]

The Anti-Federalists were not persuaded by the Federalists' promises about the limited scope of the Times, Places, and Manner Clause. Multiple state conventions demanded amendments to the clause. Virginia, for example, proposed the following:

> That Congress shall not alter, modify, or interfere in the times, places, or manner of holding elections for senators and representatives, or either of them, except when the legislature of any state shall neglect, refuse, or be disabled, by invasion or rebellion, to prescribe the same.[18]

Virginia's amendment would have left with Congress the power of self-preservation to which Hamilton referred in *Federalist* No. 59. If the states attempted to destroy the national government by refusing to hold elections, or if they were hindered by an armed foe, the federal government could set the time, place, and manner of an election. Congress would have its insurance policy, and the Anti-Federalists would have additional security to guarantee Federalist assurances about the scope of the power. Unfortunately, the first Congress did not act upon the request of Virginia and other states. Thus, the Times, Places, and Manner Clause remained unchanged.

For most of American history, Congress has not attempted to abuse this constitutional provision. Congress has not set inconvenient times, places, or manners of elections to frustrate the will of the people. But what it has done, with the aid of the Supreme Court, is to claim that the clause gives it authority to void state efforts to determine voter qualifications.

National Voter Registration Act

Congressional abuse of the Times, Places, and Manner Clause is exemplified in *Arizona v. Intertribal Council* (2013).[19] Since it became a state in 1912, Arizona has had a citizenship requirement for voters. In 2004 the people of the state, in an effort to combat voter fraud, enacted Proposition 200. This initiative requires that every application for voter registration be "accompanied by satisfactory evidence of United States citizenship."[20] Arizona statutory law further provides that various documents can serve as proper evidence. For example, a prospective voter may supply his birth certificate, passport, driver's license (if the issuing authority verifies citizenship), or naturalization documents.

Although Arizona's proof of citizenship requirement seems modest, unobtrusive, and within the states' reserved powers, the United States Supreme Court held that Proposition 200's provisions were preempted by federal law and thus void. Under the doctrine of preemption, "certain matters are of such a national, as opposed to local, character that federal laws preempt or take precedence over state laws."[21] This doctrine assumes that the national government has some delegated power to legislate in a particular field. Absent a delegation of power to the federal government, a preemption issue cannot arise.

The National Voter Registration Act ("NVRA") of 1993 requires that the states "accept and use" a federal form during the voter registration process.[22] The federal Election Assistance Commission ("EAC") is the body that designs the form. The federal form differs from state to state and contains a number of state-specific instructions. Arizona had asked the EAC to include the state's "satisfactory evidence" requirement on the federal form to be used in Arizona, but the EAC declined to do so. Instead of requiring documentation of citizenship, the EAC form simply instructs a registrant to affirm under penalty of perjury that he is a United States citizen.

In its registration process, Arizona had used the EAC form, but also required registrants to provide documentary proof of citizenship. When challenged in federal court about continuing to demand documentary proof, Arizona argued that the NVRA's "accept and use" provision merely directed the state to accept and use the EAC form as part of the voter qualification process. Arizona analogized the matter to electronic airline tickets. An airline accepts and uses an electronic ticket even if it also requires the passenger to produce an identification document to demonstrate that he is the person named on the ticket. Opponents of Proposition 200 argued that "accept and use" commands a state presented with the completed EAC form to register the prospective voter without requesting additional information.

The Supreme Court rejected Arizona's statutory construction and held that "the fairest reading of the statute is that a state-imposed requirement of evidence of citizenship not required by the Federal Form is inconsistent with the NVRA's mandate that States accept and use the Federal Form."[23] In the opinion, the Court simply assumed that the Times, Places, and Manner Clause of the Constitution permits the federal government to require use of the EAC form. The Court cited previous cases holding that this clause allows Congress "to provide a complete code for congressional elections."[24] The Court further described the effect of the Times, Places, and Manner Clause as follows: "In practice, the Clause functions as a default provision; it invests the States with responsibility for the mechanics of congressional elections, but only so far as Congress declines to pre-empt state legislative choices."[25]

While the latter statement is true to an extent, the Court spent little time explaining how a proof of citizenship requirement falls within the matters that Congress can regulate. As discussed earlier, under the Voter Qualifications Clause the states are at liberty to set the qualifications of voters for the federal House, so long as those qualifications also are imposed on voters for the popular branch of the state's legislature. The only exceptions to this, as Justice Clarence Thomas pointed out in dissent, are "the powers conferred by the Fourteenth, Fifteenth, Nineteenth, and Twenty-Sixth Amendments."[26] These amendments, in the main, guarantee blacks, women, and persons at least eighteen years old the right to vote. Those amendments do not touch the propriety of a citizenship requirement nor the documents a state can require to verify citizenship.

Unquestionably, the EAC form has nothing to do with the times when elections are held, the manner of voting (e.g., secret ballot or viva voce), or the places where ballots are cast. Instead, the EAC form regulates the qualifications of voters, which are subjects alien to the Times, Places, and Manner Clause. The citizenship qualification and the necessity of some documentary evidence are matters reserved to the states under the Voter Qualifications Clause. So long as Arizona requires the proof of citizenship for prospective voters for federal House races and state house races, no constitutional infirmity is detectable.

The media took little notice of the Court's expansion of the Times, Places, and Manner Clause. In modern America, the idea that the states are empowered to determine qualifications for voting in federal elections seems beyond the pale. Despite the unequivocal language of the Voter Qualifications Clause, the significant constitutional role played by the sovereign states is ignored or forgotten.

The Supreme Court did suggest that Arizona might have another remedy. The Court observed that Arizona could challenge, under the Administrative Procedures Act ("APA"), the EAC's rejection of its proof of citizenship requirement. The EAC has allowed other states to require additional documentation be attached to the EAC form, and the EAC's refusal to do the same for Arizona might be actionable.

Such an alternative was a mere specter because the EAC had no commissioners in 2013 to rule on an APA case. Republicans in the House were working to shut down the EAC and new commissioners were not appointed until January 2015.

The Court's decision in *Arizona v. Intertribal Council* is but the latest effort at removing vestiges of state sovereignty found in the Constitution. The sum of this decision is that the federal government is allowed to ignore the broad authority left to the states over elections. The insurance policy to prevent the states from destroying the national government has morphed into a weapon to deny the residual sovereignty promised to the states. If proof of citizenship is governed by the Times, Places, and Manner Clause, then what, if anything, is retained by the states?

II

Standing Armies

SIX OF CONGRESS'S enumerated powers in Article I deal with the common defense. Congress has the power to declare war, raise armies, maintain a navy, regulate the armed forces, call out the militia, and govern any militia units called into the service of the United States. Under the Confederation, Congress could engage in war and raise forces, but only with the assent of nine states. Military units were raised by the requisition system. The Articles provided that Congress would inform each state of its quota, and the states would be responsible for mobilizing and supplying the troops, with the promise of congressional reimbursement.

The Whig Tradition

The national legislature's enhanced powers over military concerns in the Constitution of 1787 worried many Anti-Federalists. The English Whig tradition warned against standing armies. The Whigs, of course, were champions of constitutional government and opponents of royal absolutism. For example, in their influential *Cato's Letters*, written just decades after James II attempted to turn the English army into a tool of oppression, John Trenchard and Thomas Gordon cautioned that a people could be enslaved only by superstition and force. By force, Trenchard and Gordon thought of standing armies. "It is certain, that in all Parts of Europe, which are enslaved, have been enslaved by Armies," they observed, "and it is absolutely impossible that any Nation which keeps them amongst themselves can long preserve their liberties."[1]

The Scottish reformer James Burgh echoed Trenchard's and Gordon's view of armies. In his *Political Disquisitions*, Burgh averred that "[n]o nation was enslaved but by an army" and that no nation keeping an army in times of peace maintained its liberties. A standing army, to Burgh, was "one of the most hurtful, and most dangerous of abuses" found in government.[2]

Whigs pointed to sundry instances when armies were used not to defend a realm but to control it. In his *Wealth of Nations*, Adam Smith took up the subject of armies and reminded readers of the dangers of military establishments. Smith pointed to the harm done to the Roman Republic by Julius Caesar. After he was ordered by the Senate to stand trial in Rome, Caesar marched on Rome with a legion and seized power. He centralized the governing apparatus and became a dictator in perpetuity. Smith also used an example from the English Civil War. Oliver Cromwell's New Model Army, supposedly a parliamentary army combating the evils of Charles I, forcibly dissolved the remnant of the Long Parliament and set the stage for Cromwell to become Lord Protector. Cromwell exercised supreme power and the Protectorate caused Englishmen to welcome a restoration of the monarchy in 1660.

In addition to experience, Whigs reasoned that a standing army is inimical to a free state. Soldiers typically are housed together in forts and strongholds and thus are separated from daily interaction with the common people. Soldiers also are governed by different laws than civilians and must submit to the orders of a commanding officer. Prolonged separation from the rest of society and submission to the rigors of military life, the Whigs believed, fostered a foreignness that could be abused by those in authority. Whigs did realize that many upstanding persons held commands in the army and that this provided some security against military coups d'état. But, they always reminded their opponents that good men can be dismissed from their posts and more dangerous characters promoted to positions of power.

Even the Tory William Blackstone, who along with members of his party generally favored royal authority over Parliament, believed that an army should not be a separate institution distinct from the body of the people. Blackstone urged that military units "should consist of the people, and have the same spirit with the people."[3] Soldiers should enlist for short periods and "live intermixed with the people; no separate camp, no barracks, no inland fortress should be allowed."[4] Blackstone also suggested that a general rotation in the ranks would be healthy: "by dismissing a stated number and enlisting others at every renewal of their term, a circulation could be kept up between the army and the people, and the citizen and the soldier be more intimately connected together."[5]

Whiggish principles and lessons from history taught the American colonists that constitutions should be drafted to forbid the maintenance of a standing army in peacetime. The Virginia Declaration of Rights framed the prohibition as follows: "that standing armies, in time of peace, should be avoided, as dangerous to liberty; and that, in all cases, the military should be under strict subordination to, and governed by, the civil power."[6]

Debate in America

At the end of the Revolutionary War, Americans saw firsthand the dangers of their own army. As 1783 dawned, news spread about a provisional peace treaty between the colonies and Great Britain. Officers in the continental army feared that their forces would be ordered to disband before Congress resolved the issue of back pay and pensions. Three officers left the army's winter quarters at Newburgh, New York, and demanded that Congress settle accounts. The officers made it clear that violence could erupt if Congress did not act. Alexander Hamilton and Gouverneur Morris advised the officers to use the threat of rebellion to coerce the states into approving an impost so Congress would have an independent source of revenue. Pressure from public creditors and the army, they believed, would cement a union of states.

Robert Morris, the superintendent of finance of the government, arranged for some payment to the soldiers, but this did not satisfy the officers for long. Anonymous letters circulated at Newburgh urging the army to refuse to disband if the war ended. The letters also suggested that if Great Britain decided to press on with the conflict, the army should retire to the wilderness and leave Congress at the mercy of the redcoats. Officers scheduled a meeting on March 15, 1783, to weigh their options. Just before the meeting began, General Washington appeared and addressed the gathering. He lamented that Congress had not adequately compensated the army, but he urged the officers not to tarnish accomplishments achieved during the war. He promised to lobby Congress for a satisfactory resolution. Essentially, Washington shamed the officers into abandoning any plans of mutiny to gain deserved payments. The meeting broke up and Washington ended the threatened rebellion.

Not surprisingly, Anti-Federalists inveighed against the fact that the Constitution had no specific prohibitions against a standing army. "[K]eeping a standing army, would be in the highest degree dangerous to the liberty and happiness of the community," observed Brutus.[7] "[T]he general government ought not to have authority to do it," he continued, "for no government should be empowered to do that which if done, would tend to destroy public liberty." The Pennsylvania minority declared that "[a] standing army in the hands of a government placed so independent of the people, may be made a fatal instrument to overturn the public liberties."[8] They feared that the army could "be employed to enforce the collection of the most oppressive taxes, and to carry into execution the most arbitrary measures."[9]

In the Massachusetts ratifying convention, Samuel Nason described standing armies as a "bane of republican government" and reminded his colleagues that George III used soldiers from a standing British force to perpetrate the Boston Massacre and to fight against American independence.[10] Indeed, the king's keeping of standing armies in the colonies, without the consent of the legislatures, was a grievance listed in the Declaration of Independence. Virginia patriot George Mason predicted in his state's convention that once Congress created a standing military force "the people [would] lose their liberty."[11]

The Militia

Mason also feared that "unless there be some restrictions on the power for calling forth the militia . . . we may very easily see that it will produce dreadful oppressions."[12] Mason warned that Congress had the power, for example, to require the Georgia militia to march all the way to New Hampshire on the pretext of danger. Placing such burdens on part-time soldiers would cause men to shun militia service. With the ranks depleted, the states would abolish the militia and the national government would use this as an excuse to create a standing force. To prevent this abuse of the militia, Mason and others suggested that state consent should be required before Congress could call out its militia units and/or that the militia units be required to go no further than neighboring states.

The militia in the American colonial period was part social institution, part police force, and part army. The colonial militias were typically comprised of all free male citizens able to bear arms in times of danger. When the militia mustered to drill, this turned into a community event where the people discussed political affairs and enjoyed fellowship. The muster often ended with celebration and the enjoyment of whiskey, rum, or beer. Such revelry should not induce us to believe that militia duty was not a serious matter. As historian Saul Cornell observed, "[f]or Americans living on the edge of the British Empire, in an age without police forces, the militia was essential for the preservation of public order and also protected Americans against external threats."[13] Militia service was as much a part of citizenship as jury duty or exercise of the franchise. Hence, the argument that the Constitution threatened the existence of the militia was a serious charge leveled by the Anti-Federalists.

In the face of such arguments, James Wilson and other Federalists went on the offensive by accusing the Anti-Federalists of working to strip the national government's power of defense. "I believe the *power* of raising and keeping up an army, in time of peace, is essential to every government," Wilson announced. "No government can secure its citizens against dangers, internal and external," he continued, "without possessing it, and sometimes carrying it into execution."[14]

Alexander Hamilton agreed with Wilson's assessment. In *Federalist* No. 22, he complained that the Confederation's supermajority requirement and requisition system was proven ineffectual during the war. States bid against each other with bounties for enlistments. As bounties grew higher, men delayed military service in hopes of obtaining a larger financial gain. Hamilton also bewailed that the states "near the seat of war, influenced by motives of self-preservation, made efforts to furnish their quotas, which even exceeded their abilities; while those at a distance from danger were, for the most part, as remiss as the others were diligent, in their exertions."[15]

Hamilton ridiculed the Confederation's supermajority requirement for the raising of troops. "To give a minority a negative upon the majority (which is always the case where more than a majority is requisite to a decision)," Hamilton wrote, would turn republican government into the rule of the few.[16] This requirement would make it easier for foreign powers to bribe or influence a handful of states to oppose the prosecution of a war or acceptance of peace terms. Mere majority voting, however, would limit this danger. It would become too expensive for a foreign power to attempt to pay off a majority of the states in the union.

In the Virginia convention, Madison assailed Mason's idea that the national government would abuse the militia units and thus necessitate a standing army. "The most effectual way to guard against a standing army," Madison explained "is to render it unnecessary."[17] And "[t]he most effectual way to render it unnecessary, is to give the general government full power to call forth the militia, and exert the whole natural strength of the Union, when necessary."[18] Madison also rejected the suggested state negative on calling out the militia. "If you put it in the power of the state governments to refuse the militia, by requiring their consent," Madison reasoned, "you destroy the general government, and sacrifice particular states."[19]

While the militia had on occasions during the war gained much honor in battle, the Federalists rejected the claim of some Anti-Federalists that the militia should be the primary obstacle to foreign invaders. Veterans of the war could cite multiple instances when the militia broke ranks and ran, leaving the continental army in the lurch. "The steady operation of war against a regular and disciplined army," wrote Hamilton, "can only be successfully conducted by a force of the same kind."[20] Hamilton described war as "a science to be acquired and perfected by diligence, by perseverance, by time, and by practice."[21] Hence, the militia could never be a match for a professional army.

Compromise on the Militia

The Constitution's provisions dealing with the militia and standing armies represented a compromise between the classic Whig position and Hamilton's desire for a permanent professional force. Congress could raise a professional force, but the militia remained an important component of defense. Congress could call the militia into service to repel invasions, suppress rebellions, and to execute the laws of the union. The Constitution empowered Congress to organize, arm, and to discipline the militia. The states retained the power to appoint officers and to train the units following congressional guidelines.

The first congressional measure passed governing the militia was the Militia Act of 1792. All able-bodied white men, between the ages of 18 and 45 years, were to be enrolled for militia duty. Congress required each man to provide his own musket and other necessary equipment. Congress provided that the states should organize and train the militia by the standards set by each state.[22] This law remained on the books until it was repealed by the Dick Act in 1903. The militia was officially renamed and became the National Guard. No longer would the militia be all able-bodied males of a certain age, but instead it would be a select group of volunteers organized along the lines of a regular army. In 1908, Congress further provided that when it called the National Guard into service, units could be compelled to serve abroad. This provision of overseas service contradicted the constitutional command that the militia could only be called forth to suppress insurrection, repel invasions, and to execute the laws of the Union. In 1912, the Judge Advocate General of the U.S. Army held that this overseas service requirement exceeded Congress's authority under the Constitution.

Experience in the Spanish American War, America's first major war of interventionism, persuaded the national government that it needed to be able to count on the militias to serve abroad and not limit themselves to the area prescribed by the Constitution. To circumvent the constitutional issue of foreign service identified by the Judge Advocate General, in World War I the federal government simply drafted members of the National Guard into regular army units. In 1933, Congress established a "dual enlistment" system whereby every person joining a state Guard simultaneously joins the National Guard of the United States, a wholly federal reserve force. Thus, rather than having to draft guardsmen to serve abroad, Congress simply mobilizes the National Guard of the United States.

Our armed forces (currently 1.2 million strong) have not been used as the Anti-Federalists feared to bully Americans into submission. However, we would be wrong to believe that our standing army and its frequent deployment overseas do not negatively affect our liberties. For example, the scholar Murray Rothbard, when examining the growth of national power in the twentieth century, observed that the greatest increases in governmental power occurred during our foreign wars: "It was wartime that provided the crisis situation—the spark—which enabled . . . so-called 'emergency' measures, which of course never got lifted, or rarely got lifted."[23] World War I is a prime example. According to Professor Randall G. Holcombe, during the war to make the world safe for democracy, "[t]he railroads were nationalized, waterborne shipping was regulated, and the United States Food Administration, created in 1917, controlled all aspects of the food industry, from agriculture to distribution to sales. Similar regulation was applied to fuels, and eventually to the whole economy."[24] The legacy of this "war socialism" in the United States conditioned labor and capital to accept later government intrusions in various markets and sectors of the economy.[25]

America Abroad

Depending on how one counts, the United States maintains upwards of 800 military bases overseas.[26] George Mason University's Hugh Gusterson estimates that these bases "constitute 95 percent of all the military bases any country in the world maintains on any other country's territory."[27] Granted, some of these installations are tiny with but a few personnel. Nonetheless, the 95 percent figure is shocking. According to the Pentagon, it has 80,000 troops stationed in Europe, 39,000 in Japan, and 30,000 in South Korea.[28] The numbers in Iraq and Afghanistan have been fluid, but the cost of our involvement in these two countries, adjusted for inflation, exceeds what was spent on the Revolutionary War, the War of 1812, the Mexican-American War, the Civil War, and the Spanish-American War combined.[29]

In dollars, the cost of maintaining all these bases abroad exceeds $100 billion annually.[30] The real cost, however, is the resentment level and hostility generated by our presence abroad. After the United States ejected Saddam Hussein from Kuwait in the first Gulf War, we kept bases in Saudi Arabia and supposed that a military presence there would contribute to our security and the stability of the region. In reality, our presence in the land of Mecca caused Osama bin Laden and other fundamentalists to engage in a cowardly war of terrorism against our people at home and abroad. This presence in Saudi Arabia actually undermined our security rather than enhancing it.

With our entry into the war against terror, government pushed the envelope on civil liberties in the name of national defense. Under the PATRIOT Act, Congress permitted government investigators to more easily eavesdrop on Internet activity, FBI agents to turn from crime control to gathering domestic intelligence, Treasury Department officials to gather information for use by the CIA, and the CIA, banished from the field of domestic intelligence because of abuses in the Vietnam era, to resume domestic operations. We also saw the George W. Bush administration unsuccessfully argue to the Supreme Court that it could detain American citizens and foreign nationals on U.S. soil indefinitely and without access to legal counsel—all when the writ of habeas corpus had not even been suspended. The Bush administration even defended the use of torture to glean information about terrorist activities.

Over one hundred years ago, William Graham Sumner warned that American interventionism abroad would put our system of government at risk. Just as the United States was about to go to war against Spain and obtain dominions to govern, Sumner saw that we were "throwing away some of the most important elements of the American symbol and . . . adopting some of the most important elements of the Spanish symbol."[31] By taking away Spanish possessions on the ground that Spain was failing in her colonial mission in Cuba, Sumner believed that the United States would "shrivel up into the same vanity and self-conceit of which Spain now presents an example."[32] If the United States truly believed in liberty, then Sumner suggested that it should tend to its own affairs and leave other peoples "to live out their own lives in their own way."[33] What would be in store for the United States if it succumbed to the temptations of interventionism? "The answer is: war, debt, taxation, diplomacy, a grand governmental system, pomp, glory, a big army and navy, lavish expenditures, political jobbery—in a word, imperialism."[34]

Eisenhower's Warning

Our liberties and form of government are also put at risk by the industrial establishment surrounding our standing army. President Dwight D. Eisenhower recognized this in his 1961 farewell address. Eisenhower lamented that the Cold War had prodded America to "annually spend on military security more than the net income of all United States corporations."[35] While many believed that the military Keynesianism was a boon for the economy, Eisenhower sensed great danger.

This conjunction of an immense military establishment and a large arms industry is new in the American experience. The total influence—economic, political, even spiritual—is felt in every city, every State house, every office of the Federal government. We recognize the imperative need for this development. Yet we must not fail to comprehend its grave implications. Our toil, resources and livelihood are all involved; so is the very structure of our society.

In the councils of government, we must guard against the acquisition of unwarranted influence, whether sought or unsought, by the military industrial complex. The potential for the disastrous rise of misplaced power exists and will persist.

We must never let the weight of this combination endanger our liberties or democratic processes. We should take nothing for granted. Only an alert and knowledgeable citizenry can compel the proper meshing of the huge industrial and military machinery of defense with our peaceful methods and goals, so that security and liberty may prosper together.[36]

In today's national security state, the military industrial complex enjoys even greater power than it did in the 1950s and early 1960s. The citizenry has not been alert and knowledgeable as Eisenhower urged. With the Soviet Union gone and peaceful relations maintained with China, the military industrial complex continues to prosper and exist in the memories of 9/11 and our perpetual war on terror. Boston University's Andrew Bacevich estimates that "[t]o train, equip, and maintain one American soldier in Iraq or Afghanistan for just one year costs a cool million dollars."[37] This means great profits for enterprises connected with the military. Those businesses make lucrative offers to retired general officers with the expectation that they will lobby their friends on active duty to clamor for the latest high-priced defense gadgets. If generals keep with the program, they know that once they retire they will be rewarded with six-figure salaries inside the defense industry. And so the cycle continues.

The idea of the citizen-solider who is representative of his community, a first principle of militia service, is all but dead. There is a disconnect between today's standing army, primarily composed of working class citizens, and upper class Americans, who largely avoid military service. "[T]he sons and daughters of those who occupy positions of influence in the corporate, intellectual, academic, journalistic, and political worlds," laments Bacevich, "have better things to do."[38] Even during the Cold War, when Eisenhower warned of the dangers of the military industrial complex, "citizenship and military service remained intimately connected."[39] But with the introduction of the All-Volunteer Force during the Nixon administration, the Americans who see themselves as the better sort—and this is a significant percentage of the population—have run from military service. Congress is a prime example of this. According to journalist Thomas E. Ricks, "during the Vietnam War two thirds of the members of Congress were veterans. Today almost two thirds are not."[40] This inversion is not healthy for society.

While there seems little risk of a Newburgh-type mutiny in the foreseeable future, Americans should not dismiss the Whiggish warning about the dangers of an army taking on an identity separate from the people. As we become further removed from the citizen-soldier concept of service, the dangers posed by a standing military force are more real today than in the eighteenth century. If we are to address the myriad issues raised by standing armies and the military industrial complex, Americans must divorce themselves from the mission of reshaping the world, through military power and nation building, into replicas of our governmental and economic systems. With no competing superpowers, a return to a small peacetime army with the limited mission of defense would cure much of what ails us. Non-coercive incentives for the children of middle- and upper-class families to serve in this smaller military establishment would make the armed forces more broadly representative of all levels of American society. Such a military would more closely resemble the Anti-Federalist view and be more conducive to liberty at home.

12

The Commander in Chief

THE PRESIDENCY CREATED by the Constitution had a role in the military powers inasmuch as the executive was designated as commander in chief of the armed forces. The government of the Confederation had no office comparable to the presidency proposed by the Constitution. The Confederation Congress exercised a mix of legislative and executive powers. Considering the major departure from the structure of the old government and the unpopularity of the Crown's royal governors in the 1760s and early 1770s, one might expect the Anti-Federalists to have challenged everything about the presidency from the novel electoral college to the four-year term of office. They did not.[1] We must remember that separation-of-powers principles, which were accepted widely in Anti-Federalist circles, counseled that the government of the union should have a separate executive branch. Moreover, the experience of the Confederation Congress in managing the war effort instructed that an executive department was necessary.

Many Anti-Federalists praised the idea of a unitary executive. "Reason, and the experience of enlightened nations, seem justly to assign the business of making laws to numerous assemblies," wrote the Federal Farmer, "and the execution of them, principally, to the direction and care of one man. Independent of practice, a single man seems to be peculiarly well circumstanced to superintend the execution of the laws with discernment and decision, with promptitude and uniformity. . . ."[2] The Federal Farmer also believed that the Constitution established "judicious combinations of principles and precautions" with the creation of an electoral college for the choosing of the president.[3] Fears of the evisceration of state power caused the Anti-Federalists to find comfort in the Constitution's provisions whereby the states would choose electors for the president.

A Generalissimo?

The functions delegated to the president, however, were another story. The Anti-Federalists expressed concern with such matters as the president's power to issue pardons, to make appointments with the advice and consent of the Senate, and to call either House of Congress into a special session. "[W]herein does this president invested with his powers and prerogatives, essentially differ from the king of Great-Britain?," asked Cato in his fourth letter.[4] He went on to describe the president as "the generalissimo of the nation" with "command and control of the army, navy and militia."[5]

In describing the president, Cato undoubtedly had in mind Blackstone's sketch of the king's military authority.

> The king is considered, in the next place, as the generalissimo, or the first in military command, within the kingdom. The great end of society is to protect the weakness of individuals by the united strength of the community: and the principal use of government is to direct that united strength in the best and most effectual manner, to answer the end proposed. Monarchical government is allowed to be the fittest of any for this purpose: it follows therefore, from the very end of it's institution, that in a monarchy the military power must be trusted in the hands of the prince.[6]

In defending the president's commander-in-chief power, Federalists tried to draw contrasts to the British king. In the North Carolina convention, James Iredell pointed out that the king of Great Britain "is not only the commander-in-chief of the land and naval forces, but has the power, in time of war, to raise fleets and armies. He also has the authority to declare war."[7] In the South Carolina convention, Charles Pinckney made similar points and stressed that the executive's "powers did not permit him to declare war."[8]

Writing in *Federalist* No. 24, Hamilton reminded his readers that "the whole power of raising armies was lodged in the *legislature*, not in the *executive*."[9] Moreover, the legislature cannot appropriate money for the support of an army "for any longer period than two years: a precaution, which, upon a nearer view of it, will appear to be a great and real security against the keeping of troops without evident necessity."[10]

James Wilson assured the Pennsylvania convention that the Constitution would not "hurry us into war" because "the important power of declaring war is vested in the legislature at large" and not the president.[11] Whereas the ambitions of kings are prone to carry countries into conflict, Wilson believed that "nothing but our national interest can draw us into a war."[12] This concern about the executive and war was expressed succinctly in a letter from Madison to Jefferson a decade after ratification. "The constitution supposes, what the History of all Govts demonstrates," elucidated Madison, "that the Ex. is the branch of power most interested in war, and prone to it."[13] For this reason, the Philadelphia Convention "vested the question of war in the Legisl."[14]

Madison elaborated on this decision when engaged in a debate with Hamilton about executive power in the early 1790s. Jeffersonians were concerned about President Washington's issuance of the Neutrality Proclamation in 1793. France and Great Britain were at war and the 1778 Treaty of Alliance with France bound the United States to defend the French West Indies and prohibited aiding the enemies of France. Neutrality was the prudent course for the young nation, but many worried that Washington's action was a usurpation of Congress's power to declare war. This executive action, as a practical matter, could negate or reduce Congress's options regarding hostilities.

Writing as Helvidius, Madison addressed the Philadelphia Convention's location of the war power in Congress. "In no part of the constitution is more wisdom to be found," Madison declared, "than in the clause which confides the question of war or peace to the legislature, and not to the executive department."[15] The war power in the hands of a unitary executive, Madison observed, "would be too great for any one man; not such as nature may offer as the prodigy of many centuries, but such as may be expected in the ordinary successions of magistracy."[16] Madison described war as "the true nurse of executive aggrandizement" because the executive directs the armed forces and has the opportunity to promote and benefit his associates.[17] Moreover, "[i]t is in war, finally, that laurels are to be gathered; and it is the executive brow they are to encircle. The strongest passions and most dangerous weaknesses of the human breast; ambition, avarice, vanity, the honourable or venial love of fame, are all in conspiracy against the desire and duty of peace."[18] With this conclusion Madison foresaw that presidents who are described as "great" often are wartime presidents and thus the natural drive for greatness will cause executives to commit the nation to conflict.

The Executive and War in the Early Republic

In the early years of the Republic, it was understood that Congress was su-preme in decisions about armed conflict and that presidents were charged, as the commander in chief of the armed forces, with executing congressional policy. Even the Supreme Court recognized this premise in *Little v. Barreme* (1804),[19] when adjudicating a case arising from America's Quasi-War with France in the late 1790s. The conflict between America and France arose from French outrage at (1) American neutrality as revolutionary France warred with Great Britain, and (2) American efforts to negotiate a commercial treaty with Great Britain. France felt betrayed by its ally and gave French vessels permission to seize American shipping on the high seas.

Congress directed the president to instruct American armed vessels to stop and seize American ships bound for French ports. By executive order, the president also permitted American armed vessels to stop and seize American ships sailing from France. Captain Little had stopped and seized *The Flying Fish* as it was returning from a French port. The owner of *The Flying Fish* sued Captain Little for damages. Little argued that he was following an executive order issued by the commander in chief; therefore, he should not be liable. The Supreme Court disagreed and held that because the executive order exceeded the limits expressly imposed by Congress, Little could be sued for damages relating to the seizure of *The Flying Fish*. While the president is commander in chief, the Court concluded that he is nonetheless restrained by the dictates of Congress. As noted by constitutional scholar Raoul Berger, "[t]he duty of the President is to 'take care that the laws be faithfully executed,' and nothing in the Constitution absolves him from that duty in the role of commander in chief."[20]

In 1805, the United States and Spain quarreled over the boundaries of the Louisiana Purchase. Spain asserted that Spanish Texas extended into what is modern-day Louisiana and the United States claimed that the new American territory extended to the Rio Grande or at least the Sabine River (the border existing today between the states of Louisiana and Texas). Spain severed diplomatic relations with the United States and the Sabine River was the location of much saber rattling by both sides.

In December 1805, President Thomas Jefferson sent a special message to Congress in which he informed the legislature of the disputes and Spain's apparent intent to encroach on American possessions. Jefferson explained that he was informing Congress of the disturbances because "Congress alone is constitutionally invested with the power of changing our condition from peace to war."[21] Based on this constitutional design, "I have thought it my duty to await their authority for using force in any degree which could be avoided."[22] Jefferson did take the steps of instructing "the officers stationed in the neighborhood of the aggressions to protect our citizens from violence," but he looked to Congress to authorize a more aggressive posture.[23]

Lest anyone attribute Jefferson's actions to oddly pacifistic views or an abnormally strict construction of the Constitution, we must remember that this view was no different than that articulated by George Washington. According to the Father of his country, "The constitution vests the power of declaring war in Congress; therefore no offensive expedition of importance can be undertaken until after they shall have deliberated upon the subject and authorized such a measure."[24]

The Executive and War in Modern Times

For most of the nation's history, presidents proved Cato wrong and declined to assume the mantle of generalissimo. Not even Woodrow Wilson or Franklin D. Roosevelt in the twentieth century's two world wars sent troops into combat on foreign soil until Congress had declared war. The executive certainly exercised broad authority in foreign affairs, but 1950 was the first time that a president formally adopted the position that the commander in chief designation permitted him to send troops abroad to fight without congressional authorization. President Harry S. Truman relied on a resolution of the United Nations Security Council when he sent troops to aid South Korea after it was invaded by its neighbor to the north. Secretary of State Dean Acheson specifically advised Truman against going to Congress and seeking its approval to enter the fight on the Korean peninsula.

Of course, Truman's stretching of the commander-in-chief powers did not stop with sending troops across the Pacific, but extended to the seizure of the nation's steel mills. In 1951, the mills and their employees reached an impasse when negotiating a new collective bargaining agreement. The union called for a nationwide strike. Prior to the strike, President Truman issued an executive order declaring that a work stoppage in the steel mills "would immediately jeopardize and imperil our national defense" and put troops fighting in Korea in danger.[25] To ensure that the war machine had steel products, Truman ordered the secretary of commerce to take possession of the steel mills and to operate them on behalf of the federal government.

The mill owners brought a legal action and argued that President Truman exceeded his constitutional powers. A lower court ruled against the government, and this decision made its way quickly to the Supreme Court. In his opinion for the Court, Justice Hugo Black searched the Constitution for a provision conferring such power on the president, but could find none. "[W]e cannot with faithfulness to our constitutional system," wrote Justice Black, "hold that the Commander in Chief of the Armed Forces has the ultimate power as such to take possession of private property in order to keep labor disputes from stopping production."[26] Rather than executive functions, the Court believed that the seizure was more akin to a legislative action, but separation-of-powers concerns prohibited the president from acting in this manner.

Congress has not declared war since December 8, 1941, but the United States has been involved in various military actions in Korea, Vietnam, Kuwait, Iraq, Afghanistan, and Yugoslavia. Our forces, to foster regime change, have invaded Grenada, Panama, and Haiti. In many other countries, we have offered active military assistance to various rebel groups. In some situations, the executive has consulted with Congress and received Authorization for the Use of Military Force ("AUMF"). The first AUMF was issued in 1955 when President Eisenhower requested authority to protect Formosa (now known as Taiwan) from the People's Republic of China. The AUMF permitted Eisenhower to "employ the Armed Forces of the United States as he deems necessary for the specific purpose of securing and protecting Formosa and the Pescadores against armed attack."[27] The president dispatched naval vessels to discourage a Chinese attack and the situation resolved without shots being fired.

While it is laudable that Eisenhower consulted Congress and sought some blessing for the use of the military in and around Formosa, the AUMF of 1955 established a broad and unconstitutional precedent whereby Congress abdicated its constitutional authority and gave the president *carte blanche* over the use of force—or, in the words of the AUMF, discretion to use American fighting men "as he deems necessary." Nine years later, President Lyndon B. Johnson requested an AUMF from Congress in response to North Vietnamese actions against American warships in the Tonkin Gulf. The Gulf of Tonkin Resolution authorized the president to repel any North Vietnamese attacks on American vessels as well as "to take all necessary steps, including the use of armed force, to assist any member or protocol state of the Southeast Asia Collective Defense Treaty requesting assistance in defense of its freedom."[28] Johnson and later Richard Nixon relied on this AUMF for the buildup of forces in Vietnam and the prosecution of the war there. Over 58,000 Americans died in a war that was not declared by Congress, but was merely deemed a necessary step by the executive.

Congress passed the most recent AUMF in 2001 after the 9/11 terrorist attacks. Congress authorized the president "to use all necessary and appropriate force against those nations, organizations, or persons *he determines* planned, authorized, committed, or aided the terrorist attacks that occurred on September 11, 2011, or harbored [terrorists], in order to prevent any future acts of international terrorism."[29] Congress relinquished its responsibility under the Constitution and entrusted the chief executive to use the armed forces against any nation, organization, or person that he alone deemed to bear some relation to the 9/11 attacks.

Emboldened by the broad authority granted in the AUMF, in 2002 the George W. Bush administration announced a national security policy of preemptive wars not only to protect the United States, but also to "extend the peace by encouraging free and open societies on every continent."[30] The 9/11 attacks provided the United States a "moment of opportunity to extend . . . the hope of democracy, development, free markets, and free trade to every corner of the world."[31] Hence, not only would the United States fight to eliminate emerging threats, but also to bring Americanized democratic-capitalism to the world. Such boasts could hardly be comforting to various non-belligerent nations with different governmental and economic structures from ours.

Prolonged wars and efforts at nation building are the natural result of congressional grants of power to the president that he does not possess under the Constitution. Voters are also deprived of the ability to applaud or rebuke Congress on its use of the war power during biennial elections. Members of Congress can just shrug and point to the discretionary power an AUMF gives the president to act. In other words, representatives are no longer responsible to the people for decisions to involve American forces in military actions around the globe. The president, with congressional blessing, assumes a power reminiscent of Britain's eighteenth-century monarchs.

War Powers Resolution

Of course, at times Congress has tried to act to limit the president's claims of ultimate power over the armed forces. Truman's actions in Korea and the undeclared Vietnam War led Congress to adopt the War Powers Resolution in 1973. The Resolution commands that the president should consult with Congress before "introducing United States Armed Forces into hostilities or into situations where" hostilities are likely.[32] If the president does put troops in harm's way absent a declaration of war, he has forty-eight hours in which to report to Congress about the circumstances of the action and estimated duration of the involvement. After sixty days of the use of troops, the president must terminate American involvement in the conflict unless Congress has declared war, extended the sixty-day period, or is unable to meet because of an attack on the United States. Notwithstanding the sixty-day period, the president must withdraw troops from hostilities "if the Congress so directs by joint resolution."[33]

As noted by constitutional law scholars Bruce Ackerman and Oona Hathaway, "[s]ince the adoption of the War Powers Resolution in 1973, modern presidents have repeatedly asserted the constitutional authority to commit troops without seeking congressional approval, but have nonetheless sought and received the congressional authorization that the War Powers Resolution requires (putting aside cases authorized by U.N. Security Council resolution)."[34] Even when presidents do seek congressional approval, they still are in a position to bully Congress and expand executive authority. This is because Congress no longer manages funding decisions.

In the early Republic, congressional appropriations bills specified the total number of the armed forces and what their daily rations would be. Ackerman and Hathaway have observed that "Congress provided remarkably detailed instructions" and limited the use of the appropriated funds to specific purposes.[35] Today, congressional committees no longer work with executive departments to determine what amounts are needed for what purposes. Instead, agents of the president present a budget to Congress. Even when Congress does make changes, the appropriations bills are bereft of the oversight that was the norm in early American history. This gives presidents freedom to enter conflicts with discretionary funds and to utilize "last-minute emergency supplemental appropriations to bludgeon Congress into appropriating additional funds" with the cry that a failure to act will "deprive the troops of 'bullets and body armor.'"[36]

The executive's total disregard for Congress's war powers recently was evidenced in a March 2012 exchange between Secretary of Defense Leon Panetta and Senator Jeff Sessions on possible American intervention in the Syrian civil war. Panetta told the Senate that if the Obama Administration decided that war with the Syrian government is in the country's best interests, he could not promise that Congress would be consulted. Panetta did indicate that the administration would seek an international mandate, but he made clear that Congress would not exercise veto power over the use of force in Syria.

Today, although Congress possesses the Constitution's primary delegated powers of war and peace, the president acts as the generalissimo of the nation. The president uses his designation as commander in chief as a license to do as he pleases with the armed forces. His claimed powers resemble those of the British king rather than the chief executive established by the Constitution. On too many occasions, Congress has granted broad executive actions through authorizations of military force. These declarations render Congress a spectator in our foreign adventures and make our senators and representatives unaccountable on matters of war.

In 1973, Congress tried to restore balance to the system with the War Powers Resolution, but presidents do not recognize the validity of the Resolution's framework. Presidents seek congressional approval as a matter of expediency rather than constitutional scruples. As evidenced by the 2012 exchange between Sessions and Panetta, administrations place greater value on an international mandate than a constitutional mandate from the national legislature. Anti-Federalist fears of an omnipotent commander in chief have come to pass. Federalist assurances that only Congress can lead the nation into war ring hollow.

13

The Judiciary

THE JUDICIAL POWERS under the Articles of Confederation were circumscribed. Nothing recognizable as a judicial branch of government existed. Under Article IX, Congress had the power to appoint judges to try "piracies and felonies committed on the high seas" and to hear "appeals in all cases of captures."[1] When petitioned by a state in a boundary dispute, Congress could appoint judges to hear the case if the states could not agree on arbitrators. Congress itself was "the last resort on appeal" of the matter.[2] The Articles provided for a similar mechanism for the settling of competing private claims based on conflicting state land grants. But that was the extent of the judicial structure.

The Articles did not have a judicial branch because (1) the Confederation did not operate directly upon individuals, and (2) the colonists distrusted executive power. While today we do not associate the courts with the chief executive, many of the colonists did. In England the judicial power was considered a branch of the executive department, and this view was widely accepted in America. For example, in 1776 an anonymous pamphleteer from Philadelphia discoursed on constitutions and informed his readers that "there is no more than two powers in any government, viz. the power to make the laws, and the power to execute them."[3] The judiciary, according to that pamphleteer, "is only a branch of the executive."[4] In light of bad experiences with the king and royal governors, Americans were not eager to augment executive power (which to many included the judiciary) in the state constitutions or in the Articles.

However, as Americans studied the science of government further, they began to view governmental power as divided into three separate branches so that, in Thomas Jefferson's words, "no person should exercise the powers of more than one of them at the same time."[5] The Massachusetts Constitution of 1780 stated this view as follows:

> In the government of this Commonwealth, the legislative department shall never exercise the executive and judicial powers, or either of them: The executive shall never exercise the legislative and judicial powers, or either of them: The judicial shall never exercise the legislative and executive powers, or either of them: to the end it may be a government of laws and not of men.[6]

By the time of the Philadelphia Convention, most Americans believed that a government should have three independent and separate branches. At the Convention, both the Virginia Plan and the New Jersey Plan provided for a federal judiciary. It was not so much the creation of the judiciary that vexed the Anti-Federalists, but the lack of accountability coupled with sweeping powers.

Brutus versus Hamilton

Brutus questioned "whether the world ever saw, in any period of it, a court of justice invested with such immense powers, and yet placed in a situation so little responsible."[7] Brutus was troubled by the constitutional provision whereby judges hold office during good behavior. In practice, this has meant that federal judges enjoy lifetime appointments absent removal for egregious criminal conduct. Brutus's complaint might seem odd considering that in the Declaration of Independence the colonists protested that the king had "made judges dependent on his will alone, for the tenure of their offices, and the amount and payment of their salaries."[8] In the colonies judges served at the pleasure of the king rather than during good behavior and thus were susceptible to royal influence. In the mother country, pursuant to the 1701 Act of Settlement, they served during good behavior and this was seen as a boon to English liberty.

Brutus acknowledged that British judges served during good behavior and this was appropriate under the British constitution, but the situation in America was far different. In Britain, Parliament was sovereign and no judge would ever dare to try to set aside a law passed by the Lords and Commons as contrary to the constitution. Parliament was, to a large extent, the constitution. In the words of Blackstone, Parliament has "sovereign and uncontrollable authority in making, confirming, enlarging, restraining, abrogating, repealing, reviving, and expounding laws."⁹ This parliamentary, legislative sovereignty had been rejected in the several state constitutions as well as the document drafted by the Philadelphia Convention. Hence, parliamentary sovereignty served to naturally restrain judges in a way that was not possible in America.

In addition to the principles of parliamentary sovereignty, the House of Lords served as the highest court in Great Britain. If a judge issued an erroneous opinion, this could be appealed to the Lords who could overturn or correct the decision. Brutus reminded his readers that the proposed Constitution provided for no appeal to the legislature. Unelected judges serving for good behavior would, as a practical matter, have the final say on the Constitution, statutes, and most disputes.

Brutus also showed his readers that the circumstances necessitating great judicial independence in Britain did not exist in the United States. A British judge ought to serve during good behavior because "they may be placed in a situation . . . to be influenced by the crown, to give decisions, as would tend to increase its powers and prerogatives."¹⁰ Prior to the Act of Settlement, "[i]f the crown wished to carry a favorite point" Brutus remarked, "to accomplish which the aid of the courts of law was necessary, the pleasure of the king would be signified to the judges."¹¹

An example of Brutus's point is James I. If the judges were presented with a question concerning the king's prerogative, James instructed them to "deal not with it till you consult with the king or his Council."¹² When Sir Edward Coke did not follow instructions from James, the king transferred him to a different court where Coke's earnings were reduced. Because Coke still refused to consult with the king prior to hearing certain cases, James ultimately dismissed him from the bench. Coke served at James's pleasure and had no mechanism to challenge the king's actions.

When judges began to serve during good behavior, Brutus believed that the people "got from the crown a concession, which deprived it of one of the most powerful engines with which it might enlarge the boundaries of the royal prerogative and encroach on the liberties of the people."[13] The situation in the United States was different: "we have no hereditary monarch; those who appoint the judges do not hold their offices for life, nor do they descend to their children."[14] The nature of American government does not require that "the courts should be placed beyond all account more independent, so much as to be above control."[15]

Alexander Hamilton attempted to answer Brutus's concerns about judicial independence in *Federalist* No. 78. Hamilton described good behavior as "one of the most valuable of the modern improvements in the practice of government."[16] This standard protected the people from the overreaching of the king in a monarchy, but it also could protect republican citizens from "oppressions of the representative body."[17] Hamilton did not address the distinctions raised by Brutus about the sovereignty of Parliament, the judicial functions of the Lords, or the historical development of good behavior as a check on the monarchy. Instead, Hamilton assured his readers that the judiciary "will always be the least dangerous" branch because it would remain the weakest.[18] Unlike the executive, the judiciary dispenses no honors and has no role in military matters. Unlike the legislature, the judiciary has no control over revenues and does not pass legislation. "It may be truly said to have neither Force nor Will," Hamilton wrote, "but merely judgment; and must ultimately depend on the aid of the executive arm even for the efficacy of its judgments."[19]

Brutus did not accept the argument that the court would be the weakest branch. "The power of this court is in many cases," Brutus asserted, "superior to that of the legislature."[20] He pointed out that under the proposed Article III, the Supreme Court would "be authorized to decide upon the meaning of the constitution, and that, not only according to the natural and ob. meaning of the words, but also according to the spirit and intention of it."[21] Brutus found this broad power of interpretation in the Constitution's statement that "[t]he judicial power shall extend to all cases, in law and equity, arising under this Constitution, the laws of the United States, and treaties made."[22] Equity jurisdiction in England was separate from the jurisdiction of the common law courts and permitted judges to decide cases based on general principles of fairness rather than the strict letter of the law. Brutus believed that the reference to equity in Article III opened the door for the Supreme Court to dispense with the strict legal rules of construction and to decide cases on much looser standards.

Presciently, Brutus recognized that the Supreme Court would exercise judicial review—*i.e.*, the power to review decisions of coordinate departments or levels of government.[23] American principles of popular sovereignty demanded that the courts, as co-equal branches of government, take note of constitutional provisions when deciding a case or controversy. Unlike British judges, American judges would have the authority to declare, for instance, an act of the national legislature to be incongruent with the Constitution. "If . . . the legislature pass any laws, inconsistent with the sense the judges put upon the constitution," Brutus prognosticated, "they will declare it void."[24] As agents of the people, Brutus believed that the courts would be bound to render such a decision inasmuch as "the constitution is the highest or supreme law."[25] So long as the judges recognized the sovereignty of the people, "they cannot . . . execute a law, which in their judgment, opposes the constitution, unless we can suppose they can make a superior law give way to an inferior law."[26]

Brutus did not argue with the necessity of judicial review. His concern was with judicial supremacy. The Anti-Federalists believed that "all persons who are concerned in the government [should be] made accountable to some superior for their conduct in office.—This responsibility should ultimately rest with the People."[27] Under the Constitution, representatives had to face the people every two years to account for their actions; senators had longer terms but could be replaced by the state legislatures every six years; at the end of the president's four-year term, the electors chosen by the state legislatures judged his performance if he sought reelection. The state legislatures, of course, all had a popular branch elected by the people.

Under the Constitution, Brutus explained, the judges "are independent of the people, of the legislature, and of every power under heaven. Men placed in this situation will generally soon feel themselves independent of heaven itself."[28]

Congress would soon be forced to first consider the proclamations of the courts before interpreting the constitutional text for themselves when contemplating legislation. "From the observations it appears," wrote Brutus, "that the judgment of the judicial, on the constitution, will become the rule to guide the legislature in their construction of their powers."[29] Unlike Britain and other liberal governments, "the judicial under this system have a power which is above the legislative, and which transcends any power before given to a judicial by any free government under heaven."[30]

Once Congress recognized which branch was supreme, Brutus expected that a certain partnership would arise between the national legislature and the Supreme Court. It would benefit both branches, Brutus reasoned, if the powers of the national government were expanded. "Every extension of the power of the general legislature, as well as of the judicial powers, will increase the powers of the courts; and the dignity and importance of the judges, will be in proportion to the extent and magnitude of the powers they exercise."[31] Brutus speculated that "it is highly probable the emolument of the judges will be increased, with the increase of the business they will have to transact and its importance."[32] At the expense of the states, Congress and the federal courts would prosper.

Hamilton agreed with Brutus that the Supreme Court would exercise judicial review. Perhaps forgetting about the power of the ballot box, Hamilton argued that limitations in a written constitution could only be enforced "through the medium of the courts of justice."[33] The courts were duty bound "to declare all acts contrary to the manifest tenor of the constitution void."[34] Without such a power in the courts, Hamilton said, "all the reservations of particular rights or privileges would amount to nothing."[35]

It was a product of the Anti-Federalist imagination to interpret the Constitution as granting a "superiority of the judiciary to the legislative power."[36] Hamilton went on to argue that judicial review was necessary because the people are the principals and all government actors are agents. If the courts did not strike down unconstitutional acts of Congress, then the representatives and senators could substitute "their *will* to that of their constituents."[37] This could never be. "[T]he constitution ought to be preferred to the statute," Hamilton averred, "the intention of the people to the intention of their agents."[38]

Brutus did not disagree with any of this. Hamilton's points about the people's Constitution being superior to a legislative enactment and the duty of the courts to take notice of the Constitution when deciding a case were fully congruent with Brutus's exposition of the judicial power. By repeatedly insisting that courts had to serve as bulwarks against legislative encroachments, Hamilton appeared to be dodging Brutus's central points about supremacy and accountability.

The closest Hamilton came to directly engaging with arguments about the danger of judicial supremacy is *Federalist* No. 81. In this number Hamilton addressed "judicial encroachments on the legislative authority" and described this danger as a "phantom."[39] The Court might occasionally engage in "misconstructions" but these "can never be so extensive as to amount to an inconvenience, or in any sensible degree to affect the order of the political system."[40] Why? Hamilton continued: "This may be inferred with certainty, from the general nature of the judicial power, from the objects to which it relates, from the manner in which it is exercised, from its comparative weakness, and from its total incapacity to support its usurpations by force."[41] If lack of a judicial standing army did not persuade opponents, then Hamilton instructed them to remember the power of impeachment: "And the inference is greatly fortified by the consideration of the important constitutional check which the power of instituting impeachments in one part of the legislative body, and of determining upon them in the other, would give to that body upon the members of the judicial department. This is alone a complete security."[42]

After lengthy discussions of the dangers of legislative excesses and the intrinsic weakness of the Supreme Court, Hamilton finally addressed the Anti-Federalist apprehensions about an unelected judiciary possibly claiming the ultimate right to interpret the Constitution. If a judge ever claimed to be supreme in the exposition of the Constitution and thus usurped the authority of the president, Congress, or states, the judge could be impeached.

Removal of Judges

Under the Constitution, civil officers may "be removed from office on impeachment for, and conviction of, treason, bribery, or other high crimes and misdemeanors."[43] As legal historian Raoul Berger has noted, in England impeachment for "high crimes and misdemeanors" encompassed a variety of non-indictable offenses such as abuse of office, neglect of duty, and encroach-ment upon Parliament's authority.[44] This does not mean that the English be-lieved this power to be unlimited. Solicitor General Somers, when speaking to Parliament in 1691, gave an apt description of impeachment: "the power of impeachment ought to be, like Goliath's sword, kept in the temple, and not used but on great occasions."[45] Impeachment was a broad power, often a political power, but necessary when considerable mischief was done under the color of office or authority.

Judges were certainly not immune from impeachment in England. A good example are the judges who allowed Charles I to expand his power to raise "ship money," a tax traditionally levied by the king on coastal towns in times of danger. In the 1630s, Charles was attempting to govern without calling Parliament and thus needed additional revenue. He levied ship money on coastal areas and also extended this tax to inland communities. No danger of invasion or war was present, but Charles proclaimed a national emergency to give himself cover. Several taxpayers challenged Charles's constitutional in-novations in the Court of Exchequer Chamber. The court held that the king's declaration of an emergency could not be questioned and that all subjects were bound to submit to his demand for ship money. Once Charles finally summoned the "Long Parliament" in November 1640, the ship money judges who supported expansion of royal power promptly were impeached for their rulings and found guilty.

In 1804, at the urging of President Jefferson, the United States House of Representatives impeached and the Senate convicted Judge John Pickering, a federal district judge from New Hampshire. Almost all were in agreement that Pickering was a drunkard and probably mentally ill—he took the bench drunk and then would simply disappear from his duties for weeks on end. Jefferson lamented that the Constitution did not provide for a more efficient method to remove such a judge. Jefferson believed that the Constitution should have allowed for removal of judges upon a majority vote in Congress; however, impeachment was the only option available. Members of the Federalist Party, although aware of Pickering's antics, did not pressure him to leave the bench because they did not want to give President Jefferson the opportunity to appoint a Republican in his place. Once Pickering made clear that he would not leave office voluntarily, this led to successful removal procedures in the national legislature. Some, however, had misgivings because Pickering had not engaged in criminal acts—he was simply not suited or competent to be a federal judge.

After that event the House brought articles of impeachment against Supreme Court Justice Samuel Chase. The charges dealt with a variety of misconduct, including a political harangue against Jefferson and democracy in a jury charge, tyrannical treatment of lawyers and defendants in his courtroom, and partiality during the several prosecutions brought under the Sedition Act of 1798. The case against Chase was presented to the Senate by John Randolph of Roanoke, a Republican congressman with an acerbic personality and no formal legal training. In the words of historian Gordon Wood, "Randolph was no more equipped to handle the impeachment of Chase than he was to be majority leader" of the House.[46] He bungled the presentation of the case and Chase was acquitted by the Senate. Raoul Berger has described Chase's acquittal as "a miscarriage of justice."[47] As a result of Chase's trial, impeachment of judges has been reserved for actual indictable conduct rather than erroneous legal rulings. Hence, Hamilton's stress on the power of impeachment for extra-constitutional rulings amounts to nothing. Some years after the Chase acquittal, Jefferson assessed impeachment as "scarcely a scarecrow."[48] Time has proven him correct.

Juries

The Constitution's effect on jury trials also animated Anti-Federalists. The second section of Article III gives the Supreme Court appellate jurisdiction "both as to law and fact."[49] Anti-Federalists saw this as an attempt to reduce the power of juries. "It would be a novelty in jurisprudence, as well as evidently improper to allow an appeal from the verdict of a jury, on the matter of fact," protested Centinel.[50] The Federal Farmer reminded his readers that in the Anglo-American legal system, juries had always been the masters of the facts, but in the Constitution the Supreme Court could overturn a jury's findings. "An appeal will lay in all appellate causes from the verdict of the jury," the Federal Farmer observed, "even as to mere facts, to the judges of the supreme court."[51]

The Anti-Federalists also inveighed against Article III's failure to protect jury trials in civil cases and to assure that juries, in both civil and criminal cases, would be juries of the vicinage. The judiciary provisions of the Constitution provide that "[t]he trial of all crimes, except in cases of impeachment, shall be by jury; and such trial shall be held in the State where the said crimes shall have been committed."[52] "Are there not a thousand civil cases in which the government is a party?" asked "An Old Whig."[53] The new government could be involved in myriad civil proceedings—penalties, forfeitures, demands of public debts. Jury trials, he believed, should be guaranteed in all possible civil cases. "A Maryland Farmer" (probably John Francis Mercer) contended that the Philadelphia Convention's phraseology meant that no civil case in the federal courts would involve a jury. "That where there are two objects in contemplation of any legislature," this Anti-Federalist reasoned, "the express adoption of one, is the total exclusion of the other; and that the adoption of juries in criminal cases, in every legal interpretation, amounts to an absolute rejection in civil cases."[54]

Merely promising that jury trials would be held within the state where the offense was committed, to most Anti-Federalists, provided no security. A defendant residing in New York along the Canadian border could be compelled to stand trial in New York City—a location hundreds of miles away and where he is unknown to the inhabitants. In the Massachusetts ratifying convention, Abraham Holmes concluded that under the Constitution in criminal proceedings, "a person shall not have a right to insist on a trial in the vicinity where the act was committed, where a jury of the peers would, from their local situation, have an opportunity to form a judgment of the *character* of the person charged with the crime, and also to judge the *credibility* of witnesses."[55] Samuel Spencer of North Carolina, in his state's convention, reminded his colleagues that "[o]ne reason of the resistance to the British government was, because they required that we should be carried to the country of Great Britain, to be tried by juries of that country."[56] The colonists, however, "insisted on being tried by juries of the vicinage, in our own country. I think it therefore proper that something explicit should be said with respect to the vicinage."[57]

Modern Americans undoubtedly have difficulty understanding the Anti-Federalists' emphasis on juries of the vicinage. Today, juries are pulled from large pools and are limited to factual findings. Judges are masters of the law and give the jurors lengthy instructions that jurors must follow. This was not the case in colonial times and the early days of the Republic. Juries were especially sacrosanct bodies and could not be overridden by a judge even if the judge believed the jury's decision was against the greater weight of the evidence. A "jury of peers," as originally understood, were the equals of the accused in status. Juries in pre-revolutionary America possessed virtually unlimited power to determine both law and fact.[58] According to legal history scholar William E. Nelson, "[o]n the eve of the American Revolution, the power of the jury to nullify the law was recognized up and down the Atlantic Coast, from Georgia to New Hampshire, and was fundamental to the democratic order existing on the western shore of the Atlantic."[59]

Judges often were relegated to deciding pretrial motions and other administrative matters. In the words of Thomas Jefferson, written shortly after penning the Declaration of Independence, judges should be "a mere machine" when performing their duties.[60] If judges took actions tending to undermine customary rights or republican government, citizens expected that the jurors would check them by ignoring or overturning the judges' opinions and determinations.

In Georgia, for example, the juries of the county superior courts decided issues of law and fact, turning to judges only when they desired advice.[61] Decisions of the superior courts could be appealed to special juries, not a supreme court. By placing such power in juries, the community could control the content of substantive law. A legislature could pass a statute and a judge could instruct on the common law, but juries possessed the power to veto both.

Juries empowered the people. The people's voice could be heard and they could protect themselves from legislative overreaching as well as overzealous prosecutors. Juries were the democratic branch of the judiciary. While today many speak of judges as defenders of liberty by exercising judicial review, at the time of the Revolution that task was reserved to juries of the vicinage.

Jurors who knew the accused and/or the parties to a law suit, colonial Americans believed, were better suited to adjudicate disputes than judges alone or a jury of strangers.

In *Federalist* No. 83, Hamilton denied that the Constitution threatened the right to a jury trial. He argued that Congress could choose to use juries in civil cases. The reason civil jury trials were not mentioned specifically was that in some types of civil cases, such as admiralty actions, judges typically presided without juries. Hence, representatives in the federal legislature should have discretion on this point when putting flesh on the judicial skeleton outlined in the Constitution. Moreover, Hamilton contended that liberty would most likely be threatened in criminal cases rather than civil actions; therefore, the guarantee of criminal jury trials would secure to the people their historic role. "[T]he security of liberty is materially concerned only in trial by jury in criminal cases," Hamilton averred, "which is provided for in the most ample manner in the plan of the convention."[62] Civil jury trials, of course, eventually were guaranteed by the Seventh Amendment. Judges by this same amendment also were prohibited from reexamining any fact found by a jury if such reevaluation was inconsistent with the common law.

When examining Brutus's and his compatriots' concern about the Supreme Court, one is amazed at just how accurate they were. Judges, lawyers, and lay persons accept that the Supreme Court is the ultimate judge of what the Constitution means. In the Court's own words, deciding the meaning of our fundamental law "is a responsibility of this Court as ultimate interpreter of the Constitution."[63] The Court "is supreme in the exposition of the law of the Constitution."[64] Once the judiciary interprets a constitutional provision, we are taught, no branch of the national or state governments can offer a competing interpretation in the performance of their constitutional duties. The Supreme Court might not have an army or a navy, but its pronouncements in twenty-first century America carry more weight than the branches of government that raise troops and command them in battle. The Court has the final say on a host of issues from affirmative action to abortion to capital punishment.

Furthermore, if anyone questions why unelected officials serving during good behavior can exercise such power in a republic, that person is cast to the political fringe. The heretic is warned by the likes of Sandra Day O'Connor that such a "perversion of the concept of judicial accountability threatens to undermine the safeguards of democracy and liberty that were so brilliantly conceived by those who first designed our governmental institutions and drafted our Constitution."[65]

Judicial Supremacy

Judicial supremacy was hardly carefully and "brilliantly conceived" by the Founders. It appears that after the Philadelphia Convention, Madison began to contemplate the likelihood of a supreme judiciary and realized that he and the other delegates had made a mistake. In an October 1788 letter to Jefferson, Madison observed that because courts are "generally the last in making their decisions, it results to them by refusing or not refusing to execute a law, to stamp it with its final character."[66] Unfortunately, "[t]his makes the Judiciary Department paramount in fact to the Legislature, *which was never intended and can never be proper.*"[67]

To this day, no scholar or statesman has ever satisfactorily answered Brutus's warnings about judicial supremacy. Nor has anyone explained adequately why unelected and life-tenured government officers should have the final say on the meaning of fundamental law. Judicial supremacy has meant that the courts have the ultimate say on a bevy of matters important to the average American. Because impeachment has been reserved for criminal acts rather than usurpations of power, the people and their representatives find themselves subject to the rule of the judges.

In his 1783 draft of a constitution for Virginia, Thomas Jefferson included a provision whereby a convention of the people could be summoned "for altering this constitution, or correcting breaches of it."[68] Jefferson did not believe that any one branch should be supreme in the interpretation of fundamental law. The people of Virginia, as the ultimate sovereigns, were the only body competent to resolve disputes between the branches of government on the meaning of the constitution.

Writing in *Federalist* No. 49, Madison acknowledged Jefferson's preference for a popular convention to judge disputes between the branches. He feared that frequent appeals to the people would disturb public tranquility and lessen the public's respect for the government. That number of *The Federalist* was published in February 1788—approximately eight months before Madison's epiphany expressed in his October correspondence with Jefferson regarding the unintended superiority of the judiciary. Perhaps Madison eventually had some second thoughts on his rejection of Jefferson's proposal and grimaced a bit when thinking back on *Federalist* No. 49.

If Madison did not have second thoughts, then we nonetheless should. In combating modern judicial supremacy, Americans would do well to revisit Jefferson's draft constitution and his mechanism for correcting breaches of the constitution and for judging competing claims of the co-equal branches. Judicial supremacy simply is contrary to republican government and should be reconsidered as we go forward in the experiment of self-government.

14

Treaties

UNDER THE ARTICLES of Confederation, "[t]he United States in Congress assembled, shall have the sole and exclusive right and power of . . . entering into treaties and alliances."[1] A treaty required the assent of nine of the thirteen states. The Constitution placed the treaty power with the president and senate: the executive "shall have Power, by and with the Advice and Consent of the Senate, to make Treaties, provided two thirds of the Senators present concur."[2] The Supremacy clause provides that "all Treaties made, or which shall be made, under the Authority of the United States, shall be the supreme Law of the Land."[3]

Although the Confederation Congress had broad authority to enter into treaties, it had little power to enforce them. That defect was especially evident with provisions of the Treaty of Paris, which provided for collection of all debts owed to British subjects and prohibited confiscation of loyalist property. Several states placed legislative roadblocks to prevent the recovery of debts and treated loyalist claims to property with contempt. Congress asked the states to repeal the offending legislation in a unanimous resolution, but not all states complied. John Jay, the Confederation's secretary of foreign affairs, urged that "the obvious dictates of religion, morality and national honor . . . demand a candid and punctual compliance with engagements constitutionally and fairly made."[4] He feared that the actions of a few states were threatening the safety and good name of the whole. American treaty transgressions led the British to maintain troops in forts in the trans-Appalachian region that were supposed to be turned over to the United States. If the states repealed laws contrary to the treaty of peace, the British promised that withdrawal would follow.

The Anti-Federalists did not object that the national government had a treaty power or that treaty provisions should be obeyed. The problems surrounding enforcement with the Treaty of Paris were obvious. They were instead concerned that the Constitution specified no role for the House of Representatives, which represented the people. The exclusion of the House smelled of aristocratic machinations. "And from this power of making treaties, the house of representatives, which has the best chance of possessing virtue, and public confidence, is entirely excluded," complained Hampden.[5] "Indeed, I see nothing to hinder the president and senate, at a convenient crisis, to declare themselves hereditary and supreme, and the lower house altogether useless, and to abolish what shadow of the state constitutions remain by this power alone."[6]

Another common and much more reasonable concern was the Constitution's lack of a limitation on the treaty power. The Federal Farmer complained that nothing specified that "treaties shall be made in pursuance of the constitution—nor are there any constitutional bounds set to those who shall make them."[7] He lamented that "[t]his power in the president and senate is absolute."[8] Brutus concurred with the Federal Farmer's analysis: "I do not find any limitation, or restriction, to the exercise of this power. The most important article in any constitution may therefore be repealed, even without a legislative act."[9]

George Mason believed that the treaty power under the Constitution was more powerful than that claimed by the British monarch. "Though the king can make treaties, yet he cannot make a treaty contrary to the constitution of his country," Mason observed.[10] "The President and Senate," he continued "can make any treaty whatsoever."[11] "An Old Whig" postulated that "[i]f Great Britain, for instance, were willing to enter into a treaty with us, upon terms which would be inconsistent with the liberties of the people and destructive to the very being of a Republic, the consent of our president for the time being, and of two thirds of the senators present, even though the senators present should be a very small part of the senate, will give such a treaty the validity of a law."[12] He asserted that "no treaty ought to be suffered to alter the law of the land, without the consent of the continental legislatures."[13]

To remedy the dangers flowing from the treaty power, North Carolina Anti-Federalists offered the following amendment: "That no treaties which shall be directly opposed to the existing laws of the United States in Congress

assembled shall be valid until such laws shall be repealed, or made conform-
able to such treaty; nor shall any treaty be valid which is contradictory to the
Constitution of the United States."[14]

James Madison, in the Virginia ratifying convention, attempted to calm
Anti-Federalist fears by reminding them that the "object of treaties is the
regulation of intercourse with foreign nations, and is external."[15] Hence,
treaties would not interfere with the reserved powers of the states or other
constitutional rights. George Nicholas of Virginia supported Madison on
the treaty argument: "[The president and the Senate] can . . . make no treaty
which shall be repugnant to the spirit of the Constitution, or inconsistent with
the delegated powers. The treaties they make must be under the authority
of the United States, to be within their province."[16] In the North Carolina
convention, William R. Davie assured Anti-Federalists that treaties could be
the supreme law of the land only "in cases consistent with the powers specially
granted, and not in usurpations."[17]

John Jay argued in *Federalist* No. 64 that the mechanism for choosing
the president and senators, coupled with their longer terms, made them "best
able to promote" national interests and thus "[w]ith such men the power of
making treaties may be safely lodged."[18] The expected high turnover in the
House of Representatives every two years, according to Jay, made that body
ill-equipped to exercise the treaty power. House members simply would not
have enough time in office to become acquainted with national concerns nor
would the House have the institutional memory and experience possessed
by the Senate. The president was particularly suited to exercising the treaty
power because in a unitary executive structure he could best manage foreign
intelligence and act with dispatch. If an emergency arose, Jay observed that
the executive could summon the Senate to offer him advice and consent.

An example of the desired effect of the supremacy of treaties is *Ware v.
Hylton* (1801),[19] in which a British creditor sought payment from a Virginia
debtor. A Virginia statute, enacted prior to the end of the war, allowed citizens
indebted to British creditors to extinguish their liability by making a payment
into the state treasury. The Treaty of Paris, of course, required that payments
be made to the creditors of debts contracted prior to and during the war: "It is
agreed that creditors on either side shall meet with no lawful impediment to
the recovery of the full value in sterling money of all bona fide debts heretofore

contracted."[20] The Supreme Court held that the treaty, through the Supremacy Clause, overrode the state law providing for the discharging of debts. Although prior to the treaty, Virginia as a sovereign state had the authority to nullify the debts, the Treaty of Paris, by its specific terms, revived all debts that the state statute claimed to have satisfied.

For the first century and a quarter of our government under the Constitution, it appeared that Anti-Federalist worries about the treaty power merely were political hyperbole. This changed in 1916 when the United States and Great Britain entered into a treaty that prohibited the killing, capturing, or selling of certain migratory birds. Congress feared the extermination of much of the bird population and had previously tried to protect the birds through legislation enacted pursuant to the commerce power. Two federal courts struck down the legislation as exceeding the powers delegated to Congress in Article I. To get around the limitations on its powers, Congress turned to the treaty power and enlisted the help of Great Britain. The president and senators explained to the British that constitutional limitations had stopped the national government from regulating the taking of fowl, but those restrictions could be obviated if Great Britain would sign a treaty allowing the national government to exercise greater powers. The British agreed and a treaty was signed.

The Court's Interpretation

In *Missouri v. Holland* (1920),[21] the State of Missouri challenged the constitutionality of the implementing legislation of the Migratory Bird Treaty. Missouri believed that the taking of wild birds within its borders was a matter left to the reserved powers of the states under the Constitution of 1787. In examining the state's claim, the Supreme Court noted that the Constitution expressly gave the president, with the advice and consent of the Senate, the authority to enter into treaties. Moreover, under the Supremacy Clause, treaties and statutes passed pursuant to treaties are the supreme law of the land. Because the president and the Senate followed the correct constitutional process in approving the treaty, the Court declared that the Migratory Bird Treaty was properly "made under the authority of the United States."[22] Because the treaty was valid, the Court held that "there can be no dispute about the validity of the statute [implementing the treaty] under Article I."[23] In other words, when

Congress acts to implement a treaty, constitutional restrictions that normally would apply to ordinary legislation are not in play.

Four members of the Supreme Court attempted to back away from *Holland* in *Reid v. Covert* (1957),[24] which concerned two American civilians who had been tried in military courts for murdering their servicemen-husbands overseas. The use of military courts was permitted by executive agreements between the United States and the host countries. The defendants argued that the use of military courts violated constitutional protections such as the right to a jury trial found in the Bill of Rights. A plurality of the Supreme Court agreed and held that no executive agreement or treaty could "confer power on the Congress, or any other branch of Government, which is free from the restraints of the Constitution."[25] To hold otherwise, the plurality concluded, "would permit amendment of that document in a manner not sanctioned by Article V."[26] While Americans can take some comfort in that decision, we must remember that *Reid* was a plurality opinion, that is, it did not receive a majority of votes, but more than any other opinion offered. Hence, the rules laid out in *Holland* are still good law.

One of the more recent examples of the power of treaties is *Medellín v. Texas* (2008),[27] which dealt with Texas's failure to adhere to an International Court of Justice ("ICJ") decision wherein the ICJ ordered Texas and other states to reconsider certain state-court convictions involving fifty-one Mexican nationals. Mexico brought suit in the ICJ alleging that American authorities violated the Vienna Convention by failing to timely inform the Mexican detainees of their right to speak with Mexican officials and by failing to inform the appropriate consular post of the detentions. In its opinion, the ICJ recognized that the review in some cases would conflict with the American "procedural default rule," which provides that if a criminal defendant could have raised an error (e.g., notice under the Vienna Convention) in the trial court, he is barred from raising it in future proceedings such as an appeal or petition for a writ of habeas corpus. But it held that the Vienna Convention trumped any state law to the contrary.

Medellín pled guilty to the rape and murder of two teenage girls. He confessed to the crime within hours after his arrest and signed a written statement. In considering his request for post-conviction relief, the Supreme Court recognized that the United States ratified the Vienna Convention on Consular

Relations in 1969 and that it accepted ICJ jurisdiction over disputes or applications of this treaty. The Court also acknowledged that the ICJ is the principal judicial organ of the United Nations. Under the U.N. Charter, the United States has agreed to comply with any decision of the ICJ to which it is a party. The Supreme Court even agreed that local law enforcement did not inform Medellín of his Vienna Convention rights.

However, the Court noted that "not all international law obligations automatically constitute binding federal law enforceable in United States courts."[28] The treaty stipulations of the Vienna Convention, according to the Court, were not self-executing; Congress needed to enact legislation to carry them into effect. "A non-self-executing treaty, by definition," explained the Court, "is one that was ratified with the understanding that it is not to have effect of its own force."[29] Consequently, the ICJ decision "is not automatically binding domestic law."[30] This lack of congressional action also undercut President George W. Bush's efforts to enforce the ICJ decision through executive action. Bush had ordered the state courts to give effect to the ICJ ruling, but Texas refused. Absent congressional authorization to enforce the Vienna Convention, the president's power was at its lowest ebb and he could not act.

Three dissenting justices in *Medellín* rejected the majority's characterization of the treaty as non-self-executing, and would have held that the ICJ's decision bound state courts no less than an act of Congress. The dissenters pointed to multiple treaties enforced by the judiciary when no congressional legislation had been enacted. The *Ware* case, discussed above, is but one example. Considering the clarity of the Vienna Convention and U.N. Charter, the dissenters make a compelling point. The majority appears to have latched onto the self-executing issue simply to prohibit a foreign tribunal from being erected as a court of last resort in criminal matters concerning foreign nationals. We should also not forget that Medellín, an admitted gangbanger, confessed to his role in the rape and murder of the girls. Granting relief in such a situation—especially upon the command of a U.N. court—is counter to intrinsic notions of justice. Undoubtedly, the Framers never envisioned such a patchwork of international agreements ceding authority to an international court to determine the rights and obligations of states and their residents. But this, unfortunately, is the apparent result of our zest for internationalism and the documents to which we have agreed.

Issues regarding the dangers of the treaty power came into focus in the 1950s. Frank Holman, president of the American Bar Association, believed that the Supreme Court's decision in *Holland*, coupled with the U.N. Charter and various U.N. sponsored treaties, threatened local self-government and liberties secured by the Constitution. Holman's concerns were not just isolationist chimeras. President Truman had just sent American troops into battle—not following a congressional declaration of war—but in accordance with a U.N. resolution. In 1948, the Supreme Court had struck down, on Fourteenth Amendment grounds, an illiberal California statute that prohibited land ownership by persons ineligible for citizenship. This law principally affected Japanese immigrants. In a concurring opinion, two justices stated that they also would have struck the law as violating the United Nations Charter by which the United States agreed to "promote . . . universal respect for, and observance of, human rights and fundamental freedoms for all without distinction as to race, sex, language, or religion."[31]

The concurring justices' resort to the U.N. Charter vexed Holman. Holman began to advocate adoption of a constitutional amendment to circumscribe the treaty power. No treaty, he argued, should be able to nullify provisions of the Constitution. Moreover, state laws should not be abridged absent congressional legislation grounded in an enumerated power. Holman wrote that "the domestic laws and the domestic rights of the American people, and even our form of government, could be changed and even destroyed by international pacts, covenants, [and] treaties."[32] Holman was not alone in his concern. John Foster Dulles, just a year prior to becoming Eisenhower's secretary of state, warned that treaties "can take powers away from the Congress and give them to the President."[33] He opined further that a treaty "could take away powers from the State and give them to the Federal Government or to some international body."[34]

The Bricker Amendment

Holman's arguments caught the attention of Senator John Bricker of Ohio. Bricker was a staunch anti-communist who was frightened by the centralization of power in the national government. He also shared Holman's concerns about Truman's actions in Korea and the president's attempted seizure of the nation's steel mills. He agreed with Holman that the potency of international treaties was "the great and basic issue facing the American people."[35] Bricker mobilized civic groups, veterans' organizations, the American Association of Small Business, and many others to support a constitutional restraint on the treaty power.

Largely owing to Bricker's efforts, the Committee on the Judiciary submitted to the Senate in June 1953 the following proposed amendment to the Constitution:

Section 1. A provision of a treaty which conflicts with this Constitution shall not be of any force or effect.

Section 2. A treaty shall become effective as internal law in the United States only through legislation which would be valid in the absence of treaty.

Section 3. Congress shall have power to regulate all executive and other agreements with any foreign power or international organization. All such agreements shall be subject to the limitations imposed on treaties by this article.[36]

The first section of the "Bricker Amendment" sought to solve the problem identified by the Anti-Federalists and manifested in *Holland*. The president and the Senate should not have the power to amend the Constitution by signing a treaty. The people's fundamental law, Senator Bricker believed, must take precedence over the provisions of any treaty. Otherwise, Americans elevate the president and Senate to a constituent body able to amend the Constitution so long as they can persuade a foreign power to agree.

The second section sought to curb use of treaties to modify the reserved powers of the states. For non-self-executing treaties to bind the states, Congress must enact enabling legislation pursuant to a valid enumerated power. Only if Congress could have regulated the subject matter through ordinary legislation prior to the treaty could Congress pass constitutional enabling legislation. Thus, treaties outside of war, peace, and commerce would be treated as non-self-executing. With section two neither Congress nor the state legislatures, Holman explained, could be "by-passed in their constitutional function of legislating for the people of this country."[37]

With section three, Senator Bricker took aim at the growing use of executive agreements to make policy. The *Reid* case, in which the president attempted to strip civilians of constitutional protections, is a good example of the type of conduct this section sought to thwart. If the authority is not preexisting in the Constitution, the national government may not utilize international agreements or pacts to take actions inconsistent with fundamental law. Congress, as the body the Framers directed to bear primary responsibility for war, peace, and foreign policy, would have the power under section three to regulate any agreements with foreign nations or international organizations such as the U.N.

Senator Bricker fought for this amendment throughout the 1950s. Allies of the Eisenhower administration, although they applauded Bricker for his study of the treaty power, opposed the amendment. They argued that it would hamper the president's ability to enter into proper executive agreements and to negotiate military treaties. The moderate to liberal Eisenhower Republicans (including Dulles), with one of their own in office, liked the idea of an energetic executive conducting foreign affairs. They also believed that the Cold War necessitated a strong executive with wide discretion to act when dealing with the Soviet threat. Ultimately, the Bricker Amendment did not garner enough votes to make it out of the Senate. Of course, had it done so, the amendment would have needed the support of a supermajority in the House and then ratification by three-fourths of the state legislatures.

Today, modern "treaties" touch on subjects that would shock the Framers of the Constitution. As noted by Professor Curtis A. Bradley, to the Founders treaties "were generally bilateral and regulated matters such as diplomatic immunity, military neutrality, and removal of trade barriers."[38] Now, treaties are "designed to operate as international 'legislation' binding on much of the world."[39] These treaties seek to regulate the relationship between nations and their own citizens rather than relations between nations. Most Americans are not aware of the extent of these "human rights treaties" and the possible effect on state and local laws.

A good example is the International Convention on the Elimination of All Forms of Racial Discrimination. The United States ratified this treaty in 1994. The first article of the Convention declares that "[s]pecial measures taken for the sole purpose of securing adequate advancement of certain racial or ethnic groups or individuals requiring such protection as may be necessary in order to ensure such groups or individuals equal enjoyment or exercise of human rights and fundamental freedoms shall not be deemed racial discrimination."[40] Some have argued that under this Convention, American governmental entities that reject affirmative action violate international law. The *National Catholic Reporter* has opined that the Convention "makes it clear that affirmative action is not only allowed but indeed mandated."[41]

Considering the events of the last one hundred years, it is difficult to disagree with Patrick Henry's assessment of the treaty power: "To me this power appears still destructive; for they can make any treaty."[42] The amendments proposed by the North Carolina Anti-Federalists and Senator Bricker address real problems with the scope of the treaty power. *Holland* demonstrates that constitutional protections of individual and states' rights may be rendered null and void by treaty. *Medellín* teaches that the convoluted web of international conventions we have entered can easily be interpreted to give the ICJ final say on state law matters. That was the interpretation advocated by President George W. Bush and the liberal wing of the Supreme Court. This result was avoided by describing the relevant treaty provisions as non-self-executing—an argument many commentators have called a stretch.

Americans should reconsider the scope of the treaty power. A constitutional amendment, limiting treaties to their traditional subject matter, and affirming that no treaty can override constitutional protections for states and individuals, is necessary. Such action would protect us from intentional usurpations as well as unintentional blunders brought about by the age of multi-party international conventions.

15

The Amendment Process

THE ARTICLES OF Confederation required unanimity for the passage of amendments. This allowed the legislature of the smallest state in the union to thwart a change agreed to by the other twelve. Rhode Island's opposition to the impost (a duty levied on imported goods), which would have given Congress an independent source of revenue, is the prime example of the power wielded by one state. In the words of South Carolinian Charles Pinckney, "it is to this unanimous consent, the depressed situation of the Union is undoubtedly owing."[1] The inability to make essential amendments made some sort of continental convention inevitable. Had the Articles required two-thirds or three-fourths of the states to agree to amendments, the pure federative model might have survived to present times.

From the beginning, the Constitution's Framers sought to avoid an insuperable amendment procedure. The Virginia Plan, which formed the basis of discussion in the Philadelphia Convention, averred "that provision ought to be made for the amendment of the Articles of Union whensoever it shall seem necessary, and that the assent of the National Legislature ought not to be required thereto."[2] Although this resolution is inchoate, it remains clear that the Virginians and their allies desired a workable amendment procedure with much control remaining in the several states.

Amendment Procedure Debated

Madison's *Notes* record that a few delegates questioned the need for an amendment procedure. In response, George Mason explained that a workable amendment procedure was essential. "The plan now to be formed will certainly be defective," Mason said, "as the Confederation has been found on trial to be."[3] Good judgment, he continued, counseled that "it will be better to provide for them, in an easy, regular and Constitutional way than to trust to chance and violence."[4] Mason also stressed that amendments ought not be dependent on the national government because of concerns about abuse of power and possible refusal to consent to salutary alterations in the government. Elbridge Gerry also argued that a useable amendment procedure would stabilize the new government inasmuch as "[t]he novelty & difficulty of the experiment requires periodical revision."[5]

As the Convention completed its work, the draft amendment article provided that upon "the application of the Legislatures of two thirds of the States in the Union, for an amendment of this Constitution, the Legislature of the U.S. shall call a convention for that purpose."[6] Gerry feared that the states could use the amendment procedure to "bind the Union to innovations that may subvert the State-Constitutions."[7] Gerry asked that the amendment procedure be reconsidered and his motion was seconded by Alexander Hamilton. Hamilton, however, candidly admitted that his concerns differed from Gerry's. Hamilton feared that the state legislatures would only seek amendments to preserve state powers. To promote energy in the new government, Hamilton believed that the national legislature should have a greater role in calling and structuring a convention to consider needed alterations in the form of government. Madison agreed that the amendment procedure should be reconsidered because of "the vagueness of the terms, 'call a Convention for the purpose.'"[8]

Upon further discussion, what is now Article V provided that Congress could send proposed amendments to the states for ratification if (1) two-thirds of Congress agreed to a proposed amendment, or (2) two-thirds of the state legislatures requested an amendment. Amendments would be valid only upon ratification of three-fourths of the state legislatures or conventions. Mason thought that this procedure was "exceptionable & dangerous" because "the proposing of amendments is in both the modes to depend, in the first immediately, in the second, ultimately, on Congress."[9] With Congress in charge of the amendment process, he predicted that "no amendments of the proper kind would ever be obtained by the people, if the Government should become oppressive."[10] To address Mason's concerns, Gouverner Morris of Pennsylvania and Gerry moved to amend the Article V to require a continental convention on the application of two-thirds of the states. This motion passed unanimously.

These debates and motions resulted in our present amendment procedure:

> The Congress, whenever two thirds of both houses shall deem it necessary, shall propose amendments to this Constitution, or, on the application of the legislatures of two thirds of the several states, shall call a convention for proposing amendments, which, in either case, shall be valid to all intents and purposes, as part of this Constitution, when ratified by the legislatures of three fourths of the several states, or by conventions in three fourths thereof, as the one or the other mode of ratification may be proposed by the Congress. . . ."[11]

Hence, the road to amendments must go through the Congress. Congress proposes amendments to the Constitution and reviews state requests for a convention before calling one.

Congress in Control

The Anti-Federalists believed that the amendment process was too difficult and objected to congressional control over the procedure. "An Old Whig" observed that "[p]eople once possessed of power are always loth to part with it; and we shall never find two thirds of a Congress voting or proposing any thing which shall derogate from their own authority and importance, or agreeing to give back to the people any part of those privileges which they have once parted with."[12] The Federal Farmer also expected that Congress would "be exceedingly artful and adroit in preventing any measures" limiting national power.[13] If such alterations could be obtained, they would come from "great exertions and severe struggles on the part of the common people."[14]

In the Virginia ratifying convention, Patrick Henry took aim at the amendment procedure. He echoed the words of "An Old Whig" and the Farmer regarding the likelihood that Congress would never ever agree to amendments that limited national power. Henry also objected that "four of the smallest States, that do not collectively contain one-tenth of the population of the United States, may obstruct the most salutary and necessary amendments."[15]

The minority, he averred, should not be able to prevent the majority from amending the Constitution.

Virginian Wilson Carey Nicholas challenged the Anti-Federalist critique. He agreed that if the amendment power had rested solely in Congress, then the Anti-Federalists would have grounds to object. He was keen to point out that "there is another mode provided, besides that which originates with Congress."[16] He touted the convention procedure of Article V as a guarantee that the states could procure needed constitutional alterations. In the North Carolina convention, James Iredell denied that Congress could block amendments. He averred that "it is provided that Congress shall call such convention, so that they will have no option."[17]

Edmund Pendleton believed that, on the whole, the Constitution provided "an easy and quiet method of reforming what may be found amiss."[18] If Congress ever attempted to obstruct the process, he predicted that the people of the several states would "assemble in Convention" and "wholly recall our delegated powers, or reform them so as to prevent such abuse."[19] St. George Tucker applauded the Constitution's amendment procedure and opined that the states had secured "an influence in case congress should neglect to recommend" needed alterations.[20]

Outside of the first ten amendments which were ratified in 1791 and were necessary to somewhat assuage Anti-Federalist angst, constitutional amendments (for the most part) have augmented national power rather than curtailed it. In recent years, polls have shown that large majorities of the people have favored constitutional limits on congressional power such as a balanced budget amendment, term limits, and prohibitions on imposing unfunded mandates on the states.[21] Yet Congress, a body that largely controls the amendment process, has refused to act. The Anti-Federalists foresaw this result and would not be surprised by congressional efforts to increase and secure power. Common sense dictates that seldom will those imbibing the intoxicants of power seek to reduce their intake on their own initiative.

What of the possibility of the states demanding that Congress summon a convention? There never have been enough states requesting a convention and this is for good reason. First, no one knows whether such a convention would be limited or unlimited in its scope. If the states requested a convention to consider proposing a balanced budget amendment, would the convention be prohibited from also offering amendments on matters such as abortion or capital punishment? The Constitution provides that "Congress . . . on the application of two-thirds of the Legislatures of the several States, shall call a convention for proposing amendments."[22] The plain language at the end of the sentence seems to suggest that a convention would be unrestricted and could propose amendments on a variety of subjects.

On the other hand, one could make an argument that the applications of the states should control the scope of the convention and thus Congress is duty bound to summon the convention only under the terms of the applications. If the applications requested a convention, say, to propose amendments on the federal spending power, then Congress could not constitutionally summon an unlimited convention. Both Congress and the convention delegates would be bound by the applications.

A convention could result in much chaos and constitutional uncertainty. If the applications demanded a convention to consider federal spending, but the amendment proposed and then ratified by three-fourths of the state legislatures limited the treaty power, would this be a valid amendment? Congress might refuse to recognize such an amendment on the grounds that it exceeded the subject matter of the called convention. How would the ratifying states respond? No easy answers are available.

Furthermore, what would Congress do if one-third of the states applied for a convention to consider a balanced budget amendment and another third applied for a convention to consider amendments necessary to secure the general welfare of the union? One could argue that a balanced budget might advance the general welfare of the union and thus two-thirds of the states have properly applied for a convention. Of course, one might also argue that the applications are different and thus an insufficient number of states requested the summons. The interpretation of applications is a powerful tool in the hand of Congress and is susceptible to abuse.

Another issue is Congress's power to set the rules for the convention in the call. Congress might, for example, stipulate that voting at the convention will be weighted by population and that a supermajority is required to propose an amendment. What happens if the convention delegates decide to follow the format used in Philadelphia where each state had one vote and a simple majority could carry the day on all questions? Congress might refuse to submit proposed amendments by such a convention to the states. How would the states and people react to this?

They might choose to go ahead and ratify a proposed amendment whether Congress submitted it or not. This brings up the specter of Supreme Court review. The Court, claiming to be the final arbiter of the Constitution, could hold that the amendment is void because the convention did not follow the rules laid out by Congress and/or because the amendment was not transmitted to the state legislatures from Congress. How would the ratifying states look upon an unelected branch of the national government striking an amendment that received the approval of three-fourths or more of the states?

Those unanswered questions and problems have led Professor William Quirk to conclude that "[b]ecause of uncertainty over how the convention would be organized and what its powers would be . . . the second method [provided in Article V] is not a practical alternative to an obstinate Congress."[23] The Morris-Gerry motion made in the waning days of the Philadelphia Convention removed the states from any meaningful role in initiating constitutional change. On paper they could demand a convention, but in reality Congress holds all the cards when it comes to constitutional change. The powers of our national government would likely be much reduced if the road to amendment did not require action of the national legislature.

Lessons from the Twenty-Seventh Amendment

The Twenty-Seventh Amendment is a good example of how the people and the states might place restrictions on Congress. This amendment, ratified in 1992, provides that "[n]o law varying the compensation for the services of the Senators and Representatives shall take effect, until an election of Representatives shall have intervened."[24] The amendment was submitted to the states in 1789 as one of 12 proposed alterations by the first Congress. The states had governed issues of compensation for their delegates to the Confederation Congress, and some feared that the independence of the new Congress would be tantamount to a license for Congress to make its members rich.

At the time this compensation amendment was proposed, Rhode Island and North Carolina remained out of the union. The Constitution had been ratified by very narrow margins in the critical states of Virginia and New

York. The Federalists pushed the Constitution through only with the promise that amendments would be proposed to address concerns raised in the state ratifying conventions. In this environment, Congress believed that the very survival of the national government depended upon it offering amendments pursuant to Article V. Had it not done so, Rhode Island and North Carolina would have remained independent nations and other states might have considered withdrawing from the union.

During the 1790s, the requisite three-fourths of the state legislatures did not see the need for this amendment (only six ratified it), and thus it did not become part of our Bill of Rights. Congress, however, failed to stipulate a deadline for ratification. The amendment gained traction in the 1980s in response to what many viewed as congressional misconduct. The media drew attention to Congress giving itself special tax breaks, members eating for free at the congressional cafeteria, and members nonchalantly floating checks at the congressional credit union. The significant pay raise Congress gave itself in 1989 did not help matters either. A student from the University of Texas at Austin wrote a paper on the compensation amendment and embarked on a letter-writing campaign urging the states to ratify. By 1992, a total of 38 states ratified the compensation amendment and it became part of the Constitution. In effect, the people and the states rebuked Congress for abuses of power.

Speaker of the House Tom Foley, a Democrat from Washington State, considered bringing a legal action to challenge the validity of the amendment. But the popularity of the amendment and prior case law persuaded him to submit to it. In 1938, the Supreme Court held that it would not decide the propriety of ratification of an amendment when the plaintiff complained that too much time had passed between an amendment's proposal and fulfillment of the three-fourths requirement.[25] The precedent, if honored, would have quickly disposed of Foley's lawsuit.

The Twenty-Seventh Amendment, of course, is an accident of history. But for the first Congress's failure to impose a deadline, this amendment would not be part of the Constitution. The Congress of the 1980s certainly would not have proposed such an amendment—no matter how much the people protested. As has been the case throughout American history, the states would not have risked a convention, with its myriad uncertainties, over this issue. But the uncovering of this forgotten proposal gave the states a vehicle to assert authority over the national legislature. They did not have to beg the modern Congress to submit the proposal and thus were able to take the initiative themselves.

The Twenty-Seventh Amendment is but further evidence that the states need the ability to propose and consider amendments without the involvement of the national legislature or the risks associated with a convention. In a federal system, any state should be able to propose a constitutional amendment without the involvement of Congress. If the originating state can persuade three-fourths of the others to ratify, then it should become a part of the Constitution. The result, in the words of Professor Quirk, is that "[t]he people, acting through their states, would be able, through an orderly and manageable process, to reclaim powers previously granted to, or assumed by, the federal government."[26]

Such an amendment procedure would give the states and the people a fighting chance to defend themselves against a consolidated national government that continuously operates in an extra-constitutional manner. The adoption of a new amendment procedure would open the door for constitutional change. Excluding the Bill of Rights and the exceptional circumstances under which Congress drafted it, the Constitution has been amended only seventeen times since 1791. The trials, complexities, and inadequacies of the Constitution have demonstrated the need for revisions, but Congress has not acted.

Madison warned in *Federalist* No. 43, that an amendment procedure should not "render the Constitution too mutable."[27] But he did expect that amendments, as necessary, would be proposed to augment or reduce national power. "Had the power of making treaties, for example, been omitted, however necessary it might have been," Madison explained during the national bank controversy, "the defect could only have been lamented or supplied by an amendment of the constitution."[28] As flaws became visible, the Constitution would be altered through the deliberative process outlined in Article V. But enough effort and work had to go into the procedure to interdict the passions of faction.

Unfortunately, today our Constitution is "amended" by judicial interpretations and congressional fervor for expanded power. Article V's congressionally directed amendment process has rendered the Constitution too mutable, but not because amendments are offered willy-nilly. Instead, the powerlessness of the states to police constitutional boundaries through amendments permits the national government to contort our constitutional charter.

Scholars can make the case for various amendments to the Constitution, but none is as necessary as a new procedure whereby Congress is stripped of its monopoly on constitutional change. As outlined in the Virginia Plan, the states should be able to propose amendments without the involvement of the national government. Were such a procedure in place, the national government's powers might still be few and defined rather than broad and indeterminate.

16

Rights, Amendments, and Alterations

IN THE CLOSING days of the Philadelphia Convention, George Mason urged his colleagues to preface the Constitution with a bill of rights. Mason averred that such an addition "would give great quiet to the people" and he believed a suitable declaration of rights "might be prepared in a few hours."[1] Elbridge Gerry made the formal motion to create a federal bill of rights and Mason seconded the motion. Roger Sherman asserted that the various state declarations of rights were not repealed by the Constitution and thus would be sufficient to protect the people's liberties. Mason countered that the Constitution's Supremacy Clause would make national laws "paramount to State Bills of Rights," and thus an additional security was needed.[2] Madison's *Notes* show that the debate ended here and that the Gerry–Mason motion was defeated by a vote of ten states to none (with Massachusetts abstaining).

The Philadelphia Convention blundered in its refusal to give Mason's arguments serious attention. That failure gave the Anti-Federalists much ammunition to utilize in the ratification debates. "There are certain rights which we have always held sacred in the United States," wrote the Federal Farmer, "and recognized in all our constitutions, and which, by the adoption of the new constitution in its present form, will be left unsecured."[3] The Federal Farmer did not object to national laws taking precedence over state laws. But he did believe that "national laws ought to yield to unalienable or fundamental rights."[4] A Maryland Farmer shared the Federal Farmer's concern about fundamental rights. In times of passion and heated debate, the Maryland Farmer explained, the natural rights of individuals would likely be "lost" if "not clearly and expressly ascertained" in the governing document.[5]

Brutus emphasized that the principles of the national compact "ought to have been clearly and precisely stated, and the most express and full declaration of rights to have been made—But on this subject there is almost an entire silence."[6] Universal experience, Brutus reasoned, compelled the inclusion of a declaration of rights in the Constitution. Those in power "have been found in all ages ever active to enlarge their powers and abridge the public liberty."[7] This thirst for power "has induced the people in all countries, where any sense of freedom remained, to fix barriers against the encroachments of their rulers."[8] Using England as an example, Brutus pointed to Magna Carta and the English Bill of Rights as "the boast, as well as the security, of that nation."[9] Considering the importance of such great charters in Anglo-American liberty, Brutus found it "astonishing, that this grand security, to the rights of the people, is not to be found in this constitution."[10]

Would a Bill of Rights Be Superfluous?

Staunch Federalists rejected claims that a national bill of rights was necessary. James Wilson, for example, argued that bills of rights were proper in state constitutions in which the people "invested their representatives with every right and authority which they did not in explicit terms reserve."[11] The federal constitution, Wilson averred, was different. Absent an express delegation of power, the federal government could not act. "[I]t would have been superfluous and absurd to have stipulated with a federal body of our own creation," Wilson proclaimed, "that we should enjoy those privileges of which we are not divested, either by the intention or the act that has brought the body into existence."[12] Wilson then gave the example of freedom of the press. "[W]hat control can proceed from the Federal government to shackle or destroy that sacred palladium of national freedom?" Wilson asked.[13] Had the people delegated "a power similar to that which has been granted for the regulation of commerce . . . to regulate literary publications, it would have been as necessary to stipulate that the liberty of the press should be preserved inviolate."[14] Because the Constitution contained not a word about publications, Wilson reasoned that Congress could take no action to limit the dissemination of information and opinion. An amendment declaring that Congress could not interfere with the press, Wilson claimed, would be dangerous. "[T]hat very declaration might have been construed to imply that some degree of power was given, since we undertook to define its extent."[15]

Alexander Hamilton, writing in *Federalist* No. 84, challenged the idea that a bill of rights was proper for a republican government. Hamilton pointed out that Magna Carta and the English Bill of Rights were "stipulations between kings and their subjects, abridgements of prerogative in favor of privilege, reservations of rights not surrendered to the prince."[16] Such reservations, in Hamilton's opinion, "have no application to constitutions professedly founded upon the power of the people, and executed by their immediate representatives and servants."[17] To Hamilton, the people really surrendered no powers inasmuch as the enumerated powers would be exercised by those chosen—directly or indirectly—by the people themselves. "Here is a better recognition of popular rights, than volumes of those aphorisms which make the principal figure in several of our State bills of rights, and which would sound much better in a treatise of ethics than in a constitution of government."[18]

Borrowing from Wilson's State House Yard Speech, Hamilton argued that protection for free speech was unnecessary because Congress had no power to legislate on this matter. He further speculated that something akin to our current First Amendment would be dangerous because it would imply a congressional power over speech. Amendments "would contain various exceptions to powers not granted; and, on this very account, would afford a colorable pretext to claim more than were granted. For why declare that things shall not be done which there is no power to do?"[19]

Hamilton pointed to Article I of the Constitution and crowed that the document already contained a bill of rights. Right after enumerating Congress's powers, the document sets forth limitations on the suspension of habeas corpus, the passing of bills of attainder and ex post facto laws, and the granting of noble titles. Thus, Hamilton claimed that the Constitution itself was a bill of rights. With such guarantees within the instrument, Hamilton questioned the sincerity of Anti-Federalists who clamored for a formal declaration of rights. *Federalist* No. 84 also contended that to the extent the Constitution "declare[d] and specif[ied] the political privileges of the citizens in the structure and administration of the government," it took the character of the bill of rights.[20] "Adverting therefore to the substantial meaning of a bill of rights," Hamilton concluded, "it is absurd to allege that it is not to be found in the work of the convention."[21]

The Anti-Federalists cogently replied to arguments that a bill of rights was dangerous or unnecessary. "If every thing which is not given is reserved," asked Brutus, "what propriety is there in these exceptions? Does this constitution any where grant the power of suspending the habeas corpus, to make expost facto laws, pass bills of attainder, or grant titles of nobility?"[22] If Wilson and Hamilton were correct about the reasons the Framers omitted a bill of rights, it followed that the document's drafters "would not have made certain reservations, while they totally omitted others of more importance."[23] Based on the Federalists' arguments, one could assume that without these limitations on Congress's power, by implication or otherwise, the Constitution must have permitted the grants of noble titles, the suspension of habeas corpus, and so on.

The Federal Farmer opined that the restrictions found in the ninth section of Article I obviously were included in the Constitution out of caution—as an additional security for the people. Out of caution, then, we ought to have a full bill of rights. "On the whole, the position appears to me to be undeniable," averred the Federal Farmer, "that this bill of rights ought to be carried further; and some other principles established, as part of this fundamental compact between the people of the United States and their federal rulers."[24] If the list of reserved rights was not extended, the Federal Farmer feared that enterprising rulers would conclude that the people "mean to relinquish" liberties not specified "or at least feel indifferent about them."[25]

State Conventions Make Demands

As the ratification conventions began to meet, many Anti-Federalists urged that a bill of rights and other amendments should be added before their states accepted the new Constitution. Because the people had had time to consider the work of the Philadelphia Convention, a better sense had been gained of what additional safeguards and modifications the people wanted. Accordingly, a second convention should be held where the necessary changes could be made. After this second convention, the Anti-Federalists suggested, the Constitution would be submitted to the states for ratification. In preparing for the Virginia ratifying convention, Madison wrote to Jefferson, who was serving as the American minister in Paris, that "[t]he preliminary question will be whether previous alterations shall be insisted on or not? Should this be carried in the affirmative, either a conditional ratification, or a proposal for a new Convention will ensue. In either event, I think the Constitution and the Union will be both endangered."[26]

The Anti-Federalist strategy became less viable as some states quickly ratified the Constitution without demanding previous amendments. By the end of December 1787, Delaware, Pennsylvania, New Jersey, and Georgia had ratified. Connecticut followed suit in January 1788. The earliest test for proponents of unconditional ratification came in Massachusetts. Going into the convention, it appeared that the delegates were evenly divided over the Constitution. As the debates progressed, ratification appeared unlikely. A "no" vote in an important state such as Massachusetts, the Federalists knew, would carry great influence in the others states and might preclude the Constitution from garnering the required nine states for it to go into effect.

At this critical juncture, John Hancock rose and expressed his hopes that "this Convention may adopt such a form of government as may extend its good influences to every part of the United States."[27] Hancock spoke in favor of the Constitution, but thought that the "diversity of sentiment in the gentlemen of the Convention" necessitated "introduction of some general amendments" that would "remove the doubts and quiet the apprehension" expressed on the convention's floor.[28] Hancock proposed a series of amendments that the convention would attach to its unconditional ratification. Samuel Adams questioned "whether it is best to accept this Constitution on conditional amendments, or to rely on amendments in the future, as the Constitution provides."[29] Adams, however, ultimately supported Hancock's proposal in hopes that the weight of Massachusetts behind later amendments would influence other states and yield positive results.

With old patriots such as Hancock and Adams for unconditional ratification with suggested amendments, Massachusetts ratified by a vote of 187 to 168. In its ratification message, the convention opined "that certain amendments and alterations of the said Constitution would remove fears and quiet the apprehension of many good people."[30] In addition, the proposed amendments would "more effectually guard against an undue administration of the federal government."[31] The state urged its representatives in the new Congress "to exert all their influence, and use all reasonable and legal methods, to obtain a ratification of the said alterations and provisions" in accordance with Article V.[32]

Massachusetts's Amendments

The first proposed amendment dealt with the power of the new government. Massachusetts requested that the Constitution be amended to explicitly state "that all powers not expressly delegated by the aforesaid Constitution are reserved to the several states."[33] Samuel Adams described this proposal as "a summary of a bill of rights, which gentlemen are anxious to obtain."[34] He stated further that "[i]t removes a doubt which many have entertained respecting the matter, and gives assurance that, if any law made by the federal government shall be extended beyond the power granted in the proposed Constitution" all could see the error and the courts would declare such an act "void."[35] Adams also believed that such a provision would be akin to the Confederation's second article wherein each state retained its sovereignty and independence regarding every power not delegated to the United States.

The second proposed amendment dealt with concerns about inadequate representation. Massachusetts asked that the Constitution be amended to guarantee "one representative to every thirty thousand persons . . . until the whole number of representatives amounts to two hundred."[36] The delegates objected that, as received from the Philadelphia Convention, the people could never have a more favorable ratio than one for every 30,000. They feared that representatives from large districts would have little conception of the character, hardships, and feeling of the people. A ratio in excess of one representative for every 30,000 people would not, in Massachusetts's opinion, be a true and viable representation.

In the third proposed amendment, Massachusetts asked Congress to refrain from regulating the times, places, and manners for electing senators and representatives unless a state neglected to make the necessary provisions. The Philadelphia Convention gave Congress the time-place-and-manner power so that state officials, jealous of their powers, could not abolish the national government by declining to make rules for the election of congressmen. However, Anti-Federalists feared that corrupt national officers could easily abuse this power to perpetuate themselves in office or to disenfranchise large parts of the population. For example, if Congress decreed that New York had to hold all congressional elections in New York City on a particular day, this would hinder and discourage voters from traveling from upstate New York to cast a ballot. Samuel Adams applauded Massachusetts's proposed alteration because he feared that leaving a plenary time-place-and-manner power in Congress might "infringe the sacred freedom of elections, which ought ever to be held as sacred."[37]

The fourth proposed amendment touched upon taxation. Hancock's proposal would have prohibited Congress from levying direct taxes unless (1) the funds could not be raised from imposts and excises, and (2) the states had been requisitioned for the money and had failed or neglected to raise the needed amount. As a check on the national government, Massachusetts wanted the states to retain some control on Congress's demands for revenue.

Massachusetts's fifth proposed amendment took aim at monopolies. The convention requested that Congress be prohibited from creating companies "with exclusive advantages of commerce."[38] In England during the 1600s, the great jurist and Parliamentarian Sir Edward Coke had battled against the monarch's grant of exclusive commercial privileges to a few subjects. Colonial Americans admired Coke's stand for commercial liberty and associated monopolies with royal or despotic government. Congress should not be permitted, Massachusetts averred, to follow in the footsteps of the Stuart kings by granting exclusive commercial privileges.

The sixth proposed amendment sought to preserve grand jury presentment for individuals at risk of "an infamous punishment, or loss of life."[39] Massachusetts envisioned federal crimes that could carry severe consequences. It sought to preserve the ancient institution of the grand jury in the federal criminal system. Before a charging document carrying serious consequences could issue, Massachusetts wanted a grand jury drawn from the community to hear the prosecution's evidence and to decide whether the case could go forward. Such a power in the community would shield the accused from an overzealous federal prosecutor.

In the seventh amendment Hancock sought to place a jurisdictional amount that would prohibit federal courts from resolving disputes between citizens of different states. Federal courts, Hancock believed, should not decide trifling matters just because the parties were of diverse citizenship. Massachusetts wanted to preserve the roles of the state courts and refer matters to federal judges only in very significant cases. Under the proposed amendment, state-court adjudication would be the rule and federal action the exception.

The eighth proposed amendment addressed the Philadelphia Convention's failure to explicitly preserve the right to a jury trial in federal civil cases. Massachusetts believed that either party to a civil case in federal court should have the right to demand a jury trial. The citizens' right to participate in the judicial branch was too critical not to be mentioned in the federal Constitution.

Finally, Massachusetts's ninth proposal prohibited any person serving in the United States government from accepting a title of nobility or other office from a foreign ruler. While the Constitution prohibited Congress from granting titles, it was silent on whether government officers could receive titles elsewhere while in office. Massachusetts wanted this additional safeguard to reduce the likelihood of foreign influence over the federal government.

Massachusetts's form of ratification altered the landscape of debate. By becoming the sixth state to ratify without the requirement of previous amendments, Massachusetts wounded Anti-Federalist hopes that a new convention would be held prior to acceptance of the Constitution. But the substantive amendments endorsed by the likes of Adams and Hancock caused the Federalists much concern. If and when the Constitution did go into operation, the Federalists could expect calls for a convention to consider amendments such as Hancock's or a push in the new Congress by Anti-Federalists for amendments to be offered to the several states. Federalists worried that the Constitution received from the Philadelphia Convention would not remain inviolate.

In the spring of 1788, Maryland and South Carolina both ratified the Constitution. South Carolina, following the example of Massachusetts, attached four proposed amendments to its unconditional ratification. Three of the amendments—regarding taxation, the time-place-and-manner power, and an express reservation of state power—were in the same spirit as Massachusetts's proposals. The one additional amendment requested a small change in the wording of Article VI's requirement for an oath or affirmation by certain officials to support the constitution.

On June 21, 1788, New Hampshire became the ninth state to ratify. It too attached a series of twelve amendments to the ratification message. The first nine were obtained from the work of the Massachusetts convention. The tenth proposal from New Hampshire took aim at standing armies. No such army should be maintained in peacetime, New Hampshire asserted, absent a three-fourths vote in both houses of Congress. This proposal went on to prohibit quartering soldiers in private homes in peacetime without the owner's consent. These two concerns about standing armies and quartering were no doubt taken from the English Bill of Rights, which was enacted in 1689 after James II had kept a large army in time of peace without the consent of Parliament, and had quartered his troops contrary to law.

Virginia's Ratifying Convention

The Virginia convention met at roughly the same time as New Hampshire's convention. Going into the convention, the number of Federalists and Anti-Federalists appeared to be equally divided. In modern parlance, the vote in Virginia would be a "toss-up." George Mason and Patrick Henry led the Anti-Federalist forces while James Madison and John Marshall argued in favor of ratification without prior amendments. As the oppressive June heat taxed the patience and health of many of the delegates, the Federalists estimated that they enjoyed perhaps a four-vote majority. On June 24, 1788, George Wythe rose and addressed the convention. Wythe was one of the most respected men in the state. He was a signer of the Declaration of Independence, former speaker of the Virginia house, and a beloved professor of law at William and Mary. After George Washington, Wythe was perhaps the most notable living Virginian.

Wythe urged the delegates to accept the proposed constitution without prior amendments. He spoke of the blessings of union and the defects of the Articles. He admitted that the Philadelphia Convention's work was far from perfect and suggested that a few well-designed amendments might cure the defects. Wythe believed that necessary amendments "would be easily obtained *after* ratification in the manner proposed by the Constitution."[40] He suggested that recommendatory amendments could be attached to the state's ratification message and proposed a resolution of ratification.

The debate continued. Finally, by a vote of 88 to 80, the Virginia ratifying convention rejected a motion to ratify contingent on amendments approved by the new Congress or submitted to the states in a second convention. Then, by a vote of 89 to 79, the Virginians approved a ratification motion with amendments recommended to the new Congress. Wythe headed a committee of twenty-two delegates that prepared the list of proposed amendments. The committee featured many of the Old Dominion's ablest statesmen. Patrick Henry, James Madison, George Mason, and John Marshall were among the committee's most famous members.

Virginia's ratification message declared that "the powers granted under the Constitution, being derived from the people of the United States, may be resumed by them, whensoever the same shall be perverted to their injury or oppression, and that every power not granted thereby remains with them, and at their will."[41] The message acknowledged that imperfections existed in the Constitution, but declared that these should "be examined in the mode prescribed [in Article V]," rather "than to bring the Union into danger by a delay with a hope of obtaining amendments previous to the ratifications."[42]

There followed a list of forty proposed amendments. The first twenty were aimed at "securing from encroachment, the essential and unalienable rights of the people."[43] The Wythe declaration of rights affirmed broad principles, such as the right of all persons to acquire, possess, and protect property. The declaration asserted that all power is derived from the people and that they retain the right to use force against arbitrary rulers. Public officials, the committee declared, are mere servants of the people and never should the offices of these servants be hereditary. The three branches of government "should be separate and distinct."[44] The executive and members of the legislature should be subject to term limits and "be reduced to a private station" after a fixed period of service.[45] The necessity of rotation in office aside, all elections, the committee believed, should be "free and frequent" in light of the ultimate sovereignty claimed by the people. No doubt remembering the oppressions of royal governors, the declaration observed that the executive could not suspend any duly enacted law without the consent of the legislature.

From these general principles about government and power, the declaration of rights turned to the courts and criminal procedure. A defendant in a criminal case has a right to know the nature of the charges, confront witnesses against him, introduce evidence, obtain legal counsel, and be tried by jury of the vicinage. Harkening back to chapter 39 of the Magna Carta, the declaration averred that never should government take life, liberty, or property, "but by the law of the land."[46] If a person finds himself "restrained of his liberty," he has a right to challenge the confinement in court and to be released if the detention is contrary to law.[47] Those seeking release, should not have excessive bail imposed; those found guilty should be exempt from any "cruel or unusual punishment."[48]

The committee proclaimed that in all civil cases "the ancient trial by jury is one of the greatest securities to the rights of the people."[49] In civil court, the declaration continued, the people should have access to justice without delay and independent of their wealth and status.

When the authorities undertake investigations, they may not resort to unreasonable searches or seizures. Warrants should be obtained with "information on oath . . . of legal and sufficient cause."[50] The committee decried the use of general warrants such as the British used in the colonies prior to the Revolution. A general warrant allows a law enforcement officer to search anywhere for contraband items. Those warrants required no specificity as to the place searched or a showing of probable cause for the search.

After outlining fundamental rights related to the justice system, the proposed amendments turned to certain personal rights. The committee avowed that the people should be allowed "to assemble together to consult for the common good, or to instruct their representatives."[51] Every freeman possesses "a right to petition or apply to the legislature for redress of grievances."[52] Connected with this right to petition was freedom of speech. The committee recognized this important right and noted further that "the freedom of the press is one of the greatest bulwarks of liberty, and ought not to be violated."[53]

Declarations have their places, but the committee added some insurance against usurpations by averring that "the people have a right to keep and bear arms."[54] The committee observed that standing armies in time of peace endanger liberty. The militia, rather than professional soldiers, should be relied upon for the protection of the community. In no case should soldiers in peacetime be quartered in a private home without the consent of the owner.

The proffered declaration of rights also provided protection for religion. Persons unable to bear arms because of religious convictions, the committee concluded, should be allowed to employ a substitute in wartime. Religion "can be directed only by reason and conviction, not by force or violence."[55]

It follows that the people should enjoy "the free exercise of religion" and that no denomination should be "favored or established" by the government.[56]

The next twenty proposals were styled as "amendments to the Constitution."[57] Virginia followed the example of Massachusetts regarding such matters as clarifying that the states retain what is not delegated, demanding that at least one representative be elected for every 30,000 persons, requiring Congress to requisition the states before levying direct taxes, and prohibiting Congress from altering time, place and manner regulations absent state noncompliance. In addition to these, Virginia wanted members of Congress disqualified from holding "any civil office under the authority of the United States, during the time for which they shall be . . . elected."[58] Rather than the journals of Congress being published from "time to time" as provided in Article I, the committee preferred that they be published "at least once every year."[59] Furthermore, Virginia wanted the Constitution amended to require that "a regular statement and account of the receipts and expenditures of public money" be published yearly.[60]

George Mason's hand was evident in the proposed amendments requiring two-thirds of Congress to approve commercial regulations and two-thirds of senators to approve commercial treaties. Following these proposals, Virginia offered specific prohibitions against standing armies in peacetime and wanted enlistments limited to four years "except in time of war."[61] If Congress failed to organize, arm, and discipline the militia, Virginia believed that the states should exercise this power themselves.

Members of the committee were uneasy about Congress's power to "exercise exclusive legislation in all cases whatsoever" over what would become the District of Columbia.[62] Many Anti-Federalists argued that Congress could use that broad authority to outflank the Constitution's enumeration of powers. Virginia wanted this power limited to "such regulations as respect the police and good government" of the federal city.[63]

The proposed amendments called for term limits on the presidency. "[N]o person shall be capable of being President of the United States," the committee recommended, "for more than eight years in any term of sixteen years."[64] Lengthy presidential terms were too reminiscent of hereditary monarchy for the Virginians' tastes.

Virginia offered a lengthy amendment on the judicial power. The proposal, in the main, would have limited the federal judiciary to the Supreme Court and various admiralty courts established by Congress. State courts would serve as the trial courts of the Union with the possibility of appeal to the Supreme Court. Virginia also wanted to strike the broad wording of Article III wherein the judicial power extends to all cases "arising under this constitution."[65] The amendment declared that federal court jurisdiction would not extend to a case "where the cause of action shall have originated before the ratification of the Constitution," except in certain territorial disputes and debts due to the United States.[66] Without delving into every detail of the amendment, it certainly would have circumscribed the federal judicial power.

The amendments sought to protect the criminal defendant's right to challenge or object to the jury selected to hear the case. For clauses that declared Congress "shall not exercise certain powers," Virginia wanted a constitutional statement prohibiting an interpretation that would extend rather than reduce congressional power. No pay increase for members of Congress, the committee believed, should go into effect until an election intervened. In one of the vaguer proffered amendments, Virginia declared that "some tribunal other than the Senate be provided for trying the impeachment of senators." Finally, the state's proposals concluded with an amendment prohibiting the raising or lowering of a judge's salary "during his continuance in office, otherwise than by general regulations of salary, which may take place . . . at stated periods of not less than seven years."[67]

The convention's records reflect that prior to adjourning, the Federalists (including Wythe, Marshall, and Madison) pushed to have the proposed amendment dealing with taxes and requisitions struck from the record, but the Anti-Federalists prevailed 85 to 65. The convention charged its members in the newly elected Congress to use all means to procure all amendments proposed and to ensure that federal statutes passed complied with the spirit of the amendments offered by Virginia.

New York's convention opened approximately one week prior to Virginia's ratification of the Constitution. Alexander Hamilton arranged for express riders to be at the ready to bring word of Virginia's decision to Poughkeepsie. New Hampshire had been the ninth state to ratify, but Hamilton knew that a new government would not likely succeed unless Virginia was on board. Going into the convention, Federalists were in the minority. Scholars estimate that 46 of the 65 seats at the convention were held by Anti-Federalists.[68]

New York's Ratifying Convention

New York's Anti-Federalists were adamant that amendments be added before New York joined the union. Writing as "a Plebian," Melancton Smith warned that "if alterations do not take place, a door will be left open for undue administration, and encroachments on the liberties of the people."[69] Smith pointed out that many Federalists had admitted the need for amendments, but urged the people to "confide on procuring the necessary alterations after we have received it."[70] Smith found this proposed order of things foolish:

> But it is contended, adopt first, and then amend it. I ask, why not amend, and then adopt it? Most certainly the latter mode of proceedings is more consistent with our ideas of prudence in the ordinary concerns of life. If men went about entering into a contract respecting their private concerns, it would be highly absurd for them to sign and seal an instrument containing stipulations which are contrary to their interests and wishes, under the expectation, that the parties, after its execution, would agree to make alterations agreeable to their desires.[71]

Smith conceded that a number of states already had ratified without demanding prior amendments. However, a substantial number of the people of those states were friends to amendments. Smith reasoned that those states would "cordially meet with overtures for that purpose from any state, and concur in appointing a convention to effect it."[72] With New York recovering from the trials of the Revolution and every man "sit[ting] under his own vine and under his own fig-tree," no reason existed to adopt the Constitution in its present form when needed amendments could be procured in short order.[73]

Federalists hoped that if they could prolong the debate on the Constitution, news would arrive that nine states had ratified and that Virginia was cemented to the union. Faced with such information, the Federalists believed that Anti-Federalist resolve would weaken. Anti-Federalists could not realistically argue, the Federalists reasoned, for prior amendments inasmuch as the new union would already be established. Moreover, Anti-Federal intransigence could cost New York City the opportunity to become the capital of the new nation. Without New York City in the mix, this honor would surely go to Philadelphia, Baltimore, or perhaps Richmond.

John Lansing, who had left the Philadelphia Convention early because of the consolidating tendencies of the Virginia Plan, and Melancton Smith were the chief Anti-Federalist spokesmen in the ratifying convention. Alexander Hamilton and Chancellor Robert Livingston led the Federalist delegates. During the first week of the convention both sides attacked and defended in a magnificent display of oratory. On June 25, Livingston rose and declared "an alteration of circumstances."[74] The previous day the convention received word that New Hampshire had ratified. "The Confederation," Livingston pronounced, "was now *dissolved*. The question before the committee was now a question of policy and expediency."[75] The convention should not waste time debating prior or subsequent amendments, but rather contemplate whether New York would join the new union or suffer the dangers of wilderness wandering. Smith retorted that the news from New Hampshire "had not altered his feelings or wishes" concerning prior amendments and that he "had long been convinced that nine states would receive the Constitution."[76] Lansing supported Smith on this point. He "insist[ed] that it is still our duty to maintain our rights" despite the actions of the other states.[77] Lansing acknowledged that New York's "dissent cannot prevent the operation of the government," but urged the convention to "let [the nine] make the experiment."[78] Despite the actions of the sister states, New York should not "adopt a system which is dangerous to liberty."[79]

When the convention learned that Virginia had ratified, the news had little immediate effect on the Anti-Federalists. They continued to discuss the Constitution and to propose multiple substantive amendments. The Federalists, on the other hand, altered their strategy. They had made grand speeches and arguments in hopes of keeping the convention in session until the express riders from Virginia and New Hampshire reached Poughkeepsie. The Federalists achieved this objective, but without the desired results. Exasperated, the Federalists declined to continue with the debate and, for a while, became spectators.

The convention enjoyed a respite as Anti-Federalist leaders took time to organize the amendments that had been offered and to formally offer a report.

During this suspension of debate, fractures developed in the Anti-Federalist façade. Smith's cohort began to contemplate what it meant for New York to be out of the union. Perhaps the state should ratify, follow the course of the Virginia Anti-Federalists, and demand that Congress or a new convention propose needed amendments and a bill of rights. Anti-Federalists initially proposed a conditional ratification contingent upon Congress not exercising certain powers and the adoption of requested amendments. The Federalists, feeling confident after Virginia's ratification, refused to countenance a conditional ratification. Congress would not accept New York's qualifications, they argued, and would deem the state to be a foreign territory.

Despite his earlier demands for prior amendments, Smith began to change his mind. He conceded that Congress would not accept any conditions on ratification. To the chagrin of many Anti-Federalists, Smith met with Federalists to reach an accommodation. Smith knew that prior amendments and conditional ratification were inadmissible; however, he still had reservations about many constitutional provisions. The best chance New York would have for meaningful amendments, Smith deduced, would be as a part of the union with the seat of government in New York City. The state's representatives and senators could work within the new Congress to hammer out a bill of rights and to revise some of the Constitution's most troubling provisions. As July reached its end, Smith persuaded just enough Anti-Federalists to join him.

On July 26, 1788, New York—by a vote of 30 to 27—chose to ratify the Constitution. The form of ratification was the most complicated submitted by any of the states. The first part of the ratification document was a twenty-five-paragraph explanation and declaration of rights. These paragraphs dealt with diverse subjects such as popular sovereignty, the right of the people to resume the delegated powers, the importance of juries, and the right to bear arms. The convention then averred that because these rights and explanations, in its opinion, "are consistent with the said Constitution," and because it believed that proposed amendments would "receive an early and mature consideration" in the new government, New York could "assent to and ratify" the Constitution.[80]

But immediately following that assent language, New York expressed its confidence that until a new convention assembled to deliberate upon amendments, Congress would refrain from taking certain actions. Congress would not send the militia outside of the state for a period longer than six weeks unless the state's legislature consented. No time, place, and manner regulations would be adopted "unless the legislature of this state shall neglect or refuse to make" the necessary enactments.[81] Congress would not impose any excise taxes on New York's produce—"ardent spirits excepted."[82] If Congress needed revenue, it would not impose direct taxes until after the state's legislature had an opportunity to raise the money itself and submit the funds to Congress. Only if the state failed to come up with the money could Congress take the extraordinary step of imposing a direct tax.

The convention then instructed its representatives to the new Congress to "use all reasonable means" to obtain ratification of thirty-two proposed amendments attached to the conclusion of the ratification document. Many of these amendments were restatements of ideas appearing in the proposals from Massachusetts, New Hampshire, South Carolina, and Virginia. However, several novel amendments were suggested. Fearful that Congress would drive the nation into greater debt, New York wanted an amendment requiring two-thirds of Congress to approve any borrowing on the credit of the United States. The convention objected to Congress's power to levy capitation or "head taxes" upon the people and believed that the Constitution should be altered to prevent such taxation.

New York questioned whether the Constitution provided adequate protection for the writ of habeas corpus, which permits any person detained by the government to demand a hearing in front of a judge to test the lawfulness of the confinement. Article I permits Congress to suspend habeas corpus in case of rebellions or invasions, but says nothing about the duration of the suspension. New York wanted the suspension limited to six months "or until twenty days after the meeting of the Congress next following the passing of the act for such suspension."[83]

The convention sought to have senators limited to serving "six years in any term of twelve years."[84] New York expressed concern that senators might not properly represent their states once the senators arrived at the seat of government. Hence, New York proposed that states should have the power to recall their senators at any time and to elect new senators to fill the unexpired terms. New York also asked that the Article I "authority given to the executives of the states to fill up vacancies of the senators be abolished, and that such vacancies be filled by the respective legislatures."[85]

Turning to executive power, the convention suggested that the president be limited to two terms in office and that his power to grant pardons be circumscribed. In no case, the convention believed, should the president be allowed to grant a pardon for treason absent the assent of Congress. The president could grant a reprieve to the traitor, but only until the matter could "be laid before the Congress."[86]

New York objected to the Senate's "sole power" to try impeachments.[87] Instead, New York recommended that "the court for the trial of impeachments shall consist of the Senate, the judges of the Supreme Court, and the first or senior judge, for the time being, of the highest court of general and ordinary common-law jurisdiction in each state."[88]

The convention thought that the Constitution erred in not having some tribunal to review Supreme Court decisions when the High Court heard cases pursuant to its original jurisdiction. In these types of cases, the Court would act as a trial court with no body to correct any errors. Accordingly, New York suggested that litigants aggrieved by such a decision "shall, upon application, have a commission, to be issued by the President of the United States to such men learned in the law as he shall nominate" with the advice and consent of the Senate to review the case.[89]

New York implored that the Constitution be amended to prevent any federal Supreme Court judge from holding any other federal or state office. The delegates likely believed that such office holding could create conflicts of interest affecting the impartiality of the judges. The convention believed that federal court jurisdiction should not extend to land claims "unless it relate to claims of territory or jurisdiction between states, and individuals under the grants of different states."[90]

Evincing concern about the abuse of its militia, New York believed that the militia should not be required to serve more than six weeks outside its home state unless the state legislature gave consent. As discussed previously, many citizens feared that the federal government would destroy the citizens' militia by calling it forth for long stints far away from home.

The final piece of the New York ratification package was a circular letter from the convention to the governors of the several states. The letter was far from a glowing endorsement of the Constitution as ratified. In the letter's first lines, the delegates observed that multiple constitutional provisions "appear so exceptionable to a majority of us, that nothing but the fullest confidence of obtaining a revision of them by a general convention, and an invincible reluctance to separating from our sister states, could have prevailed upon a sufficient number to ratify it, without stipulating for previous amendments."[91] After noting that several states had suggested amendments, New York urged that "effectual measures be immediately taken for calling a convention, to meet at a period not far remote."[92] To operate well, the letter continued, government must possess "the confidence and good will of the body of the people."[93] This confidence could be garnered only if the subject of amendments was addressed immediately in the new Congress. Otherwise, a "numerous class of American citizens" would remain anxious about their liberties and abuse of power in government.[94]

North Carolina's Ratifying Convention

North Carolina's convention met on July 21, 1788, and concluded on August 4. Similar to New York, North Carolina Anti-Federalists began the convention with a substantial majority. Anti-Federalist Willie Jones, comfortable that the numbers were on his side, quickly moved that "the question upon the Constitution should be immediately put."[95] Jones believed that the delegates "had had ample opportunity to consider" the merits of the Constitution.[96] The document had been debated in newspapers, taverns, and copies of the Philadelphia Convention's work had long been in circulation. Inasmuch as the state was in an impecunious position, it would be a waste of public funds to prolong the convention any longer than absolutely necessary.

Federalist James Iredell rose and expressed astonishment at the motion made by Jones. "A Constitution like this," he urged, "ought not to be adopted or rejected in a moment."[97] The subject was too important and complicated to be decided without significant debate. Only from a full discussion of the Constitution and the principles of free governments could the delegates "form a proper judgment."[98] Iredell implied that the Anti-Federalists were afraid to engage in meaningful debate; his speech caused the Anti-Federalists to relent. The convention formed itself into a committee of the whole and began to discuss the Constitution.

The Federalists praised clause after clause of the Constitution in lengthy speeches. For the most part, the Anti-Federalists remained quiet and spoke up only when, in their view, the most troublesome provisions (such as taxation and the lack of a bill of rights) were discussed. By July 30, the Federalists had been through the entire Constitution. Governor Samuel Johnston moved that the convention ratify the Constitution and propose amendments as Massachusetts and other states had done. Jones rose and demanded that Johnston's motion be voted on. Jones expected Johnston's motion to be defeated easily. He further planned to introduce an Anti-Federalist motion requiring prior amendments before North Carolina would ratify. Thomas Person supported Jones. Further delay was useless, he said, because the Federalists "had all the debating to themselves, and would probably have it again, if they insisted on further argument."[99]

Federalists urged Jones and his colleagues to rethink their desired course. North Carolina, the Federalists argued, would be out of the union and have no members in the new Congress to contend for amendments. Jones pushed aside these concerns. "It is objected we shall be out of the Union," Jones said. "So I wish to be. We are left at liberty to come in at any time."[100] Jones doubted that the new Congress would do anything "of importance till a convention be called" to revise the Constitution.[101] Timothy Bloodworth supported Jones's analysis. A "temporary exclusion" from the union was a "trifling" matter.[102] He doubted that "political advantages" in the new government should "be put in competition with our liberties."[103] Matthew Locke also expressed his desire for disunion rather than the embracing of "tyrannical government."[104]

Much different from the New York convention, the Federalists were unable to break the Anti-Federalists' resolve. The Constitution, to the majority of the North Carolina convention, was simply too ill-crafted to accept without prior amendments. They believed that refusal to join the union would be a more powerful statement than ratification and a plea for subsequent changes in the Constitution. In a way, they were following the advice of Thomas Jefferson, who, when he initially studied the Constitution, wished "that the first 9 conventions may receive, and the 4. last reject it. The former will secure it finally, while the latter will oblige them to offer a declaration of rights in order to complete the union."[105] The convention resolved (by a vote of 184 to 83) that a bill of rights "together with amendments to the most ambiguous and exceptionable parts of the said Constitution" were necessary "previous to the ratification of the Constitution aforesaid on the part of the state of North Carolina."[106]

The convention proposed the same declaration of rights as suggested by the Virginia convention. It also proposed twenty-six amendments to the Constitution. Twenty of the amendments were borrowed from Virginia's recommendations. The remaining six aimed to circumscribe Congress's powers as well as protect certain state prerogatives. Section nine of the Constitution permits Congress to suspend the writ of habeas corpus in the case of rebellion. North Carolina wanted the Constitution amended so that Congress could not declare any state to be in rebellion "without the consent of at least two thirds of all the members present in both houses."[107] Apparently, North Carolina wanted some additional check on this power so that Congress would not abuse it and suspend the writ absent a manifest necessity.

Similar to a Massachusetts proposal, North Carolina desired an explicit statement that Congress could not create a "company of merchants with exclusive advantages of commerce."[108] As discussed in the chapter dealing with the treaty power, North Carolina demanded that no treaty be enacted that would contradict the Constitution. The convention foresaw that rights might be endangered by agreements with foreign powers. The convention also did not want a treaty to be self-executing. Congressional statutes would not be voided by a treaty until Congress repealed or otherwise altered the statutes in question.

North Carolina appreciated the Constitution's intent to foster free trade among the states by prohibiting preferences to certain ports and by declaring that ships traveling to or from a state are not "obliged to enter, clear, or pay Duties in another."[109] However, the convention wanted this provision strengthened or clarified with the following: "Nor shall vessels bound to a particular state be obliged to enter or pay duties in any other; nor, when bound from any one of the states, be obliged to clear another."[110]

The convention also expressed angst over provisions in Article I, Section 10 that restricted state issuance of fiat money and limited state regulation of economic affairs. Paper money, and the inflation caused by it, aided debtors inasmuch as they could pay creditors with depreciated currency. Many Anti-Federalists feared that restrictions in Article I, Section 10 would benefit the creditor class while leaving the debtor class in financial ruin. Rhode Island even refused to send delegates to the Philadelphia Convention because of worries that a new Constitution would limit state issuance of paper money. North Carolina understood that the states would be limited on currency expansions, but it also wanted some additional security so that it could liquidate the paper already in circulation without interference from the national government. North Carolina asked that neither Congress nor the federal courts "interfere with any one of the states in the redemption of paper money already emitted and now in circulation, or in liquidating and discharging the public securities of any one of the states."[III]

In its final proposed amendment, North Carolina suggested that a two-thirds vote take place in Congress before foreign troops were deployed in the United States. The state feared that Congress might hire foreign mercenaries to oppress the states. North Carolina patriots certainly remembered the clamor in the 1770s when George III hired Germans to wage war against the colonies.

At the end of July 1788, the Federalists could boast that 11 of the 13 states had ratified the Constitution. Only North Carolina and troublesome Rhode Island remained outside the union. The national government, with new and invigorated powers, would go into operation in 1789. While the Federalists certainly felt a sense of vindication, they also realized that many of the state ratification messages were not glowing endorsements of the Constitution. Important states such as Virginia, Massachusetts, and New York had requested a bill of rights and substantive amendments to the Constitution. Those states contemplated that changes would be proposed in the first Congress or in a constitutional convention. The Constitution had been ratified not because it was a magnificent charter of liberty, but rather because the majorities in the ratifying conventions believed it somewhat better than the Articles of Confederation. Some also voted to adopt the Constitution because they believed that alterations would be more likely if their states were in the union rather than outside it. Amendments and alterations, most observers concluded, seemed to be a given. The only real question was the extent of the changes and how soon they would occur.

17

A Tub to a Whale

TO THE CHAGRIN of Federalists, demands for a bill of rights and substantive amendments did not die after ratification of the Constitution. Anti-Federalists continued to express serious concerns about the lack of safeguards for individual liberty and the broadly worded provisions granting powers to the new government. For example, in September 1788 delegates from Philadelphia and thirteen Pennsylvania counties met in Harrisburg to consider a course of action in light of ratification. The delegates agreed that the citizenry should acquiesce in the formation of the national government, but they worried about the Constitution's effects on future generations. The national charter, they averred, "contains in it some principles which may be perverted to purposes injurious to the rights of free citizens."[1] The document also contained "some ambiguities which may probably lead to contentions incompatible with order and good government."[2] Hence, the delegates resolved that "early" and "considerable amendments are essentially necessary."[3] It recommended that the Pennsylvania legislature petition Congress for a second convention to convene and consider revision of the Constitution.

In November 1788, Virginia's General Assembly shocked Federalists when it formally called upon Congress, which would not assemble until the spring of 1789, to summon a general convention. Patrick Henry's forces controlled the lower house and easily pushed this measure through. Virginia Federalists attempted to persuade the lower house to simply suggest that Congress consider amendments, but they were defeated 85 to 39.

Virginia's application for a new convention stressed that the state's ratifying body "dreaded [the Constitution's] operation under the present form" and

had accepted it "from motives of affection to our sister States."[4] The application expressed that the misgivings outlined in Virginia's ratification message
were "not founded in speculative theory, but deduced from principles which
have been established by the melancholy example of other nations in different
ages."[5] Until the flaws in the Constitution were addressed, Virginia opined,
the public would be anxious and have little confidence in the national government. It recommended a general convention "with full power to take into
their consideration the defects of this Constitution that have been suggested
by the state Convention."[6]

In February 1789, New York submitted its own application for a second
convention. The legislature declared that "several articles of the Constitution
[were] so exceptionable" that it would never have ratified but for a love for
the sister states.[7] Hence, it called for a second convention to meet "as early
as possible" to consider amendments "best calculated to promote our common interests, and secure to ourselves and our latest posterity, the great and
unalienable rights of mankind."[8]

James Madison was disappointed in North Carolina's refusal to ratify and
the persistent demands for a new convention. He believed that New York's
July 28 circular letter had reinvigorated Anti-Federalists. He feared that an
early convention would be "composed of men who will essentially mutilate the
system, particularly in the article of taxation, without which in my opinion
the system cannot answer the purposes for which it was intended."[9] Writing
to Jefferson, Madison complained that Patrick Henry and his followers "enter
with great zeal into the scheme."[10] George Washington had urged Madison
to run for a seat in the General Assembly to fight against Henry's efforts that
culminated in the application for a convention, but Madison did not heed
this advice.

Madison's decision to remain in New York and to decline to participate in
state politics almost cost him a role in drafting what would become the United
States Bill of Rights. Federalists suggested that the legislature elect Madison to
the new national Senate, but Henry's partisans instead chose Richard Henry
Lee and William Grayson. Madison later would claim that this decision suited
him because he doubted that he had enough wealth to maintain a residence
sufficient to entertain various foreign dignitaries. He believed senators would

regularly host feasts and other functions at great personal expense. The House of Representatives, he contended, was better suited for a person of his means.

Madison's Campaign

Garnering a House seat, however, was not easy. In a bit of gerrymandering, Henry crafted Madison's district to give Anti-Federalists a strong advantage. Of the sixteen delegates from the newly created district that had attended the Virginia ratifying convention, only five had voted to accept the Constitution. Moreover, the war hero and young Anti-Federalist James Monroe also resided in this district and would run against Madison.

To prevent Madison from seeking election in a Federalist congressional district, the General Assembly passed a law requiring that any candidate for a congressional seat be a resident of the district in which he was running for at least twelve months prior to the election. To further make it difficult for Madison, the General Assembly reappointed him to the lame-duck Confederation Congress to keep Madison out of the state and unable to campaign for office.

In Madison's district, as well as throughout the country, the only real national issue was amendments. The people demanded alterations and a bill of rights. Thus, in the words of historian Pauline Maier, "[s]ometimes Federalist candidates had to promise—or at least indicate, even disingenuously—that they favored amendments."[11] Madison was no exception. At the behest of friends, Madison returned to the congressional district just five weeks before the scheduled elections. In the cold and snow, he traveled around asking for votes and making speeches to gatherings both large and small.

Madison asserted that he was a friend to amendments and that he had urged several amendments at the Philadelphia Convention that had been rejected. He said that he did believe that consideration of amendments was premature until the Constitution had been ratified. But now that it was in place, Madison pledged that he was in favor of amendments and would work in the first Congress to present amendments to the states. Madison had made similar statements in correspondence to Thomas Jefferson. "My own opinion has always been in favor of a bill of rights," Madison wrote, "provided it be so framed as not to imply powers not meant to be included in the enumeration."[12]

Madison further confided to Jefferson that the lack of a bill of rights was not "a material defect," but that he would support one because "it is anxiously desired by others."[13]

Madison's rhetoric on the campaign trail was, to put it charitably, stretching the truth. When George Mason beseeched the Philadelphia Convention to add a bill of rights, Madison did nothing to support his fellow Virginian. When Jefferson expressed his hope that "a bill of rights will be formed to guard the people against the federal government," Madison challenged his old friend.[14] Madison responded that "experience proves the inefficacy of bills of rights on those occasions when its control is most needed."[15] Even in the Old Dominion, Madison thought that the "parchment barrier" that was the Declaration of Rights is "violated in every instance where it has been opposed to a popular current."[16] Although he agreed that James Wilson had somewhat overstated the security provided by enumerated powers, Madison believed that Wilson was more right than wrong. An enumeration of powers, to Madison, was far more valuable than a list of rights.

The real danger to rights, Madison wrote Jefferson, came not from the central government created by the Constitution, but from "the majority of the Community."[17] Because he was living in France, which was governed by a monarch, Jefferson's views of the danger of government were clouded, Madison lectured. The differences between popular government and monarchial government were too great to draw lessons from one and apply them to the other. Nonetheless, Madison conceded, a bill of rights in the United States could have some benefit inasmuch as the "truths declared in that solemn manner acquire by degrees the character of fundamental maxims of free Government," and are incorporated into the national psyche.[18] In the unlikely event that government rather than the majority became tyrannical, Madison agreed that a bill of rights could serve as a rallying point for the people.

In responding to Madison's arguments, Jefferson admitted that a bill of rights "is like all other human blessings alloyed with some inconveniences, and not accomplishing fully it's object."[19] But, because the Constitution formed the people "into one state as to certain objects," the instrument should "guard us against . . . abuses of power within the field submitted" to national officers.[20] Jefferson believed that a bill of rights would "be the text whereby [the people] will try all the acts of the federal government."[21] Certainly not all rights could be agreed upon by the drafters and ratifiers of amendments, but "[h]alf a loaf," Jefferson observed, "is better than no bread."[22]

Madison's national reputation and campaign-trail endorsement of amendments earned him victory over Monroe. The Federalists as a whole did very well in the elections. The public's willingness to give the political experiment a chance, the promises of amendments, and pro-Federalist election statutes in some states proved insurmountable for Anti-Federalist candidates. As a result, the Federalists held forty-nine seats in the fifty-nine-man House. In the Senate, Virginia's Lee and Grayson were the only Anti-Federalist members. With these small numbers, any amendments proposed would likely be conservative in character. Madison expressed this sentiment in a letter to Jefferson: the Federalists, he asserted, "wish the revisal to be carried no farther than to supply additional guards for liberty, without abridging the sum of power transferred from the States to the general Government."[23]

Madison's Amendments

On April 1, 1789, the first federal House of Representatives achieved a quorum and began the business of organizing the new government. Congress had to organize a court system, tackle the issue of finance, and deal with foreign affairs matters such as American navigation of the Mississippi. George Washington delivered his inaugural address at the end of April. The address, drafted by Madison, reminded the senators and representatives that "it will remain with your judgment to decide, how far an exercise of the occasional power delegated by the fifth article of the Constitution, is rendered expedient at the present juncture by the nature of objections which have been urged against the system, or by the degree in inquietude which has given birth to them."[24] Washington then advised that Congress should "carefully avoid every alteration which might endanger the benefits of an united and effective government."[25]

Just a few days later, Madison rose from his seat and informed the House that he would introduce a discussion of amendments on May 25. Though Madison never believed that amendments were necessary, he had made a promise to his constituents. Despite the pressing business of the Congress,

Madison wanted time allotted to proposed amendments. Such a move, Madison surely hoped, would halt other states from following Virginia and New York in calling for a second convention. Madison also must have been influenced by his friend Jefferson's dogged insistence that the people were entitled to a declaration of rights.

Because the House remained preoccupied with pressing business at the end of May, Madison waited until June 8 to offer his proposals. Madison acknowledged that the House was busy, but he urged that the members "should commence the enquiry, and place the matter in such a train as to inspire a reasonable hope and expectation, that full justice would eventually be done to so important a subject."[26] He assured Federalists that he "had no design to propose any alterations which . . . could affect its main structure of principles, or do it any possible injury."[27] Madison's proposals for amendments were met with skepticism. Roger Sherman of Connecticut thought that "the necessity of amendments would be best pointed out by the defects, which experience may discover in the constitution."[28] Georgia's James Jackson compared the Constitution to a ship "that has never been put to sea." Until the voyage was undertaken and ocean conditions were experienced "we can not determine with any precision, whether she sails upon an even keel or no."[29] Hence, he believed that any amendments offered would be "speculative and theoretical."[30] John Vining of Delaware recognized that the people had agitated for amendments, but he believed that the best way to quiet the public mind would be "to pass salutary laws" grounded in wisdom and equity.[31]

Massachusetts's Elbridge Gerry, who had supported Mason's desire for a bill of rights in Philadelphia, stepped forward to support Madison. Gerry said he was "in favor of an early day, on account of North-Carolina and Rhode-Island, as the accession of these States to the Union was very desirable, and good policy dictated that every proper step should be taken to expedite that event."[32] In addition to the states outside of the union, Benjamin Goodhue of Massachusetts thought it "proper to attend to the subject earlier; because it is the wish of many of our constituents that something should be added to the constitution to secure in a stronger manner their liberties from the inroads of power."[33]

Fearing that his proposals would be exiled to a committee, Madison addressed the House and began making the case for his amendments, which would be inserted into the body of the Constitution. In his first resolution, Madison proposed a prefix to the Constitution stating that all power is derived from the people and that they have the right to reform or change the government. The prefix also stated that government was instituted for the benefit of the people and to permit them to enjoy their lives, liberties, and property. In the second resolution, Madison addressed representation. Rather than the Constitution's declaration that no district could be smaller than one representative for every 30,000 people, Madison proposed that after "the first actual enumeration, there shall be one representative for every thirty thousand."[34] However, after an unspecified number of representatives joined the House, then the ratio would be regulated by Congress. Thirdly, Madison proposed that no congressional pay increase should go into effect until after an intervening election.

In the fourth resolution, Madison enumerated certain rights of the people and restrictions on the national government. At base, the substance of the first eight amendments of our current bill of rights was included in this resolution. Madison also incorporated a statement into this resolution that the mention of specific rights should not be construed to limit unenumerated liberties or to enlarge the power of the national government.

Although no ratifying convention had asked for further restrictions on state power, in the fifth resolution Madison sought to prohibit state laws that "violate the equal rights of conscience, or the freedom of the press, or the trial by jury in criminal cases."[35] Madison's Virginia Plan had sought a national negative over state laws. Deprived of this veto, Madison in the first Congress attempted to limit the power of tyrannical majorities to injure fundamental rights.

The sixth and seventh resolutions endeavored to protect the right to a jury trial. In addition, Madison sought to limit the Supreme Court's appellate jurisdiction to cases where a significant monetary amount was in controversy.

The eighth resolution contained an amendment guaranteeing the separation of powers. The final clause of this resolution contained the forerunner of the current Tenth Amendment: "The powers not delegated by the constitution, nor prohibited by it to the states, are reserved to the states respectively."[36] Madison declined to include the word "expressly" as had been demanded by several state conventions.

The House did not devote significant time to Madison's resolutions until mid-August. The House ultimately accepted the proposed amendments with relatively small additions and changes. However, during the course of debates, some Anti-Federalist members protested that the House was not considering all the proposals offered by the states, but rather was limiting itself to Madison's resolutions. A broader consideration, South Carolina's Thomas Tudor Tucker said, would "tend to give a greater degree of satisfaction to those who are desirous of" material changes.[37] Otherwise, the states "would feel some degree of chagrin at having misplaced their confidence in the general government."[38] The Federalists, enjoying a substantial majority, countered that the lion's share of state proposals were untrustworthy and contradictory. When the Anti-Federalists attempted to introduce substantive amendments dealing with such matters as taxation and Congress's power over elections, the Federalists easily defeated the proposals.

The biggest change to Madison's handiwork was in form rather than substance. Roger Sherman and others urged that the original constitutional text be preserved inviolate. Rather than weaving amendments into the text, Sherman suggested that they "be annexed to the constitution."[39] Madison protested that a supplement to the Constitution would be confusing to the people. They would be unsure which portions of the text were in force and which ones were void. Sherman and his colleagues eventually overcame Madison's opposition by arguing that just as the Magna Carta and other great documents were supplemented rather than altered, so should the House treat the Constitution.

The debate on the Bill of Rights in the Senate is a mystery because the upper chamber met in secret. The product returned to the House, however, was reorganized and some language altered. Of most significance, the Senate deleted Madison's restrictions on state power and thus targeted the full Bill of Rights at the national government. The final version sent to the states contained twelve amendments. Ten were ratified and became a part of the Constitution in 1791. The amendment restricting congressional pay increases from going into effect was not ratified until 1992. The amendment regarding the size of House districts has never been ratified.

Flourish and Dressing

Today, scholars describe the Bill of Rights "as the high temple of our constitutional order—America's Parthenon."[40] It was not so viewed by the Anti-Federalists or the average citizen. According to Gordon Wood, "[a]fter ratification, most Americans promptly forgot about the first ten amendments to the Constitution."[41] The Anti-Federalists felt betrayed that Congress, in the main, limited the amendments to statements of personal liberties. There was little, if anything, in the amendments touching upon substantive matters such as taxation, the treaty power, control over elections, implied powers, or a host of other issues raised by the state ratifying conventions.

Of course, that was the Federalists' plan all along. Writing to Edmund Randolph, Madison indicated that his goal was to leave "[t]he structure & stamina of the Govt. . . . as little touched as possible."[42] George Clymer described Madison as "a sensible physician" giving his "malades imaginaires bread pills powder of paste & neutral mixtures to keep them in play."[43] Samuel Johnston, serving as governor of North Carolina, had advised Madison that amendments should be "a little Flourish & Dressing without injuring the substantial part" of the Constitution.[44] Roger Sherman assured Federalist colleagues that the amendments emanating from Congress "will probably be harmless" and hopefully would be "Satisfactory to those who are fond of a Bill of rights."[45]

In light of the Federalists' description of the amendments, it is no surprise that the Anti-Federalists were deeply disappointed. William Grayson, writing to Patrick Henry, complained that the proposed amendments "are so mutilated & gutted that in fact they are good for nothing."[46] Theodorick Bland of Virginia lamented that the congressmen "have not made one single material" alteration to the Constitution.[47] Thomas Tudor Tucker thought the amendments sent to the states were "calculated merely to amuse, or rather to deceive."[48]

Using colorful imagery, Aedanus Burke of South Carolina opined that the amendments "are little better than whip-syllabub, frothy and full of wind, formed only to please the palate, or they are like a tub thrown out to a whale, to secure the freight of the ship and its peaceable voyage."[49] (Whip-syllabub was an extremely light and sweet dessert or refresher made with whipped cream, white wine, and sugar.) As for throwing tubs to whales, this reference comes from Jonathan Swift. Allegedly, mariners crossing the Atlantic, when coming across a large sea creature, tossed a tub into the ocean to distract the whale so the ship could safely pass.

Valuable rights had been declared, observed Richard Henry Lee, but unfortunately "the powers that remain are very sufficient to render them nugatory at pleasure."[50] Stepping back and dissecting the ratification battlefield, Lee further observed that "the idea of subsequent Amendments was a delusion altogether, and so intended by the greater part of those who arrogated themselves the name of Federalists."[51]

Writing in 1801, Alexander Hamilton candidly summed up our vaunted Bill of Rights. These amendments, Hamilton said, "scarcely [met] any of the important objections which were urged" and left "the structure of the government, and the mass and distribution of its powers where they were."[52] The changes were "too insignificant to be with any sensible man a reason for being reconciled to the system if he thought it originally bad."[53]

One must question the efficacy of the Bill of Rights offered by Congress to the people. For instance, the protections for speech and the press, just seven years after ratification of the First Amendment, were ignored by a Federalist Congress that criminalized criticism of the national government in the Sedition Act of 1798. The Federalists argued that inherent powers, the Necessary and Proper Clause, and the General Welfare Clause gave them the right to pass such a law. Those clauses and theories of power had been the concerns of Anti-Federalists and the proposed amendments by the state conventions. Unfortunately, Madison and the first Congress declined to offer any amendments dealing with these substantive matters.

On the other hand, the First Amendment did serve as a rallying cry for Americans who opposed the Sedition Act. In resolutions and protests adopted in state and local gatherings, the people pointed to the First Amendment and demanded a repeal of the Sedition Act. The First Amendment might not have stopped the Federalists from acting unconstitutionally, but it did serve as a beacon to guide the people in their protests of constitutional violations. Ultimately, the protests led to the election of Jefferson to the presidency and likeminded men to the House. The Sedition Act expired and the new Congress declined to reenact it.

Judicial Actions

Proponents of a bill of rights expected that the courts would assist the people and states in enforcing the first ten amendments against the national government. Thomas Jefferson, for instance, believed that "the legal check which it puts into the hands of the judiciary" was one of the greatest reasons the Constitution needed a declaration of rights.[54] However, the Supreme Court did not use a provision of the Bill of Rights to strike a national law until 1857. In *Dred Scott v. Sandford* (1857),[55] the Court, in a fateful decision, used the Fifth Amendment's Due Process Clause to declare the anti-slavery provision of the Missouri Compromise unconstitutional.

Today, when we think of the Bill of Rights and landmark cases, we typically think of restrictions on state power. It does not occur to modern Americans that the Bill of Rights applied only to the national government. As the preamble to the Bill of Rights declares, "further declaratory and restrictive clauses" were adopted because the state conventions wanted some security to "prevent misconstruction and abuse of" powers delegated to the national government.[56] The people of the states were satisfied with their own bills of rights and restrictions on state power appearing in the various state constitutions. As mentioned earlier, of the more than 200 proposed amendments submitted by the various ratification conventions, none requested additional restrictions on state power.

Even the Supreme Court in 1833 recognized the limited applicability of the federal Bill of Rights. Writing for the Court in *Barron v. Baltimore* (1833), Chief Justice Marshall observed that during the late 1780s "fears were extensively entertained that" certain powers "might be exercised in a manner dangerous to liberty."[57] He continued:

In almost every convention by which the Constitution was adopted, amendments to guard against the abuse of power were recommended. These amendments demanded security against the apprehended encroachments of the General Government—not against those of the local governments. In compliance with a sentiment thus generally expressed, to quiet fears thus extensively entertained, amendments were proposed by the required majority in Congress and adopted by the States. These amendments contain no expression indicating an intention to apply them to the State governments. This court cannot so apply them.[58]

From the 1920s to the present, the Supreme Court has "incorporated" most of the rights found in the first eight amendments and applied them against the states. To do so, the Court has held that the Fourteenth Amendment, enacted after the Civil War, was intended to nationalize fundamental rights. Hence, the Court holds that these rights have been "incorporated" by the Fourteenth Amendment's Due Process Clause. Scholars continue to debate the propriety of incorporation, but it is now a fact of American law.

The modern controversy over incorporation is not so much about the application of the clear provisions of the Bill of Rights to the states, but the stretching of language to apply to various situations. To create a general right to privacy so that it could strike a state law regulating possession of contraceptives, the Court in *Griswold v. Connecticut* (1965), claimed that "specific guarantees in the Bill of Rights have penumbras, formed by emanations from those guarantees that help give them life and substance."[59] In creating a general right of privacy the Court cited the Third Amendment's prohibition against quartering troops, the First Amendment's right of association, the criminal law protections of the Fourth and Fifth Amendment, and the Ninth Amendment's declaration that not all rights are enumerated in the Constitution. Such a cobbling together of these provisions is not likely what the states had in mind when they petitioned in 1788–89 for a declaration of rights. *Griswold's* central holding led to *Roe v. Wade* (1973),[60] and the controversy over abortion jurisprudence that endures well into the twenty-first century.

Looking back, the Bill of Rights certainly fulfilled its role as a tub to a whale. North Carolina and Rhode Island ratified the Constitution and joined the union. Demands for a second convention died away. After submitting the Bill of Rights to the states, Congress moved on to other matters and was never forced to wrestle with substantive changes to the Constitution.

While the courts prior to the incorporation debate took no great interest in the Bill of Rights, instances arose when it served as a rallying point for the people. Over time, it would be fair to say that such things as the guarantee of free speech and an accused's right to certain safeguards have become part of our national psyche.

But when we measure the first ten amendments against what was asked for by the states and the dangerous provisions of the Constitution discussed in previous chapters, we can hardly argue with Aedanus Burke's whip-syllabub comparison. We are better off for our Bill of Rights, but, in the final analysis, poorer for the first Congress's refusal to discuss and offer the states amendments of substance.

18

Mending the Venerable Fabric

HISTORIANS HOLD *The Federalist Papers* in high regard. Those essays and the Constitution they expound upon, we are told, are the crown jewels of American political theory. Indeed, *The Federalist Papers* are a coherent series of essays masterfully employing rhetoric. They are also, from a global perspective, often wrong. The Federalists promised that the Constitution of 1787 would bring just enough energy to the national government to address the pressing issues of foreign affairs, trade, and security. That could be done, they assured the people, without destroying what was won in the American Revolution and preserved in the Articles of Confederation—the right of self-government in the thirteen states and their various counties, townships, and villages. Yes, the Federalists said, the new national government was more powerful than that of the Confederation, but it would be a government of few and defined powers. The lion's share of authority would rest in the states and localities just as it did with the Articles.

With astonishing perspicacity, Brutus, the Federal Farmer, and the other Anti-Federalist writers foresaw how the national government would use the General Welfare Clause, the Necessary and Proper Clause, and the treaty power to aggrandize itself at the states' expense. They raised valid concerns about scale, meaningful representation, and consolidation. They also saw how standing armies could be built and then used by the executive for imperial purposes. They cautioned that congressional control of the amendment process would prevent future restrictions on national power. In particular, Brutus's warnings about judicial supremacy proved so true that one might be tempted to attribute supernatural powers to him. The unelected Supreme

Court controls the people's Constitution and is not checked by the states or any branch of the national government. It is constitutionally omnipotent.

The Anti-Federalists, far from just complaining, offered substantive amendments to address many of the problems they identified. The state conventions spent time organizing, editing, and presenting over 200 proposed amendments to the new Congress with the understanding that they would be considered and acted on early in the life of the government. Unfortunately, the various amendments were ignored by Madison and the first Congress as they prepared the smokescreen of the Bill of Rights. Important personal rights were safeguarded, but nothing was done to curtail the expansive and vague provisions of the Constitution.

Jefferson and the Articles

The failure of the Constitution and Bill of Rights to create a truly limited national government brings up the question of the Articles. Could the Articles of Confederation have been revised to meet the exigencies of the union without destroying the self-government won in the Revolution? Thomas Jefferson and other republicans thought so. Writing in 1786, Jefferson described the Articles as a "wonderfully perfect instrument, considering the circumstances under which it was formed."[1] In a letter to Edward Carrington, Jefferson was even more complimentary and described the Articles as "without comparison the best [form of government] existing or that ever did exist."[2] When comparing the Confederation, with its foibles, to the centralized governments of Europe, Jefferson found the Articles to be closer to "Heaven" than to the "Hell" existing in European statecraft.[3] Because of the good government of the Articles, Americans, in Jefferson's view, "may certainly be considered as in the happiest political situation which exists."[4] True to his admiration of the Articles, Jefferson's initial reaction to the work of the Philadelphia Convention was one of lamentation. He wrote to John Adams that "all the good of this new constitution might have been couched in three or four new articles to be added to the good, old, and venerable fabrick, which should have been preserved even as a religious relique."[5]

Critics are quick to point out that Jefferson made these comments while in France and distanced from the troubles at home. How easy it was for Jefferson, they say, to view such things as Shays' Rebellion in a positive light when he was an ocean away and not involved in the failed continental effort to raise troops. From France, one could believe that a rebellion every twenty years or so was necessary to manufacture the "natural manure" (*i.e.*, blood) for the tree of liberty.[6] Critics forget that Jefferson did have a front-row seat to the defects of the Confederation. As the American minister in France, Jefferson was repeatedly stymied by the Confederation's inability to pay its debts. Jefferson and John Adams (the minster to Great Britain) regularly dealt with the Confederation's creditors and the reluctance of many to lend any more money to the United States. Jefferson was also frustrated in efforts to negotiate favorable commercial treaties. Both he and the Europeans knew that the American states had poor track records of abiding by treaties and that Congress was unable to compel obedience.

Jefferson often explained to his correspondents that reform was absolutely necessary. The three principal areas where Jefferson saw problems were foreign affairs and foreign commerce, separation of powers, and state non-compliance with continental obligations.[7] Regarding foreign commerce, Jefferson had, while a member of Congress, participated in drafting instructions to American diplomats who were negotiating trade pacts. Jefferson instructed the diplomats to view the United States as one nation regarding treaty obligations and to reject the idea of state authority over international commerce. Jefferson also championed greater power in Congress to retaliate against Great Britain and other nations that restricted American trade. In the area of trade and foreign affairs, Jefferson had always been very continental in his thinking.[8]

Jefferson was also troubled by the Confederation Congress exercising both executive and legislative power. "I think it very material to separate in the hands of Congress," Jefferson wrote, "the Executive & Legislative powers, as the Judiciary already are in some degree."[9] The lack of independent branches of government, Jefferson said, "has been the source of more evil than we have experienced from any other cause."[10] He complained that Congress spent more time on the smallest details of execution than it did on drafting "the most important act of legislation"[11]

In the matter of state non-compliance, Jefferson became so frustrated that he dabbled with the idea of implied powers. Writing to Carrington, Jefferson urged that Congress should claim the power to enforce its enactments "by the law of nature."[12] Viewing the Confederation as a compact between the states, Jefferson asserted that the parties had an implied power to compel execution. If one state refused to comply, say, with a congressional requisition of funds, the other twelve states in Congress could demand obedience. Jefferson believed that Congress would "probably exercise long patience before they would recur to force," but insisted that Congress had such a right.[13]

With the proper alterations, Jefferson believed the Confederation would serve the union well. Writing to George Washington before learning that the Philadelphia Convention planned to jettison the Articles, Jefferson urged amendments to "make our States one as to all foreign concerns, preserve them several as to all merely domestic, to give to the Federal head some peaceable mode of enforcing its just authority, to organize that head into legislative, executive, and judiciary departments."[14]

Many Anti-Federalist writers made similar points about revisions to the Articles. Centinel began his fourth letter with the observation that "the present confederation is inadequate to the objects of the union, seems to be universally allowed."[15] He thought the chief problems related to "commerce and maritime affairs."[16] The Federal Farmer unequivocally stated that it "must . . . be admitted, that our federal system is defective" and that Congress's powers "are inadequate to the exigencies of the union."[17] He pointed to commerce and servicing of the public debt as the critical issues facing the Confederation.[18] The Impartial Examiner joined the chorus and identified the chief failings as commercial regulation and the inability of Congress to obtain "the requisite contributions for all expences, that may be incurred" for continental purposes.[19] "An Old Whig" concluded that the very real problems of the Confederation could be "alleviated, if not wholly removed, by devolving upon Congress the power of regulating trade and laying and collecting duties and imposts."[20] Very similar to Jefferson, the Anti-Federalists, in the words of the Federal Farmer, affirmed that the desired reforms would yield "a system in which national concerns may be transacted in the centre, and local affairs in the state or district governments."[21]

After the ratification struggle, Jefferson denied that he had any connection with either the Federalists or Anti-Federalists. "I am not a federalist," Jefferson wrote, "because I have never submitted the whole system of my opinions to the creed of any party of men whatever . . . where I was capable of thinking for myself."²² Jefferson continued: "If I could not go to heaven but with a party, I would not go there at all."²³ When Jefferson denied any Federalist affiliation, he quickly added that his opinions were even further from the Anti-Federalists. Of course, those remarks were made after the Anti-Federalist defeat in the state conventions and just prior to the Constitution going into operation. Nothing was to be gained by identifying with the losing side, especially when his friends Madison and George Washington had pushed so hard for the Constitution's ratification. Madison also persistently had advocated for ratifying the Constitution in various letters to Jefferson. Certainly, Madison's efforts caused Jefferson to warm to the idea of the new Constitution. Nonetheless, whether he would admit it or not, Jefferson's regret that the Constitution had no bill of rights plus the other criticisms found in his correspondence placed him in closer kinship with the Anti-Federalists than he would claim.

Three or Four Revisions

So what "three or four" revisions might have saved the federative principle in American governance? Beginning with Jefferson's framework, Congress needed the power to regulate commerce with foreign nations. Without the ability to present a united front to the world, the United States was forced to accept whatever trade restrictions European nations chose to impose. So long as one recalcitrant state failed to go along with the other twelve in matters of import duties and trade, foreign powers could circumvent state restrictions. Moreover, friction from internal barriers to commerce needed to be removed so the Confederation could flourish as a free trade zone.

Consequently, Article IX required amending to give Congress the full authority over treaties concerning duties and trade. In addition to this deletion, the Confederation government required the sole and exclusive right of governing the trafficking in commodities among the states and with all foreign nations. In light of modern abuse of the Constitution's Commerce Clause, a statement reserving state power over intrastate trade and other productive activity would have been prudent.

As for separation of powers, Jefferson's 1783 draft constitution for Virginia is an excellent starting point. Jefferson created this constitution in expectation of a state constituent assembly that did not take place. Fortunately, Jefferson's draft is preserved in his *Notes on the State of Virginia.* Immediately after declaring that Virginia "shall ever hereafter be governed as a commonwealth," Jefferson addressed separation of powers:[24]

> The powers of government shall be divided into three distinct departments, each of them to be confided to a separate body of magistracy; to wit, those which are legislative to one, those which are judiciary to another, and those which are executive to another. No person, or collection of persons, being one of these departments, shall exercise any power properly belonging to either of the others, except in circumstances hereinafter expressly permitted.[25]

Jefferson went on to provide for a bicameral legislature with "the one [chamber] to be called the House of Delegates, the other the Senate."[26] Elsewhere in his *Notes*, Jefferson stated that "[t]he purpose of establishing different houses of legislation is to introduce the influence of different interests or different principles."[27] Montesquieu also advanced a similar rationale for bicameralism: "The legislative power is therefore to be committed to the body of nobles, and to that which represents the people, each having their assemblies and deliberations apart, each with their own separate views and interest."[28] As a democrat, Jefferson would have objected to the idea of "nobles" in the Virginia legislature, but appreciated the benefits of bodies having different interests. Indeed, Jefferson's support of bicameralism was more rooted in fears of consolidation. When all or a large portion of power is united into a single body, Jefferson believed that this resulted in "despotic government."[29] Hence, a bicameral legislature served to further the diffusion of power.[30]

To execute the laws passed by the legislature, Jefferson's constitution provided for a governor "chosen by joint ballot of both houses of the assembly."[31] The governor would serve a single five-year term and was delegated "those powers . . . necessary to execute the laws (and administer the government) and which are not in their nature either legislative or judiciary."[32] The draft made clear that powers delegated to the Confederation such as declaring war and contracting alliances remained with the Confederation and could not be exercised by the governor. The governor would have a council of state appointed by the legislature to advise him on various matters concerning executive functions.

Jefferson's judiciary consisted of three superior courts divided into legal, equitable, and maritime jurisdiction. Judges of the superior courts would be chosen by joint ballot of the legislature and serve during good behavior. The county courts, and any others created by the legislature, served as the state's inferior courts. The judges of the three superior courts, when assembled together, constituted "the Court of Appeals whose business shall be to receive and determine appeals from the three superior courts."[33]

The division of powers in Jefferson's draft was based on the idea that "the powers of government should be so divided and balanced among several bodies of magistracy, as that no one could transcend their legal limit, without being effectually checked and restrained by the others."[34] In line with this sound reasoning, the government of the Confederation needed a similar structure so that not all power rested in one assembly. Rather than Congress managing the "general interests of the United States" as set forth in Article V, reform was needed to make it a mere legislative body.[35] A bicameral body, much like that created by the Philadelphia Convention, would solve the issue of the weight of each state's vote, which had been plaguing the states since the First Continental Congress. An equality of votes in one chamber and then a second chamber based on a state's population or wealth would be the logical resolution to the question of state power in the general government. A governor, similar to Jefferson's, and a judicial branch deciding cases and controversies relating to the Confederation, would be the final pieces in the separation-of-powers design.

The final issue in Jefferson's framework of revision was state obedience to federal obligations. As mentioned earlier, Jefferson at one point was so frustrated that he countenanced military action by the Confederation. However, Jefferson came up with a much more peaceable approach when discussing with Madison the proposed national veto on all state legislation found in the Virginia Plan. Madison was a champion of this veto power. Without it, he feared that "however ample the federal powers may be made, or however Clearly their boundaries delineated, on paper, they will be easily and continually baffled by the Legislative sovereignties of the States."[36] Madison believed that the national veto was essential to protecting the general government from state encroachments and "to prevent instability and injustice in the legislation of the States."[37] The defeat of the national veto in the Philadelphia Convention created much consternation for him.

In responding to Madison's praise of a national veto, Jefferson told him "[p]rimâ facie I do not like it."[38] It was overkill: "It fails in an essential character, that the hole and the patch should be commensurate."[39] Madison's proposal sought "to mend a small hole by covering the whole garment."[40] Jefferson then proposed a more moderate solution: "Would not an appeal from the state judiciaries to a federal court, in all cases where the act of Confederation controuled the question, be as effectual a remedy, and exactly commensurate to the defect?"[41] Jefferson gave the example of legislation improperly impeding the collection of British debts. If a creditor sued in state court and lost the case because of state legislation counter to provisions of the Treaty of Paris, the creditor ought to have a right to appeal to a Confederation court to set the matter right. Jefferson recognized that a Confederation court might encroach on the jurisdiction of the state courts, but he believed that this problem could be solved if the Congress had the power "to watch and restrain" the court's exercise of jurisdiction.[42]

Jefferson's Confederation court appears to be the answer to state recalcitrance. In addition to hearing appeals in cases such as that of the hypothetical British creditor, if the court was granted original jurisdiction over disputes between Congress and the state legislatures, it could decide disputes over non-payment of requisitions and issue judgments against delinquent states. The court could order specific performance of obligations owed to the Confederation and possibly craft other remedies through its power to hold states in contempt. A state that refused to abide by a congressional ordinance might, for example, have its voting power suspended in Congress until the state fulfilled its obligations.

Additional Amendments

Outside of Jefferson's framework two additional alterations would have perhaps allowed the Articles to survive. The first is the amendment process. As mentioned previously, but for the stubbornness of Rhode Island and later New York on another occasion, Congress would have been granted an independent source of revenue by levying imposts. That would have been a giant step toward restoring public credit and might have derailed any attempt to hold a grand convention at which the Articles were abandoned. One state should not be permitted to hold the other twelve hostage to its selfish interests. Rather than requiring unanimity to revise the Articles as set out in Article XIII, some lesser number such as two thirds or three fourths of the states would be appropriate. Such a provision would be especially needed if the union grew to more than thirteen states.

Finally, the Confederation Congress needed an independent source of revenue for its ordinary expenses. An impost would be the natural source of this and had been agreed to by twelve states. The impost would allow the Congress to pay the interest on the debt and to eventually pay down the principal. Extraordinary situations certainly might arise where more revenue was needed. Requisitions, backed by the power to levy direct taxes if a state failed to comply, would have satisfied the need for emergency funding. That solution was proposed by various Anti-Federalists and would have given the states the discretion to craft additional taxes as they deemed best, but provided Congress an alternative if a state was non-compliant. Such an amendment, coupled with the authority of a Confederation court, likely would have solved the financial problems of the Confederation and also have remedied state recalcitrance without making Congress totally independent of the states in all financial circumstances. The lack of a state check on congressional spending is one of our chief problems today.

Would these amendments have supplied the Confederation government with the power to address continental concerns, but left state and local government relatively untouched? We cannot know for sure, but we can be fairly confident that those amendments—unlike the wholesale change wrought in Philadelphia—would not have recreated a central government reminiscent of that thrown off in 1776. We must remember that the purpose of the Revolution was not to replace the British central government with an American central government. In declaring the states independent, the Americans expressed their preference for governing themselves by their own laws in their own assemblies. Historian Merrill Jensen has observed that "[c]entralized government with a legal veto on state laws, the power to enact general and uniform legislation, and the power to use arms to subdue rebellious social groups within the states, had disappeared with the Declaration of Independence."[43] Indeed, Jensen has aptly described the Articles as "a constitutional expression of the philosophy of the Declaration of Independence."[44] The Articles were crafted to prevent the resurrection of centralization in the newly independent states. This they did—along with providing enough structure to permit the thirteen states to defeat a superpower.

Modern Americans have for too long been taught that the government under the Articles was doomed to fail. One historian even has claimed that we are fortunate that the Articles could not be amended easily because "[i]f it had been workable, the United States might have struggled along with a patched-up Articles of Confederation rather than an effective new Constitution."[45] At best, our historians describe the Confederation as a stepping stone to a lasting and effective government.

Americans must rediscover that the Articles are much more than brittle rock along the path to good government. As we tackle issues plaguing our country in the twenty-first century, it might do us good to look back to the Articles of Confederation. Has the pooling of power at the center brought us great blessings or has it contributed to our national bankruptcy, militarism, and dependence on the nanny state? Perhaps it would benefit us to reexamine the decentralized system of the Articles as we consider reforms in government.

The Confederation's structure, and the Anti-Federalist objections to the Constitution, are worthy of reconsideration. Although we cannot return to the rural and agrarian world of 1776, there is no reason we cannot aspire to govern ourselves in communities—or wards, as Jefferson called them. Not every problem has to be a national issue requiring presidential task forces and congressional legislation. The states and their subdivisions, serving as laboratories of democracy, should be able to experiment with a variety of solutions based on local circumstances and resources.

Going forward, let us take pride in the Articles of Confederation and the men who defended the principles of decentralization and limited government. The system it created was born from the same stock as the Declaration of Independence. The Articles were not perfect, but they mark the way back to the self-government that so many patriots fought and died for. The Articles, along with the Anti-Federalist thought of the ratification period, bear greater study as we continue the American experiment.

19

Lessons for Today

ALTHOUGH THE CONFEDERATIVE form of government likely could have endured with a few modifications, it was abandoned for the framework crafted by the Philadelphia Convention. We have been governed by the Constitution of 1787 for two centuries and a quarter. Considering the path of history, one might question why the Articles and Anti-Federalism retain any relevancy to government in the twenty-first century. Although the story of our first continental constitution and the challenges lodged against the Constitution of 1787 might be interesting to historians, what possible lessons do they contain for the issues that face modern Americans?

That is a fair question. To answer it, we must remember that the goal of the American Revolution was to overthrow centralized power and to permit the diverse American states to govern themselves in their various town, county, and state-wide assemblies. Moreover, we should take notice that a central purpose of the Articles was to preserve self-government and to inhibit the rise of a homegrown central government that would rule the states much like Parliament and George III ruled the colonies. Therefore, so long as Americans debate and consider the balance of power between Washington and the states, the lessons of the Articles and Anti-Federalists will be informative.

In the book of *Ecclesiastes*, Solomon observes that "[w]hat has been will be again, what has been done will be done again; there is nothing new under the sun."[1] Although Solomon certainly was not thinking of the American system of government, he could very well have been describing our continuing dialog about the division of power between the center and the peripheries of the country. This issue was debated prior to the Revolution when colonists chaffed under British imperial restructuring that circumscribed colonial home rule. When the colonies declared independence, their delegates debated the Dickinson draft of the Articles of Confederation and rejected broad wording that arguably could have given Congress control of myriad state and local concerns. At the urging of Thomas Burke the final draft of the Articles contained a clear and express reservation of state prerogatives and sovereignty.

During the debates on the Constitution of 1787, the overwhelming Anti-Federalist concern was consolidation. The Federalists spent much of their time assuring Americans that the new Constitution would preserve state power and that the national government could act only in a few carefully delineated areas. In an effort to silence Anti-Federalist critics, the first Congress offered amendments to the states, one of which declared that "[t]he powers not delegated to the United States by the Constitution, nor prohibited by it to the states, are reserved to the states respectively, or to the people."[2]

In the early days of George Washington's administration, Alexander Hamilton urged the creation of a national bank. The debate that erupted focused not so much on monetary policy, but whether Hamilton's interpretation of the delegated powers would effectively delete the newly adopted Tenth Amendment from the constitutional charter. At the close of the 1790s, the Federalist Party supporters and Jeffersonians clashed over the Sedition Act of 1798, which made it a crime to criticize the national government. While the Jeffersonians articulated a libertarian approach to speech, their primary concern was the precedent that would be set with the national government legislating on a matter (i.e., speech) that was nowhere mentioned in enumerated powers.

In the 1820s and 1830s, Andrew Jackson and his followers battled against aspects of Henry Clay's "American System" focused on internal improvements. Jackson believed that the building of canals and roads was a subject reserved to the states. Allowing Congress to spend on these projects, Jackson feared, would aggrandize the national government. Jackson also vetoed a bill that would have extended the charter of the Second Bank of the United States. Although the Supreme Court had found the bank to be a valid exercise of Congress's power, Jackson maintained that the national government's powers should be strictly construed.

The nullification controversy, secession, and the Civil War brought a multitude of moral, economic, and constitutional issues to the national debate. Was the union indissoluble? Could sections with deeply disparate economic systems coexist? Was slavery within the purview of Congress's powers? Certainly multiple causes and motives underpinned the sectional clashes that occurred from the 1820s to the 1860s. But an impartial observer must admit that the division of power between the states and the nation was one of the taller trees in the forest of causation.

In 1832, South Carolina faced possible invasion by federal forces because of its nullification of the Tariff of Abominations. Passed in 1828, the law raised duties to 50 percent of the value of imported goods and threatened to destroy the Southern economy. Americans averted a civil war when Congress agreed to lower duties and South Carolina rescinded its ordinance of nullification. The tariff controversy caused division to grow between North and South with the latter convinced that manufacturing interests were determined to dominate them politically and financially.

Indeed, the men who framed the government of the Confederate States of America, in the words of historian William C. Davis, believed "they were the keepers of the original flame of 1776" and the promise that the states should be allowed to govern their own internal affairs.[3] While we fortunately have difficulty grasping how some Southerners could defend the peculiar institution of slavery as a moral good, we should not let our revulsion at that system drown out the constitutional assertions drawn from the American Revolution. "The states' rights interpretation of the Constitution was not, as its enemies have alleged, a mere theoretical rationalization made up for the defense of slavery," writes Clyde N. Wilson, the editor of *The Papers of John C. Calhoun*.[4] "It is, rather, a living heritage of great power, absolutely central to the understanding of the American liberty."[5]

Arguments surrounding the expansion of national authority during the Progressive Era and the New Deal centered around the balance of state and national power.[6] For instance, the administration of Franklin D. Roosevelt created a bevy of national programs that regulated wages, labor relations, and the production of manufactured goods and agricultural commodities. The New Deal, according to Robert P. Sutton, "established an unprecedented expansion of the constitutional power of the federal government. It could now permanently regulate the nation's economy. Congress could legislate as a social engineer under the fiscal power . . . and take responsibility for curing social as well as economic ills. . . ."[7]

Opponents of the New Deal appealed repeatedly to the limits of national authority. In the early 1930s, the conservatives on the Supreme Court recoiled at New Deal legislation. In *United States v. Butler* (1936), the majority objected that the Agricultural Adjustment Act "invades the reserved rights of the states."[8] The Court chaffed at the idea that Congress could "ignore the constitutional limitations upon its own powers and usurp those reserved to the states" when the Constitution disallowed such meddling.[9] The Court's opposition was short-lived, as FDR petitioned Congress to increase the number of justices, which would have permitted him to pack the judiciary with his favorites. Although FDR's court-packing plan failed, after facing this attack from a popular president, the Court relented and began to sign off on various New Deal programs.

In its 1936 platform, the Republican Party voiced support for the early 1930s Court decisions and accused Roosevelt of "dishonor[ing] American traditions" and "constantly seek[ing] to usurp the rights reserved to the States and to the people."[10] Hence, the Republicans pledged to "maintain the American system of constitutional and local self government"[11] by returning to the states and localities the responsibility for poor relief and other such internal matters.

In the 1970s, the Supreme Court revived the age-old question about the powers of the states and nation with a jurisprudence that scholars called "the New Federalism."[12] Since the triumph of the New Deal, most scholars had assumed that congressional power had no effective limit. In *National League of Cities v. Usery* (1976),[13] the Court held that Congress exceeded its authority when it extended the minimum wage and maximum hour requirements of the Fair Labor Standards Act to the states. The Court found that such legislation targeting the states qua states unconstitutionally limited the residual sovereignty left to the states after ratification of the Constitution. The Court retreated from its holding in *Usery* ten years later, but *Usery* signaled a willingness to more closely examine national claims of power.

In 1995, the New Federalism reached its zenith with *United States v. Lopez* (1995),[14] when the Court struck down a federal law prohibiting possession of firearms near school premises. The possession of a firearm in school zones, the government contended, could affect the functioning of the American economy by hindering classroom education and thus result in an unproductive workforce. The Court rejected the government's argument, fearing that such reasoning would permit Congress to "regulate any activity that it found was related to the economic productivity of individual citizens."[15] The Constitution delegated to Congress only a few and defined powers, the Court announced, and those constitutional limits were transgressed by passing a criminal statute disguised as commercial regulation.

Much of the debate regarding the 2010 Patient Protection and Affordable Care Act's national requirement that individuals purchase health insurance has been colored by federalism concerns. For example, Robert E. Moffit, a senior fellow at the Heritage Foundation, observed that "[r]egardless of the wisdom of the policy, if a state wants to experiment with a health insurance mandate, as most do with auto insurance, it has the constitutional right to do so. But Congress, in this instance, is invading the traditional authority of the states in regulating health insurance within their own borders."[16]

Yes, from Parliament's imposition of the Stamp Act to the fight over Obamacare, the debate has focused on the division of power between the colonies/states and the general government of the empire/union. Chief Justice John Marshall was correct in 1819 when he commented that "the question respecting the extent of the powers actually granted [to the union] is perpetually arising, and will probably continue to arise so long as our system shall exist."[17]

Having established that the Articles of Confederation and the Anti-Federalists are relevant to our modern world and current constitutional debate, we must draw lessons for today. Our ship of government has been at sea for well over 200 years. Experience is a great teacher and shows that the fears articulated about aspects of the Constitution of 1787 were not speculative. Madison and the Federalists gave short shrift to the substantive amendments presented to the first Congress. Governmentally, we have been impoverished because of the Federalists' treatment of amendments as tubs to whales. The Federalists secured a safe passage but did little to improve the substance of the system.

If we look closely at the neglected amendments offered by the state conventions and Anti-Federalist writers, perhaps we can find the answers to some of our most vexing modern problems. In what follows, we will consider application of the principles of the Articles and Anti-Federalists to profligate borrowing and spending, an unrepresentative House, and the political careerism that has replaced the citizen-legislator with a ruling class.

The National Debt

Undoubtedly, the national fiscal situation is one of the most critical issues we will face in the coming years. As of this writing, our national debt stands at $18 trillion. Each citizen's share of the debt is approximately $56,000. China currently owns in excess of seven percent of our federal debt in the form of U.S. treasury securities. If the Chinese decided to dump those securities, they could cause a currency crisis and plunge our economy into recession or worse. Hence, we can't even jokingly write off our debt because "we owe it to ourselves."

Some economists fear that the United States quickly is reaching a fiscal tipping point where our economy cannot grow fast enough to support the debt load. According to the Independent Institute's *MyGovCost* blog, that point will be here in the next few years.[18] The debt will be growing faster than gross domestic product ("GDP"). While Congress might succeed in buying some more time with a combination of spending cuts and revenue increases, the fact remains that we are dangerously close to a critical fiscal tipping point.

Even if the tipping point can be staved off for a few years, the inevitable retirement of baby boomers and their claims to government pensions and Medicare will impel us toward a debt crisis. The first of the boomers retired in 2008 and every year more will be joining their ranks and collecting Social Security benefits. According to researchers at the Heritage Foundation, in "net-present-value terms, Social Security owes $11.3 trillion more in benefits than it will receive in taxes. This 2012 number consists of $2.7 trillion to re-pay the special-issue bonds in the trust fund and $6.5 trillion to pay benefits after the trust fund is exhausted in 2033."[19] Just looking at Social Security alone, "[a]fter adjusting for inflation, annual deficits will reach $95 billion in 2020 and $318.7 billion in 2030."[20] Such results are inevitable inasmuch as the worker-to-beneficiary ratio (which was 4.9 in 1960 and 2.8 in 2010) is projected to be 1.9 in 2035.[21] Even with significant tax increases, one or two workers simply cannot cover the retirement benefits for one boomer.

Medicare is even a more serious fiscal issue than Social Security. Right now, we spend approximately four percent of GDP on the Medicare program. With boomers rapidly aging and retiring, this percentage will double by 2045.[22] Experts predict that by 2030, Medicare alone will dwarf other entitlement programs such as Social Security, Medicaid and Obamacare.[23] Just a decade after the 2030 benchmark, Medicare spending could account for as much as 81 percent of the federal deficit. This percentage could grow even larger, and many American liberals still hold out hope for an expansion of Obamacare that will lead to a national single-payer health care system.

Our fiscal plight compels serious discussion about our welfare state and the federal government's role in providing pensions and health care for the entire population. Along the way to answering this ultimate question, the country will debate various stopgap measures such as means testing Social Security and perhaps privatization. We will also discuss healthcare spending accounts and similar mechanisms to address rising healthcare costs. In short, there will be a mad scramble and multiple proposals to avoid default such as occurred in Greece in 2012 and the national economic catastrophe that followed.

While our world of welfarism is not one recognizable to the Anti-Federalists, they fully understood the dangers of deficit spending. The Articles of Confederation imposed the requisition system on Congress in an effort to check the general government's power. By issuing paper money during the war years, Congress tried to outmaneuver this restriction on its authority. In the short-term it enjoyed some success, but soon the paper issued became almost valueless. From this experience, most Americans agreed that Congress needed some independent source of revenue. Paper money was no panacea and real issues were encountered in persuading all the states to make their payments of funds and items requisitioned by Congress.

The Constitution of 1787 sought to remedy that budgetary problem by providing Congress with the power to tax as well as to spend for enumerated purposes. Anti-Federalists rightly sensed that the demise of the requisition system and the general government's power to levy its own taxes might lead to pernicious fiscal results. The New York convention, for example, recommended an amendment by which "[n]o money [may] be borrowed on the credit of the United States without the assent of two thirds of the senators and representatives present in each house."[24] Under such an amendment, Congress would have full discretion—so far as permitted by the Constitution—to spend the revenues generated by taxation. But, to the extent Congress wants to live beyond its means and borrow, a supermajority in both houses would have to agree to that course. Such a provision would give fiscally responsible senators and representatives a club to beat back our profligate spending. If a real emergency arose, borrowing could occur so long as the supermajority requirement was satisfied.

Representative Government

Representation is another area where we can learn from the Anti-Federalists. Throughout the 2012 political season, attention was fixed on the contest between President Barack Obama and Republican candidate Mitt Romney. A few other races garnered some media attention, but Americans treated the presidential election as the Super Bowl of politics. The winner, they were told, would chart the nation's future and have an effect for years to come.

Predominantly lost in the presidential hype were the biennial elections for the House of Representatives. Every two years Americans trudge to the polls and select a federal representative. These representatives, unlike the president, actually have the power to originate legislation. The president can recommend that certain policies assume legislative form, but without action from a member of the House or Senate nothing will move forward. The president might opine that tax rates should be raised or lowered on a certain class of citizens, but under the Constitution only the House of Representatives can originate revenue bills.

In light of these basic civics lessons, one would think that House races should have dominated the political discussion. But from local diners to talk radio stations, Americans preferred to chatter about the White House. Incumbency rates are indicative of this indifference to the House of Representatives. Since 1998, the reelection rate of incumbent candidates for the House has dipped below 94 percent just once (85 percent in 2010). That has been a steady pattern going back several decades. Despite our crushing national debt and myriad other problems, once a person is elected to the House they enjoy excellent odds of staying there.

The mainstream media certainly bears some of the blame for our fixation with the presidency. Packs of reporters follow the candidates around as they give the same stump speech day after day. Talking heads weigh in each night on the significance of a candidate's lunch order or his claimed favorite ice cream flavor. This coverage begins at least a year before the earliest primaries and caucuses actually take place. The hype intensifies with the national conventions and finally election night.

The 24-hour news cycle brings little good, but the genesis of our apathy for the House races predates the founding of CNN. The real issue goes to the House's standing as a representative institution. Is the House of Representatives, as it is currently constituted, capable of providing actual representation for the people of the country? If not, could this explain our seeming indifference to the popular branch of the national legislature?

Based on the 2010 census, each of the 435 House members is chosen from an average district of 710,767 persons. The ratio of one representative for every 710,767 Americans would have shocked the Framers of the Constitution and the Anti-Federalists. Under accepted understandings of representation, such a body as today's House would have been anathema to the revolutionary generation.

Under Article I, Section 2 "[t]he number of representatives shall not exceed one for every thirty thousand" and each state is guaranteed at least one representative.[25] This Section further provides for a decennial census after which there is supposed to be a reapportionment of representatives. At the Philadelphia Convention the original number was 40,000 inhabitants for each representative until George Washington spoke up and expressed his concern that the ratio of 1:40,000 was too large to secure "the rights & interests of the people."[26] The Convention quickly addressed this issue and the Constitution was modified to provide for a smaller ratio of inhabitants to representatives.

At the beginning of the Republic there were sixty-five members of the House. That original number was specified in Article I. It was also short-lived. After the first scheduled census and the admissions of Vermont and Kentucky to the Union, the number of representatives rose to 105 in 1793.

Even with the change adopted on George Washington's advice during the Philadelphia Convention, opponents of the Constitution were concerned that one representative for every 30,000 people was insufficient to foster a true representative body. They also complained that 1:30,000 was not a constitutional requirement, but rather was the smallest ratio achievable under the Constitution.

The simple fact of the people voting, the candidates campaigning, and the winner sharing legal citizenship with his constituents did not amount to true representation. In the Anti-Federalist view, the representative should be someone who is one of the people. He should worship among his constituents, engage in commerce with them, and socialize with them. He should have similar views and inclinations as his constituents that come from a common upbringing and pattern of life.

Prior to the first census, Virginia had a population of approximately 747,550 and was allotted ten representatives in the first Congress. This meant that each representative represented 74,755 souls. The Anti-Federalists saw no way that a representative from such a large body of people could have any real connection with them. The larger and more diverse body of the people, the more difficult it would be for the representative to share the mind of the people.

In the main, the Federalists did not disagree with the Anti-Federalist concept of representation, but argued that the Constitution guarded a true representation of the people sufficiently. "It is a sound and important principle," wrote James Madison in *Federalist* No. 56, "that the representative ought to be acquainted with the interests and circumstances of his constituents."[27] Because the national government's powers were few and limited to objects concerning the Union, Madison argued that a larger representative body, such as would be needed in a state legislature, was not required.

Madison also expected that the number of representatives would rise above 100 with the first census (which it did) and estimated that within fifty years the House would have 400 members (which it did not—only 242). Madison assured the Anti-Federalist critics that "the number of representatives will be augmented from time to time in the manner provided by the constitution."[28] Thus, Madison predicted that as the population grew, the number of representatives would also grow.

This was the pattern into the 1900s. After the 1910 census, the number of representatives was increased from 393 to 435. At the time our population was 91 million and the average district contained almost 210,000 people. After the 1920 census, Congress failed to reapportion the House in violation of the Constitution. In 1929, after much debate and politicking, Congress fixed the number of representatives permanently at 435. The House remains this size today even though our population has exceeded 300 million.

Not even the staunchest Federalist could argue that the current House adequately represents the people of the United States. This is especially so because Madison's promise that the national government would have limited authority has proven to be untrue. Various local matters are now within Washington's purview and this makes knowledge of local circumstances necessary.

Furthermore, vast electoral districts preclude the people from rubbing shoulders with their congressmen and make it less likely that representatives can truly identify with their constituents. On average, the winning candidate for a congressional seat in the 2010 election spent $1.6 million on campaigning. Studies show that the margin of victory is often tied to the challenger's level of funding. This price of admission precludes all but the richest persons from running for Congress. Not surprisingly, 46 percent of House members are millionaires. The economics of politics mean that the victor in a House race probably will have little idea of what life is like for the typical person in the district.

Defenders of the arbitrary 435 seat number might concede that the people are not as well represented as they once were, but they contend that significant enlargement of the House will make it too unwieldy. Would not a debate involving, say, 800 congressmen be chaos? Such an objection assumes that meaningful debate takes place on the floor of Congress even now. In reality, most of the work is done in committees. Congressmen appear to vote on bills and then scurry back to their offices. There are unfortunately no great debates and unparalleled oratory taking place on the floor that will be fouled up because of increased membership. Expansion of the House would not significantly affect the committee process.

Moreover, new technologies make the casting of ballots easier and can speed the work of the House even with increased membership. To the extent that opponents cite space concerns, there is no reason why congressmen could not telecommute like so much of the workforce does today. With a computer, internet access, and a phone, a congressman can work just as easily from his home district as from Washington.

Opponents also ignore that other countries with representative government have larger representative bodies (and perhaps less dysfunction than ours) in addition to more favorable ratios. For example, the 62 million people of the United Kingdom elect 650 members of Parliament— a ratio of 1:95,000. Japan's 127 million people elect 480 members to its representative assembly—1:264,000. In Germany, 81 million people elect 620 members to the Bundestag—1:130,000. The French National Assembly has 577 members representing 64,000,000 persons—1:117,636. Americans should be ashamed that so few House members represent such large districts in our country.

Besides simply reducing the ratio of citizens to representatives, expansion could have numerous salutary benefits for the health of American democracy. First, it would make it easier for third parties to compete in elections. Under the current state of affairs, congressional races present the people with two options: a Republican and a Democrat. Third parties struggle to raise monies to reach the 710,767 persons in an average district. To effectively campaign in our mega-districts, a candidate needs a sizeable war chest to pay for television and radio advertisements, direct mailing, and thousands of unsightly signs. In smaller districts, the price of candidacy would drop. A community-sized district would permit alternative candidates to go door-to-door and to spread their messages in small meetings. Voters might actually be offered a meaningful choice instead of the ins and the outs.

Second, House expansion could also reduce the power of lobbyists and special interests. PACs and other interests with no connection to a district contribute a significant amount to incumbents. During the 2010 election, House winners received an average of $665,000 from PACs. It is much more feasible to buy a "controlling interest" in a majority of a 435-member House than an 800 or 1000 member body. The larger the body the less bang-for-the-buck enjoyed by interest groups.

Finally, research shows a correlation between the size of legislative districts and the activities of government. States with bicameral legislatures and small districts for the lower house tend to rank higher on various freedom indices. The larger the average district, the more likely that big-government policies are enacted in the state.

Of course, we must be mindful that an assembly can become too big. Madison believed that "the number [in the House] ought at most to be kept within a certain limit, in order to avoid the confusion and intemperance of a multitude." He also observed that "[h]ad every Athenian citizen been a Socrates, every Athenian assembly would still have been a mob." This is no doubt true. While caution and reflection should be used if we expand the House of Representatives, the danger that it might one day become too big is no argument for maintaining it at 435 seats.

We can gradually increase the membership and observe the effects on the House's operation. An initial step might be to increase the number of House members by 215, which would equal the numbers in the British House of Commons. From this point, 100 members could be added after the next census. Hence, after the 2020 census the House would be comprised of 750 members. Projections indicate that by 2020, our population will be roughly 336 million. This means that with the augmentation suggested, the average congressional district would contain 448,000 constituents—smaller than the current districts but still a far cry from a district that George Washington or the other Founders would consider appropriate. But that would be a start.

If the House can function with 750 members, perhaps another 250 could be added after the 2030 census and thereby further reduce the size of congressional districts. This would give us an even 1000. Or if some critical mass is reached where the House cannot be augmented but the ratio of members to constituents remains "unrepresentative," then perhaps we should seriously consider whether Montesquieu was correct that only in a small territory can republican government subsist.

The bottom line is that one House member for a supersized district of 710,767 persons is counter to the fundamentals of meaningful representation. We have been stuck at 435 since the apportionment after the 1910 census. The population has grown significantly, but the size of the House has remained constant. The principles of representation as communicated by the Anti-Federalists cannot be met with today's House. It is little wonder that the people focus on the "main event" of presidential politics rather than on the choice of representatives. The House bears so little resemblance to a representative body that the people have ceased to care. The prediction of Brutus has come to pass: "the people do not govern, but the sovereignty is in a few."[29]

Rotation in Office

In conjunction with Anti-Federalist concerns about the number of representatives, we should consider the principle of rotation in office. Rotation in office, what we would call term limits, dates back to ancient Athenian democracy. In the fourth and fifth centuries B.C., Athenians prohibited anyone from serving on the 500-person ruling council for longer than two years.[30] Aristotle held that in a constitutional state "citizens rule and are ruled by turns" inasmuch as "the natures of the citizens are equal."[31] Hence, this vaunted philosopher was an early champion of term limits.

Rotation in office was a critical part of the Articles of Confederation's efforts to limit congressional power. Under Article V, "no person shall be capable of being a delegate for more than three years in any term of six years."[32] According to historian Gordon Wood, motivating factors for this provision were fears of establishment of an American ruling aristocracy and the belief that public service should be open to men equally talented as (or perhaps more so than) the old guard.[33]

Terms limits were part of the Virginia Plan at the Philadelphia Convention, but were rejected "as entering too much into detail for general propositions."[34] When the Constitution of 1787 omitted the term limits of the Articles, Anti-Federalists protested. "ROTATION, that noble prerogative of liberty, is entirely excluded from the new system of government, and great men may and probably will be continued in office during their lives," predicted An Officer of the Late Continental Army.[35] Similarly, a Columbian Patriot abjured that "[t]here is no provision for a rotation, nor any thing to prevent the perpetuity of office in the same hands for life; which by a little well timed bribery, will probably be done, to the exclusion of men of the best abilities from their share in the offices of the government." Melancton Smith believed that rotation in office has "a tendency to diffuse a more general spirit of emulation, and to bring forward into office the genius and abilities of the continent."[36] He further averred that "a numerous body of enlightened citizens" stood ready to serve if the Constitution, through rotation, would limit the power of the rich and influential.[37] Not surprisingly, Smith supported proposed amendments to limit Senators to six years of service in any period of twelve years and to limit the president to two terms. Second only to the omission of a bill of rights, the failure to provide for rotation was to Thomas Jefferson the greatest defect in the Constitution. Jefferson scolded Madison because the Constitution "abandon[ed] in every instance the necessity of rotation in office."[38]

Until the twentieth century, the Anti-Federalist insistence on term limits seemed misplaced. However, in 1951 Americans added the Twenty-Second Amendment to the Constitution. This amendment prohibited any person from being elected to the presidency more than twice. Until FDR, American presidents had honored George Washington's precedent and stepped aside after two terms. FDR, however, stood for election and was elected four times to the presidency. His lengthy service caused Americans to reconsider executive term-limit proposals voiced by the Anti-Federalists.

In the early years of the Republic, rotation in office was common and members of Congress rarely served lengthy stints. According to the Congressional Research Service, "[m]ost lawmakers in the 18th and early 19th centuries can be characterized as 'citizen legislators,' holding full-time non-political employment and serving in Congress on a part-time basis for a short number of years. During the twentieth century, congressional careers lengthened as turnover decreased and Congress became more professionalized."[39] The data show that in the nineteenth century, it was not uncommon for 40 or 50 percent of representatives to choose private life over seeking an additional term.[40] Today, that number is down to about 10 percent.[41]

As mentioned in the previous section, for incumbents seeking reelection, the odds of success are excellent. In the 2012 elections, 91 percent of the serving members of the House and Senate were reelected.[42] Although this rate seems and is high, it is about 2 percent below the historical average since 1954.[43] It does show that incumbency is a huge advantage in an election and this, in turn, means that political careerism is alive and well. Incumbents have stronger name recognition than challengers and are known commodities. They appear on the local news, radio, and often have their names in the newspaper. Also, many voters choose incumbents because seniority in Congress means greater influence and power. In the scramble for pork, voters reason that the more seniority a member of Congress has, the more benefits he will send back to the district. Voters also know that if they throw their bum out, a more senior congressman from another district will help his district to tax dollars that otherwise would have gone to the incumbency-rejecting district. The rise of the seniority system, which did not exist for much of congressional history, has certainly contributed to the new pattern of lengthy congressional service.

Americans cannot pretend that the Congress is composed of citizen legislators who briefly step out of private life to serve the people. Congress is a group of professional politicians whose main goal is often the extension of their own careers. And careerism creates problems in our Republic. In the words of Patrick Basham, "[o]nce in office careerist legislators pay less attention to the needs and wishes of their constituents. Moreover, careerist elected officials become a political class attentive to their own interests."[44] Studies show that the longer a person serves in the House or Senate, the more likely he is to vote for pork and special-interest spending.[45]

Faced with the rise of congressional careerism, in the early 1990s, Americans strongly backed the movement for term limits. In 1992, nine states enacted provisions to restrict multi-term congressional incumbents from having their names printed on state ballots.[46] Momentum increased, and by 1995, twenty-three states had adopted term limits for their members of Congress. Unfortunately, the United States Supreme Court stepped in and, in a 5 to 4 decision, held that states may not impose qualifications for the offices of federal representative and federal senator.[47] That ruling stopped the grassroots efforts aimed at Congress.

However, it did not affect the term limits movement aimed at the state legislatures and local bodies. According to U.S. Term Limits, in the 2012 election ninety jurisdictions placed various forms of term limits on the ballot.[48] The people voted for term limits in eighty-seven of those ninety opportunities. Indeed, term limits are in place in fifteen state legislatures, eight of the ten largest American cities limit the terms of the city council and/or mayor, and thirty-seven states have term limits on their constitutional officers.

While the Constitution is not easy to amend, Americans would do well to focus on an amendment limiting representatives to three terms in office and senators to two terms. Even Joseph Lieberman, who served in the Senate for twenty-four years, expressed his support of term limits upon his return to private life. Lieberman said that he had always contended that senators and representatives were term limited by elections, but that now he has rethought his position. With term limits in place, Lieberman speculated that Congress "might be healthier and less partisan . . . if it turned over more often."[49] Warren Rudman, who represented New Hampshire in the Senate, expressed a similar sentiment when he retired in 1993: "the longer you stay in public office, the more distant the outside world becomes."[50]

In January 2013, Senators David Vitter (R-La.) and Pat Toomey (R-Pa.) sponsored legislation to back a constitutional amendment imposing term limits on Congress. "Call it Potomac Fever," Vitter said, "or whatever you'd like, but the longer some folks are in Washington, the more taxpayer money they want to spend."[51] Vitter and others supporting the bill believe that term limits would help members of Congress reconnect with the people and restore confidence in the legislative branch. They understand that political careerism is inimical to a national government of few and defined powers. The Vitter and Toomey proposal should be supported by all Americans who want to end political careerism and the baggage attendant with this malady.

Unrestrained borrowing, representation, and term limits are but three examples where we can find guidance and wisdom from the Anti-Federalist mind and the Articles of Confederation. The nature and extent of Washington's power remains a critical issue for American governance. Central authority has grown, but our troubles seem more insurmountable. Perhaps the problem is not that Washington lacks authority to deal with certain issues, but that a general government is not suited to decree one-size-fits-all solutions for matters that are either inherently local by nature or susceptible to wide experimentation in state laboratories of democracy. Today, our national government looks more like the powerful British central government from which the colonies rebelled than the limited general government established by the Confederation. While the Articles did withhold necessary powers from Congress, the pendulum has swung far in the opposite direction. In the first decades of the twenty-first century, almost nothing is denied Washington. Careerist legislators spend billions of dollars in excess of tax revenues on matters that have little or no constitutional basis. In super-sized districts, it appears that special interests are the real constituencies rather than the people of the districts. Matters are fast getting out of hand.

Before we continue further down this current road, let us listen to the Cassandras of the 1770s and 1780s. They predicted the future and offered concrete proposals that would have allowed us to avoid our current predicament. Their principles can guide us back to stability and limited government. Let us open our ears and hear what they have to say.

Appendix A
Articles of Confederation (1778)

TO ALL TO whom these Presents shall come, we the undersigned Delegates of the States affixed to our Names send greeting.

Articles of Confederation and perpetual Union between the states of New Hampshire, Massachusetts-bay, Rhode Island and Providence Plantations, Connecticut, New York, New Jersey, Pennsylvania, Delaware, Maryland, Virginia, North Carolina, South Carolina and Georgia.

ARTICLE I. The style of this Confederacy shall be "The United States of America."

ARTICLE II. Each state retains its sovereignty, freedom, and independence, and every power, jurisdiction, and right, which is not by this Confederation expressly delegated to the United States, in Congress assembled.

ARTICLE III. The said States hereby severally enter into a firm league of friendship with each other, for their common defense, the security of their liberties, and their mutual and general welfare, binding themselves to assist each other, against all force offered to, or attacks made upon them, or any of them, on account of religion, sovereignty, trade, or any other pretense whatever.

ARTICLE IV. The better to secure and perpetuate mutual friendship and intercourse among the people of the different States in this Union, the free inhabitants of each of these States, paupers, vagabonds, and fugitives from justice excepted, shall be entitled to all privileges and immunities of free citizens in the several States; and the people of each State shall free ingress and regress to and from any other State, and shall enjoy therein all the privileges of trade and commerce, subject to the same duties, impositions, and restrictions as the inhabitants thereof respectively, provided that such restrictions shall not extend so far as to prevent the removal of property imported into any State, to any other State, of which the owner is an inhabitant; provided also that no imposition, duties or restriction shall be laid by any State, on the property of the United States, or either of them.

If any person guilty of, or charged with, treason, felony, or other high misdemeanor in any State, shall flee from justice, and be found in any of the United States, he shall, upon demand of the Governor or executive power of the State from which he fled, be delivered up and removed to the State having jurisdiction of his offense.

Full faith and credit shall be given in each of these States to the records, acts, and judicial proceedings of the courts and magistrates of every other State.

ARTICLE V. For the most convenient management of the general interests of the United States, delegates shall be annually appointed in such manner as the legislatures of each State shall direct, to meet in Congress on the first Monday in November, in every year, with a power reserved to each State to recall its delegates, or any of them, at any time within the year, and to send others in their stead for the remainder of the year.

No State shall be represented in Congress by less than two, nor more than seven members; and no person shall be capable of being a delegate for more than three years in any term of six years; nor shall any person, being a delegate, be capable of holding any office under the United States, for which he, or another for his benefit, receives any salary, fees or emolument of any kind.

Each State shall maintain its own delegates in a meeting of the States, and while they act as members of the committee of the States.

In determining questions in the United States in Congress assembled, each State shall have one vote.

Freedom of speech and debate in Congress shall not be impeached or questioned in any court or place out of Congress, and the members of Congress shall be protected in their persons from arrests or imprisonments, during the time of their going to and from, and attendance on Congress, except for treason, felony, or breach of the peace.

ARTICLE VI. No State, without the consent of the United States in Congress assembled, shall send any embassy to, or receive any embassy from, or enter into any conference, agreement, alliance or treaty with any King, Prince or State; nor shall any person holding any office of profit or trust under the United States, or any of them, accept any present, emolument, office or title of any kind whatever from any King, Prince or foreign State; nor shall the United States in Congress assembled, or any of them, grant any title of nobility.

No two or more States shall enter into any treaty, confederation or alliance whatever between them, without the consent of the United States in Congress assembled, specifying accurately the purposes for which the same is to be entered into, and how long it shall continue.

No State shall lay any imposts or duties, which may interfere with any stipulations in treaties, entered into by the United States in Congress assembled, with any King, Prince or State, in pursuance of any treaties already proposed by Congress, to the courts of France and Spain.

No vessel of war shall be kept up in time of peace by any State, except such number only, as shall be deemed necessary by the United States in Congress assembled, for the defense of such State, or its trade; nor shall any body of forces be kept up by any State in time of peace, except such number only, as in the judgment of the United States in Congress assembled, shall be deemed requisite to garrison the forts necessary for the defense of such State; but every State shall always keep up a well-regulated and disciplined militia, sufficiently armed and accoutered, and shall provide and constantly have ready for use, in public stores, a due number of filed pieces and tents, and a proper quantity of arms, ammunition and camp equipage.

No State shall engage in any war without the consent of the United States in Congress assembled, unless such State be actually invaded by enemies, or shall have received certain advice of a resolution being formed by some nation of Indians to invade such State, and the danger is so imminent as not to admit of a delay till the United States in Congress assembled can be consulted; nor shall any State grant commissions to any ships or vessels of war, nor letters of marque or reprisal, except it be after a declaration of war by the United States in Congress assembled, and then only against the Kingdom or State and the subjects thereof, against which war has been so declared, and under such regulations as shall be established by the United States in Congress assembled, unless such State be infested by pirates, in which case vessels of war may be fitted out for that occasion, and kept so long as the danger shall continue, or until the United States in Congress assembled shall determine otherwise.

ARTICLE VII. When land forces are raised by any State for the common defense, all officers of or under the rank of colonel, shall be appointed by the legislature of each State respectively, by whom such forces shall be raised, or in such manner as such State shall direct, and all vacancies shall be filled up by the State which first made the appointment.

ARTICLE VIII. All charges of war, and all other expenses that shall be incurred for the common defense or general welfare, and allowed by the United States in Congress assembled, shall be defrayed out of a common treasury, which shall be supplied by the several States in proportion to the value of all land within each State, granted or surveyed for any person, as such land and the buildings and improvements thereon shall be estimated according to such mode as the United States in Congress assembled, shall from time to time direct and appoint.

The taxes for paying that proportion shall be laid and levied by the authority and direction of the legislatures of the several States within the time agreed upon by the United States in Congress assembled.

ARTICLE IX. The United States in Congress assembled, shall have the sole and exclusive right and power of determining on peace and war, except in the cases mentioned in the sixth article—of sending and receiving ambassadors—entering into treaties and alliances, provided that no treaty of commerce shall be made whereby the legislative power of the respective States shall be restrained from imposing such imposts and duties on foreigners, as their own people are subjected to, or from prohibiting the exportation or importation of any species of goods or commodities whatsoever—of establishing rules for deciding in all cases, what captures on land or water shall be legal, and in what manner prizes taken by land or naval forces in the service of the United States shall be divided or appropriated—of granting letters of marque and reprisal in times of peace—appointing courts for the trial of piracies and felonies committed on the high seas and establishing courts for receiving and determining finally appeals in all cases of captures, provided that no member of Congress shall be appointed a judge of any of the said courts.

The United States in Congress assembled shall also be the last resort on appeal in all disputes and differences now subsisting or that hereafter may arise between two or more States concerning boundary, jurisdiction or any other causes whatever; which authority shall always be exercised in the manner following. Whenever the legislative or executive authority or lawful agent of any State in controversy with another shall present a petition to Congress stating the matter in question and praying for a hearing, notice thereof shall be given by order of Congress to the legislative or executive authority of the other State in controversy, and a day assigned for the appearance of the parties by their lawful agents, who shall then be directed to appoint by joint consent, commissioners or judges to constitute a court for hearing and determining the matter in question: but if they cannot agree, Congress shall name three persons out of each of the United States, and from the list of such persons each party shall alternately strike out one, the petitioners beginning, until the number shall be reduced to thirteen; and from that number not less than seven, nor more than nine names as Congress shall direct, shall in the presence of Congress be drawn out by lot, and the persons whose names shall be so drawn or any five of them, shall be commissioners or judges, to hear and finally determine the controversy, so always as a major part of the judges who shall hear the cause shall agree in the determination: and if either party shall neglect to attend at the day appointed, without showing reasons, which Congress shall judge sufficient, or being present shall refuse to strike, the Congress shall proceed to nominate three persons out of each State, and the secretary of Congress shall strike in behalf of such party absent or refusing; and the judgment and sentence of the court to be appointed, in the manner before prescribed, shall be final and conclusive; and if any of the parties shall refuse to submit to the authority of such court, or to appear or defend their claim or cause, the court shall nevertheless proceed to pronounce sentence, or judgment, which shall in like manner be final and decisive, the judgment or sentence and other proceedings being in either case transmitted to Congress, and lodged among the acts of Congress for the security of the parties concerned: provided that every commissioner, before he sits in judgment, shall take an oath to be administered by one of the judges of the supreme or superior court of the State, where the cause shall be tried, 'well and truly to hear and determine the matter in question, according to the best of his judgment, without favor, affection or hope of reward': provided also, that no State shall be deprived of territory for the benefit of the United States.

All controversies concerning the private right of soil claimed under different grants of two or more States, whose jurisdictions as they may respect such lands, and the States which passed such grants are adjusted, the said grants or either of them being at the same time claimed to have originated antecedent to such settlement of jurisdiction, shall on the petition of either party to the Congress of the United States, be finally determined as near as may be in the same manner as is before prescribed for deciding disputes respecting territorial jurisdiction between different States.

The United States in Congress assembled shall also have the sole and exclusive right and power of regulating the alloy and value of coin struck by their own authority, or by that of the respective State—fixing the standards of weights and measures throughout the United States—regulating the trade and managing all affairs with the Indians, not members of any of the States, provided that the legislative right of any State within its own limits be not infringed or violated—establishing or regulating post offices from one State to another, throughout all the United States, and exacting such postage on the papers passing through the same as may be requisite to defray the expenses of the said office—appointing all officers of the land forces, in the service of the United States, excepting regimental officers—appointing all the officers of the naval forces, and commissioning all officers whatever in the service of the United States—making rules for the government and regulation of the said land and naval forces, and directing their operations.

The United States in Congress assembled shall have authority to appoint a committee, to sit in the recess of Congress, to be denominated 'A Committee of the States', and to consist of one delegate from each State; and to appoint such other committees and civil officers as may be necessary for managing the general affairs of the United States under their direction — to appoint one of their members to preside, provided that no person be allowed to serve in the office of president more than one year in any term of three years; to ascertain the necessary sums of money to be raised for the service of the United States, and to appropriate and apply the same for defraying the public expenses—to borrow money, or emit bills on the credit of the United States, transmitting every half-year to the respective States an account of the sums of money so borrowed or emitted—to build and equip a navy—to agree upon the number of land forces, and to make requisitions from each State for its quota, in proportion to the number of white inhabitants in such State; which requisition shall be binding, and thereupon the legislature of each State shall appoint the regimental officers, raise the men and clothed, arm and equip them in a solid-like manner, at the expense of the United States; and the officers and men so clothed, armed and equipped shall march to the place appointed, and within the time agreed on by the United States in Congress assembled. But if the United States in Congress assembled shall, on consideration of circumstances judge proper that any State should not raise men, or should raise a smaller number of men than the quota thereof, such extra number shall be raised, officered, clothed, armed and equipped in the same manner as the quota of each State, unless the legislature of such State shall judge that such extra number cannot be safely spread out in the same, in which case they shall raise, officer, clothe, arm and equip as many of such extra number as they judge can be safely spared. And the officers and men so clothed, armed, and equipped, shall march to the place appointed, and within the time agreed on by the United States in Congress assembled.

The United States in Congress assembled shall never engage in a war, nor grant letters of marque or reprisal in time of peace, nor enter into any treaties or alliances, nor coin money, nor regulate the value thereof, nor ascertain the sums and expenses necessary for the defense and welfare of the United States, or any of them, nor emit bills, nor borrow money on the credit of the United States, nor appropriate money, nor agree upon the number of vessels of war, to be built or purchased, or the number of land or sea forces to be raised, nor appoint a commander in chief of the army or navy, unless nine States assent to the same: nor shall a question on any other point, except for adjourning from day to day be determined, unless by the votes of the majority of the United States in Congress assembled.

The Congress of the United States shall have power to adjourn to any time within the year, and to any place within the United States, so that no period of adjournment be for a longer duration than the space of six months, and shall publish the journal of their proceedings monthly, except such parts thereof relating to treaties, alliances or military operations, as in their judgment require secrecy; and the yeas and nays of the delegates of each State on any question shall be entered on the journal, when it is desired by any delegates of a State, or any of them, at his or their request shall be furnished with a transcript of the said journal, except such parts as are above excepted, to lay before the legislatures of the several States.

ARTICLE X. The Committee of the States, or any nine of them, shall be authorized to execute, in the recess of Congress, such of the powers of Congress as the United States in Congress assembled, by the consent of the nine States, shall from time to time think expedient to vest them with; provided that no power be delegated to the said Committee, for the exercise of which, by the Articles of Confederation, the voice of nine States in the Congress of the United States assembled be requisite.

ARTICLE XI. Canada acceding to this confederation, and adjoining in the measures of the United States, shall be admitted into, and entitled to all the advantages of this Union; but no other colony shall be admitted into the same, unless such admission be agreed to by nine States.

ARTICLE XII. All bills of credit emitted, monies borrowed, and debts contracted by, or under the authority of Congress, before the assembling of the United States, in pursuance of the present confederation, shall be deemed and considered as a charge against the United States, for payment and satisfaction whereof the said United States, and the public faith are hereby solemnly pledged.

ARTICLE XIII. Every State shall abide by the determination of the United States in Congress assembled, on all questions which by this confederation are submitted to them. And the Articles of this Confederation shall be inviolably observed by every State, and the Union shall be perpetual; nor shall any alteration at any time hereafter be made in any of them; unless such alteration be agreed to in a Congress of the United States, and be afterwards confirmed by the legislatures of every State.

And Whereas it hath pleased the Great Governor of the World to incline the hearts of the legislatures we respectively represent in Congress, to approve of, and to authorize us to ratify the said Articles of Confederation and perpetual Union. Know Ye that we the undersigned delegates, by virtue of the power and authority to us given for that purpose, do by these presents, in the name and in behalf of our respective constituents, fully and entirely ratify and confirm each and every of the said Articles of Confederation and perpetual Union, and all and singular the matters and things therein contained: And we do further solemnly plight and engage the faith of our respective constituents, that they shall abide by the determinations of the United States in Congress assembled, on all questions, which by the said Confederation are submitted to them. And that the Articles thereof shall be inviolably observed by the States we respectively represent, and that the Union shall be perpetual.

In Witness whereof we have hereunto set our hands in Congress. Done at Philadelphia in the State of Pennsylvania the ninth day of July in the Year of our Lord One Thousand Seven Hundred and Seventy-Eight, and in the Third Year of the independence of America.

Appendix B
Constitution of the United States (1787)

WE THE PEOPLE of the United States, in Order to form a more perfect Union, establish Justice, insure domestic Tranquility, provide for the common defence, promote the general Welfare, and secure the Blessings of Liberty to ourselves and our Posterity, do ordain and establish this Constitution for the United States of America.

Article I

Section 1. All legislative Powers herein granted shall be vested in a Congress of the United States, which shall consist of a Senate and House of Representatives.

Section 2. The House of Representatives shall be composed of Members chosen every second Year by the People of the several States, and the Electors in each State shall have the Qualifications requisite for Electors of the most numerous Branch of the State Legislature.

No Person shall be a Representative who shall not have attained to the Age of twenty five Years, and been seven Years a Citizen of the United States, and who shall not, when elected, be an Inhabitant of that State in which he shall be chosen.

Representatives and direct Taxes shall be apportioned among the several States which may be included within this Union, according to their respective Numbers, which shall be determined by adding to the whole Number of free Persons, including those bound to Service for a Term of Years, and excluding Indians not taxed, three fifths of all other Persons. The actual Enumeration shall be made within three Years after the first Meeting of the Congress of the United States, and within every subsequent Term of ten Years, in such Manner as they shall by Law direct. The Number of Representatives shall not exceed one for every thirty Thousand, but each State shall have at Least one Representative; and until such enumeration shall be made, the State of New Hampshire shall be entitled to chuse three, Massachusetts eight, Rhode-Island and Providence Plantations one, Connecticut five, New-York six, New Jersey four, Pennsylvania eight, Delaware one, Maryland six, Virginia ten, North Carolina five, South Carolina five, and Georgia three.

When vacancies happen in the Representation from any State, the Executive Authority thereof shall issue Writs of Election to fill such Vacancies.

The House of Representatives shall chuse their Speaker and other Officers; and shall have the sole Power of Impeachment.

Section 3. The Senate of the United States shall be composed of two Senators from each State, chosen by the Legislature thereof, for six Years; and each Senator shall have one Vote.

Immediately after they shall be assembled in Consequence of the first Election, they shall be divided as equally as may be into three Classes. The Seats of the Senators of the first Class shall be vacated at the Expiration of the second Year, of the second Class at the Expiration of the fourth Year, and of the third Class at the Expiration of the sixth Year, so that one third may be chosen every second Year; and if Vacancies happen by Resignation, or otherwise, during the Recess of the Legislature of any State, the Executive thereof may make temporary Appointments until the next Meeting of the Legislature, which shall then fill such Vacancies.

No Person shall be a Senator who shall not have attained to the Age of thirty Years, and been nine Years a Citizen of the United States, and who shall not, when elected, be an Inhabitant of that State for which he shall be chosen.

The Vice President of the United States shall be President of the Senate, but shall have no Vote, unless they be equally divided.

The Senate shall chuse their other Officers, and also a President pro tempore, in the Absence of the Vice President, or when he shall exercise the Office of President of the United States.

The Senate shall have the sole Power to try all Impeachments. When sitting for that Purpose, they shall be on Oath or Affirmation. When the President of the United States is tried, the Chief Justice shall preside: And no Person shall be convicted without the Concurrence of two thirds of the Members present.

Judgment in Cases of Impeachment shall not extend further than to removal from Office, and disqualification to hold and enjoy any Office of honor, Trust or Profit under the United States: but the Party convicted shall nevertheless be liable and subject to Indictment, Trial, Judgment and Punishment, according to Law.

Section 4. The Times, Places and Manner of holding Elections for Senators and Representatives, shall be prescribed in each State by the Legislature thereof; but the Congress may at any time by Law make or alter such Regulations, except as to the Places of chusing Senators.

The Congress shall assemble at least once in every Year, and such Meeting shall be on the first Monday in December, unless they shall by Law appoint a different Day.

Section 5. Each House shall be the Judge of the Elections, Returns and Qualifications of its own Members, and a Majority of each shall constitute a Quorum to do Business; but a smaller Number may adjourn from day to day, and may be authorized to compel the Attendance of absent Members, in such Manner, and under such Penalties as each House may provide.

Each House may determine the Rules of its Proceedings, punish its Members for disorderly Behaviour, and, with the Concurrence of two thirds, expel a Member.

Each House shall keep a Journal of its Proceedings, and from time to time publish the same, excepting such Parts as may in their Judgment require Secrecy; and the Yeas and Nays of the Members of either House on any question shall, at the Desire of one fifth of those Present, be entered on the Journal.

Neither House, during the Session of Congress, shall, without the Consent of the other, adjourn for more than three days, nor to any other Place than that in which the two Houses shall be sitting.

Section 6. The Senators and Representatives shall receive a Compensation for their Services, to be ascertained by Law, and paid out of the Treasury of the United States. They shall in all Cases, except Treason, Felony and Breach of the Peace, be privileged from Arrest during their Attendance at the Session of their respective Houses, and in going to and returning from the same; and for any Speech or Debate in either House, they shall not be questioned in any other Place.

No Senator or Representative shall, during the Time for which he was elected, be appointed to any civil Office under the Authority of the United States, which shall have been created, or the Emoluments whereof shall have been encreased during such time; and no Person holding any Office under the United States, shall be a Member of either House during his Continuance in Office.

Section 7. All Bills for raising Revenue shall originate in the House of Representatives; but the Senate may propose or concur with Amendments as on other Bills.

Every Bill which shall have passed the House of Representatives and the Senate, shall, before it become a Law, be presented to the President of the United States; If he approve he shall sign it, but if not he shall return it, with his Objections to that House in which it shall have originated, who shall enter the Objections at large on their Journal, and proceed to reconsider it. If after such Reconsideration two thirds of that House shall agree to pass the Bill, it shall be sent, together with the Objections, to the other House, by which it shall likewise be reconsidered, and if approved by two thirds of that House, it shall become a Law. But in all such Cases the Votes of both Houses shall be determined by yeas and Nays, and the Names of the Persons voting for and against the Bill shall be entered on the Journal of each House respectively. If any Bill shall not be returned by the President within ten Days (Sundays excepted) after it shall have been presented to him, the Same shall be a Law, in like Manner as if he had signed it, unless the Congress by their Adjournment prevent its Return, in which Case it shall not be a Law.

Every Order, Resolution, or Vote to which the Concurrence of the Senate and House of Representatives may be necessary (except on a question of Adjournment) shall be presented to the President of the United States; and before the Same shall take Effect, shall be approved by him, or being disapproved by him, shall be repassed by two thirds of the Senate and House of Representatives, according to the Rules and Limitations prescribed in the Case of a Bill.

Section 8. The Congress shall have Power To lay and collect Taxes, Duties, Imposts and Excises, to pay the Debts and provide for the common Defence and general Welfare of the United States; but all Duties, Imposts and Excises shall be uniform throughout the United States;

To borrow Money on the credit of the United States;

To regulate Commerce with foreign Nations, and among the several States, and with the Indian Tribes;

To establish an uniform Rule of Naturalization, and uniform Laws on the subject of Bankruptcies throughout the United States;

To coin Money, regulate the Value thereof, and of foreign Coin, and fix the Standard of Weights and Measures;

To provide for the Punishment of counterfeiting the Securities and current Coin of the United States;

To establish Post Offices and post Roads;

To promote the Progress of Science and useful Arts, by securing for limited Times to Authors and Inventors the exclusive Right to their respective Writings and Discoveries;

To constitute Tribunals inferior to the supreme Court;

To define and punish Piracies and Felonies committed on the high Seas, and Offenses against the Law of Nations;

To declare War, grant Letters of Marque and Reprisal, and make Rules concerning Captures on Land and Water;

To raise and support Armies, but no Appropriation of Money to that Use shall be for a longer Term than two Years;

To provide and maintain a Navy;

To make Rules for the Government and Regulation of the land and naval Forces;

To provide for calling forth the Militia to execute the Laws of the Union, suppress Insurrections and repel Invasions;

To provide for organizing, arming, and disciplining, the Militia, and for governing such Part of them as may be employed in the Service of the United States, reserving to the States respectively, the Appointment of the Officers, and the Authority of training the Militia according to the discipline prescribed by Congress;

To exercise exclusive Legislation in all Cases whatsoever, over such District (not exceeding ten Miles square) as may, by Cession of particular States, and the Acceptance of Congress, become the Seat of the Government of the United States, and to exercise like Authority over all Places purchased by the Consent of the Legislature of the State in which the Same shall be, for the Erection of Forts, Magazines, Arsenals, dock-Yards, and other needful Buildings; —And

To make all Laws which shall be necessary and proper for carrying into Execution the foregoing Powers, and all other Powers vested by this Constitution in the Government of the United States, or in any Department or Officer thereof.

Section 9. The Migration or Importation of such Persons as any of the States now existing shall think proper to admit, shall not be prohibited by the Congress prior to the Year one thousand eight hundred and eight, but a Tax or duty may be imposed on such Importation, not exceeding ten dollars for each Person.

The Privilege of the Writ of Habeas Corpus shall not be suspended, unless when in Cases of Rebellion or Invasion the public Safety may require it.

No Bill of Attainder or ex post facto Law shall be passed.

No Capitation, or other direct, Tax shall be laid, unless in Proportion to the Census or Enumeration herein before directed to be taken.

No Tax or Duty shall be laid on Articles exported from any State.

No Preference shall be given by any Regulation of Commerce or Revenue to the Ports of one State over those of another: nor shall Vessels bound to, or from, one State, be obliged to enter, clear, or pay Duties in another.

No Money shall be drawn from the Treasury, but in Consequence of Appropriations made by Law; and a regular Statement and Account of the Receipts and Expenditures of all public Money shall be published from time to time.

No Title of Nobility shall be granted by the United States: And no Person holding any Office of Profit or Trust under them, shall, without the Consent of the Congress, accept of any present, Emolument, Office, or Title, of any kind whatever, from any King, Prince, or foreign State.

Section 10. No State shall enter into any Treaty, Alliance, or Confederation; grant Letters of Marque and Reprisal; coin Money; emit Bills of Credit;

make any Thing but gold and silver Coin a Tender in Payment of Debts; pass any Bill of Attainder, ex post facto Law, or Law impairing the Obligation of Contracts, or grant any Title of Nobility.

No State shall, without the Consent of the Congress, lay any Imposts or Duties on Imports or Exports, except what may be absolutely necessary for executing it's inspection Laws: and the net Produce of all Duties and Imposts, laid by any State on Imports or Exports, shall be for the Use of the Treasury of the United States; and all such Laws shall be subject to the Revision and Controul of the Congress.

No State shall, without the Consent of Congress, lay any Duty of Tonnage, keep Troops, or Ships of War in time of Peace, enter into any Agreement or Compact with another State, or with a foreign Power, or engage in War, unless actually invaded, or in such imminent Danger as will not admit of delay.

Article II

Section 1. The executive Power shall be vested in a President of the United States of America. He shall hold his Office during the Term of four Years, and, together with the Vice President, chosen for the same Term, be elected, as follows:

Each State shall appoint, in such Manner as the Legislature thereof may direct, a Number of Electors, equal to the whole Number of Senators and Representatives to which the State may be entitled in the Congress: but no Senator or Representative, or Person holding an Office of Trust or Profit under the United States, shall be appointed an Elector.

The Electors shall meet in their respective States, and vote by Ballot for two Persons, of whom one at least shall not be an Inhabitant of the same State with themselves. And they shall make a List of all the Persons voted for, and of the Number of Votes for each; which List they shall sign and certify, and transmit sealed to the Seat of the Government of the United States, directed to the President of the Senate. The President of the Senate shall, in the Presence of the Senate and House of Representatives, open all the Certificates, and the Votes shall then be counted. The Person having the greatest Number of Votes shall be the President, if such Number be a Majority of the whole Number of Electors appointed; and if there be more than one who have such Majority, and have an equal Number of Votes, then the House of Representatives shall immediately chuse by Ballot one of them for President; and if no Person have a Majority, then from the five highest on the List the said House shall in like Manner chuse the President. But in chusing the President, the Votes shall be taken by States, the Representation from each State having one Vote; A quorum for this purpose shall consist of a Member or Members from two thirds of the States, and a Majority of all the States shall be necessary to a Choice. In every Case, after the Choice of the President, the Person having the greatest Number of Votes of the Electors shall be the Vice President. But if there should remain two or more who have equal Votes, the Senate shall chuse from them by Ballot the Vice President.

The Congress may determine the Time of chusing the Electors, and the Day on which they shall give their Votes; which Day shall be the same throughout the United States.

No Persons except a natural born Citizen, or a Citizen of the United States, at the time of the Adoption of this Constitution, shall be eligible to the Office of President; neither shall any Person be eligible to that Office who shall not have attained to the Age of thirty five Years, and been fourteen Years a Resident within the United States.

In Case of the Removal of the President from Office, or of his Death, Resignation, or Inability to discharge the Powers and Duties of the said Office, the Same shall devolve on the Vice President, and the Congress may by Law provide for the Case of Removal, Death, Resignation or Inability, both of the President and Vice President, declaring what Officer shall then act as President, and such Officer shall act accordingly, until the Disability be removed, or a President shall be elected.

The President shall, at stated Times, receive for his Services, a Compensation, which shall neither be increased nor diminished during the Period for which he shall have been elected, and he shall not receive within that Period any other Emolument from the United States, or any of them.

Before he enter on the Execution of his Office, he shall take the following Oath or Affirmation:—"I do solemnly swear (or affirm) that I will faithfully execute the Office of President of the United States, and will to the best of my Ability, preserve, protect and defend the Constitution of the United States."

Section 2. The President shall be Commander in Chief of the Army and Navy of the United States, and of the Militia of the several States, when called into the actual Service of the United States; he may require the Opinion, in writing, of the principal Officer in each of the executive Departments, upon any Subject relating to the Duties of their respective Offices, and he shall have Power to grant Reprieves and Pardons for Offences against the United States, except in Cases of Impeachment.

He shall have Power, by and with the Advice and Consent of the Senate, to make Treaties, provided two thirds of the Senators present concur; and he shall nominate, and by and with the Advice and Consent of the Senate, shall appoint Ambassadors, other public Ministers and Consuls, Judges of the supreme Court, and all other Officers of the United States, whose Appointments are not herein otherwise provided for, and which shall be established by Law: but the Congress may by Law vest the Appointment of such inferior Officers, as they think proper, in the President alone, in the Courts of Law, or in the Heads of Departments.

The President shall have Power to fill up all Vacancies that may happen during the Recess of the Senate, by granting Commissions which shall expire at the End of their next Session.

Section 3. He shall from time to time give to the Congress Information of the State of the Union, and recommend to their Consideration such Measures as he shall judge necessary and expedient; he may, on extraordinary Occasions, convene both Houses, or either of them, and in Case of Disagreement between them, with Respect to the Time of Adjournment, he may adjourn them to such Time as he shall think proper; he shall receive Ambassadors and other public Ministers; he shall take Care that the Laws be faithfully executed, and shall Commission all the Officers of the United States.

Section 4. The President, Vice President and all civil Officers of the United States, shall be removed from Office on Impeachment for, and Conviction of, Treason, Bribery, or other high Crimes and Misdemeanors.

Article III

Section 1. The judicial Power of the United States, shall be vested in one supreme Court, and in such inferior Courts as the Congress may from time to time ordain and establish. The Judges, both of the supreme and inferior Courts, shall hold their Offices during good Behaviour, and shall, at stated Times, receive for their Services, a Compensation, which shall not be diminished during their Continuance in Office.

Section 2. The judicial Power shall extend to all Cases, in Law and Equity, arising under this Constitution, the Laws of the United States, and Treaties made, or which shall be made, under their Authority;—to all Cases affecting Ambassadors, other public Ministers and Consuls;—to all Cases of admiralty and maritime Jurisdiction;—to Controversies to which the United States shall be a Party;—to Controversies between two or more States;—between a State and Citizens of another State;—between Citizens of different States;—between Citizens of the same State claiming Lands under Grants of different States, and between a State, or the Citizens thereof, and foreign States, Citizens or Subjects.

In all Cases affecting Ambassadors, other public Ministers and Consuls, and those in which a State shall be Party, the supreme Court shall have original Jurisdiction. In all the other Cases before mentioned, the supreme Court shall have appellate Jurisdiction, both as to Law and Fact, with such Exceptions, and under such Regulations as the Congress shall make. The Trial of all Crimes, except in Cases of Impeachment, shall be by Jury; and such Trial shall be held in the State where the said Crimes shall have been committed; but when not committed within any State, the Trial shall be at such Place or Places as the Congress may by Law have directed.

Section 3. Treason against the United States, shall consist only in levying War against them, or in adhering to their Enemies, giving them Aid and Comfort. No Person shall be convicted of Treason unless on the Testimony of two Witnesses to the same overt Act, or on Confession in open Court.

The Congress shall have Power to declare the Punishment of Treason, but no Attainder of Treason shall work Corruption of Blood, or Forfeiture except during the Life of the Person attained.

Article IV

Section 1. Full Faith and Credit shall be given in each State to the public Acts, Records, and judicial Proceedings of every other State. And the Congress may by general Laws prescribe the Manner in which such Acts, Records and Proceedings shall be proved, and the Effect thereof.

Section 2. The Citizens of each State shall be entitled to all Privileges and Immunities of Citizens in the several States.

A Person charged in any State with Treason, Felony, or other Crime, who shall flee from Justice, and be found in another State, shall on Demand of the executive Authority of the State from which he fled, be delivered up, to be removed to the State having Jurisdiction of the Crime.

No Person held to Service or Labour in one State, under the Laws thereof, escaping into another, shall, in Consequence of any Law or Regulation therein, be discharged from such Service or Labour, but shall be delivered up on Claim of the Party to whom such Service or Labour may be due.

Section 3. New States may be admitted by the Congress into this Union; but no new State shall be formed or erected within the Jurisdiction of any other State; nor any State be formed by the Junction of two or more States, or Parts of States, without the Consent of the Legislatures of the States concerned as well as of the Congress.

The Congress shall have Power to dispose of and make all needful Rules and Regulations respecting the Territory or other Property belonging to the United States; and nothing in this Constitution shall be so construed as to Prejudice any Claims of the United States, or of any particular State.

Section 4. The United States shall guarantee to every State in this Union a Republican Form of Government, and shall protect each of them against Invasion; and on Application of the Legislature, or of the Executive (when the Legislature cannot be convened) against domestic Violence.

Article V

The Congress, whenever two thirds of both Houses shall deem it necessary, shall propose Amendments to this Constitution, or, on the Application of the Legislatures of two thirds of the several States, shall call a Convention for proposing Amendments, which, in either Case, shall be valid to all Intents and Purposes, as Part of this Constitution, when ratified by the Legislatures of three fourths of the several States, or by Conventions in three fourths thereof, as the one or the other Mode of Ratification may be proposed by the Congress; Provided that no Amendment which may be made prior to the Year One thousand eight hundred and eight shall in any Manner affect the first and fourth Clauses in the Ninth Section of the first Article; and that no State, without its Consent, shall be deprived of its equal Suffrage in the Senate.

Article VI

All Debts contracted and Engagements entered into, before the Adoption of this Constitution, shall be as valid against the United States under this Constitution, as under the Confederation.

This Constitution, and the Laws of the United States which shall be made in Pursuance thereof; and all Treaties made, or which shall be made, under the Authority of the United States, shall be the supreme Law of the Land; and the Judges in every State shall be bound thereby, any Thing in the Constitution or Laws of any State to the Contrary notwithstanding.

The Senators and Representatives before mentioned, and the Members of the several State Legislatures, and all executive and judicial Officers, both of the United States and of the several States, shall be bound by Oath or Affirmation, to support this Constitution; but no religious Test shall ever be required as a Qualification to any Office or public Trust under the United States.

Article VII

The Ratification of the Conventions of nine States, shall be sufficient for the Establishment of this Constitution between the States so ratifying the Same.

Done in Convention by the Unanimous Consent of the States present the Seventeenth Day of September in the Year of our Lord one thousand seven hundred and Eighty seven and of the Independence of the United States of America the Twelfth In Witness whereof We have hereunto subscribed our Names.

Appendix C
Amendments to the Constitution
of the United States of America

Amendment I
Ratified December 15, 1791

Congress shall make no law respecting an establishment of religion, or prohibiting the free exercise thereof; or abridging the freedom of speech, or of the press; or the right of the people peaceably to assemble, and to petition the Government for a redress of grievances.

Amendment II
Ratified December 15, 1791

A well regulated Militia, being necessary to the security of a free State, the right of the people to keep and bear Arms, shall not be infringed.

Amendment III
Ratified December 15, 1791

No Soldier shall, in time of peace be quartered in any house, without the consent of the Owner, nor in time of war, but in a manner to be prescribed by law.

Amendment IV
Ratified December 15, 1791

The right of the people to be secure in their persons, houses, papers, and effects, against unreasonable searches and seizures, shall not be violated, and no Warrants shall issue, but upon probable cause, supported by Oath or affirmation, and particularly describing the place to be searched, and the persons or things to be seized.

Amendment V

Ratified December 15, 1791

No person shall be held to answer for a capital, or otherwise infamous crime, unless on a presentment or indictment of a Grand Jury, except in cases arising in the land or naval forces, or in the Militia, when in actual service in time of War or public danger; nor shall any person be subject for the same offence to be twice put in jeopardy of life or limb, nor shall be compelled in any criminal case to be a witness against himself, nor be deprived of life, liberty, or property, without due process of law; nor shall private property be taken for public use, without just compensation.

Amendment VI

Ratified December 15, 1791

In all criminal prosecutions, the accused shall enjoy the right to a speedy and public trial, by an impartial jury of the State and district wherein the crime shall have been committed, which district shall have been previously ascertained by law, and to be informed of the nature and cause of the accusation; to be confronted with the witnesses against him; to have compulsory process for obtaining witnesses in his favor, and to have the assistance of counsel for his defence.

Amendment VII

Ratified December 15, 1791

In Suits at common law, where the value in controversy shall exceed twenty dollars, the right of trial by jury shall be preserved, and no fact tried by a jury, shall be otherwise reexamined in any Court of the United States, than according to the rules of the common law.

Amendment VIII

Ratified December 15, 1791

Excessive bail shall not be required, nor excessive fines imposed, nor cruel and unusual punishments inflicted.

Amendment IX
Ratified December 15, 1791

The enumeration in the Constitution, of certain rights, shall not be construed to deny or disparage others retained by the people.

Amendment X
Ratified December 15, 1791

The powers not delegated to the United States by the Constitution, nor prohibited by it to the States, are reserved to the States respectively, or to the people.

Amendment XI
Ratified February 7, 1795

The Judicial power of the United States shall not be construed to extend to any suit in law or equity, commenced or prosecuted against one of the United States by Citizens of another State, or by Citizens or Subjects of any Foreign State.

Amendment XII
Ratified June 15, 1804

The Electors shall meet in their respective states, and vote by ballot for President and Vice President, one of whom, at least, shall not be an inhabitant of the same state with themselves; they shall name in their ballots the person voted for as President, and in distinct ballots the person voted for as Vice-President, and they shall make distinct lists of all persons voted for as President, and of all persons voted for as Vice-President, and of the number of votes for each, which lists they shall sign and certify, and transmit sealed to the seat of the government of the United States, directed to the President of the Senate;—The President of the Senate shall, in the presence of the Senate and House of Representatives, open all the certificates and the votes shall then be counted;—The person having the greatest number of votes for President, shall be the President, if such number be a majority of the whole number of Electors appointed; and if no person have such majority, then from the persons having the highest numbers not exceeding three on the list of those voted for as President, the House of Representatives shall choose immediately, by ballot, the President. But in choosing the President, the votes shall be taken by states, the representation from each state having one vote; a quorum for this purpose shall consist of a member or members from two-thirds of the states, and a majority of all the states shall be necessary to a choice. And if the House of Representatives shall not choose a President whenever the right of choice shall devolve upon them, before the fourth day of March next following, then the Vice-President shall act as President, as in the case of the death or other constitutional disability of the President. The person having the greatest number of votes as Vice-President, shall be the Vice-President, if such number be a majority of the whole number of Electors appointed, and if no person have a majority, then from the two highest numbers on the list, the Senate shall choose the Vice-President; a quorum for the purpose shall consist of two-thirds of the whole number of Senators, and a majority of the whole number shall be necessary to a choice. But no person constitutionally ineligible to the office of President shall be eligible to that of Vice-President of the United States.

Amendment XIII
Ratified December 6, 1865

Section 1. Neither slavery nor involuntary servitude, except as a punishment for crime whereof the party shall have been duly convicted, shall exist within the United States, or any place subject to their jurisdiction.

Section 2. Congress shall have the power to enforce this article by appropriate legislation.

Amendment XIV
Ratified July 9, 1868

Section 1. All persons born or naturalized in the United States, and subject to the jurisdiction thereof, are citizens of the United States and of the State wherein they reside. No State shall make or enforce any law which shall abridge the privileges or immunities of citizens of the United States; nor shall any State deprive any person of life, liberty, or property, without due process of law; nor deny to any person within its jurisdiction the equal protection of the laws.

Section 2. Representatives shall be apportioned among the several States according to their respective numbers, counting the whole number of persons in each State, excluding Indians not taxed. But when the right to vote at any election for the choice of electors for President and Vice President of the United States, Representatives in Congress, the Executive and Judicial officers of a State, or the members of the Legislature thereof, is denied to any of the male inhabitants of such State, being twenty-one years of age, and citizens of the United States, or in any way abridged, except for participation in rebellion, or other crime, the basis of representation therein shall be reduced in the proportion which the number of such male citizens shall bear to the whole number of male citizens twenty-one years of age in such State.

Section 3. No person shall be a Senator or Representative in Congress, or elector of President and Vice President, or hold any office, civil or military, under the United States, or under any State, who, having previously taken an oath, as a member of Congress, or as an officer of the United States, or as a member of any State legislature, or as an executive or judicial officer of any State, to support the Constitution of the United States, shall have engaged in insurrection or rebellion against the same, or given aid or comfort to the enemies thereof. But Congress may by a vote of two-thirds of each House, remove such disability.

Section 4. The validity of the public debt of the United States, authorized by law, including debts incurred for payment of pensions and bounties for services in suppressing insurrection or rebellion, shall not be questioned. But neither the United States nor any State shall assume or pay any debt or obligation incurred in aid of insurrection or rebellion against the United States, or any claim for the loss or emancipation of any slave; but all such debts, obligations and claims shall be held illegal and void.

Section 5. The Congress shall have power to enforce, by appropriate legislation, the provisions of this article.

Amendment XV

Ratified February 3, 1870

Section 1. The right of citizens of the United States to vote shall not be denied or abridged by the United States or by any State on account of race, color, or previous condition of servitude.

Section 2. The Congress shall have power to enforce this article by appropriate legislation.

Amendment XVI

Ratified February 3, 1913

The Congress shall have power to lay and collect taxes on incomes, from whatever source derived, without apportionment among the several States, and without regard to any census or enumeration.

Amendment XVII

Ratified April 8, 1913

The Senate of the United States shall be composed of two Senators from each State, elected by the people thereof, for six years; and each Senator shall have one vote. The electors in each State shall have the qualifications requisite for electors of the most numerous branch of the State legislatures.

When vacancies happen in the representation of any State in the Senate, the executive authority of such State shall issue writs of election to fill such vacancies: Provided, That the legislature of any State may empower the executive thereof to make temporary appointments until the people fill the vacancies by election as the legislature may direct.

This amendment shall not be so construed as to affect the election or term of any Senator chosen before it becomes valid as part of the Constitution.

Amendment XVIII

Ratified January 16, 1919

Section 1. After one year from the ratification of this article the manufacture, sale, or transportation of intoxicating liquors within, the importation thereof into, or the exportation thereof from the United States and all territory subject to the jurisdiction thereof for beverage purposes is hereby prohibited.

Section 2. The Congress and the several States shall have concurrent power to enforce this article by appropriate legislation.

Section 3. This article shall be inoperative unless it shall have been ratified as an amendment to the Constitution by the legislatures of the several States, as provided in the Constitution, within seven years from the date of the submission hereof to the States by the Congress.

Amendment XIX
Ratified August 18, 1920

The right of citizens of the United States to vote shall not be denied or abridged by the United States or by any State on account of sex.

Congress shall have power to enforce this article by appropriate legislation.

Amendment XX
Ratified January 23, 1933

Section 1. The terms of the President and Vice President shall end at noon on the 20th day of January, and the terms of Senators and Representatives at noon on the 3d day of January, of the years in which such terms would have ended if this article had not been ratified; and the terms of their successors shall then begin.

Section 2. The Congress shall assemble at least once in every year, and such meeting shall begin at noon on the 3d day of January, unless they shall by law appoint a different day.

Section 3. If, at the time fixed for the beginning of the term of the President, the President elect shall have died, the Vice President elect shall become President. If a President shall not have been chosen before the time fixed for the beginning of his term, or if the President elect shall have failed to qualify, then the Vice President elect shall act as President until a President shall have qualified; and the Congress may by law provide for the case wherein neither a President elect nor a Vice President elect shall have qualified, declaring who shall then act as President, or the manner in which one who is to act shall be selected, and such person shall act accordingly until a President or Vice President shall have qualified.

Section 4. The Congress may by law provide for the case of the death of any of the persons from whom the House of Representatives may choose a President whenever the right of choice shall have devolved upon them, and for the case of the death of any of the persons from whom the Senate may choose a Vice President whenever the right of choice shall have devolved upon them.

Section 5. Sections 1 and 2 shall take effect on the 15th day of October following the ratification of this article.

Section 6. This article shall be inoperative unless it shall have been ratified as an amendment to the Constitution by the legislatures of three-fourths of the several States within seven years from the date of its submission.

Amendment XXI
Ratified December 5, 1933

Section 1. The eighteenth article of amendment to the Constitution of the United States is hereby repealed.

Section 2. The transportation or importation into any State, Territory, or possession of the United States for delivery or use therein of intoxicating liquors, in violation of the laws thereof, is hereby prohibited.

Section 3. This article shall be inoperative unless it shall have been ratified as an amendment to the Constitution by conventions in the several States, as provided in the Constitution, within seven years from the date of the submission hereof to the States by the Congress.

Amendment XXII
Ratified February 27, 1951

Section 1. No person shall be elected to the office of the President more than twice, and no person who has held the office of President, or acted as President, for more than two years of a term to which some other person was elected President shall be elected to the office of the President more than once.

But this Article shall not apply to any person holding the office of President when this Article was proposed by the Congress, and shall not prevent any person who may be holding the office of President, or acting as President, during the term within which this Article becomes operative from holding the office of President or acting as President during the remainder of such term.

Section 2. This article shall be inoperative unless it shall have been ratified as an amendment to the Constitution by the legislatures of three-fourths of the several States within seven years from the date of its submission to the States by the Congress.

Amendment XXIII
Ratified March 29, 1961

Section 1. The District constituting the seat of Government of the United States shall appoint in such manner as the Congress may direct:

A number of electors of President and Vice President equal to the whole number of Senators and Representatives in Congress to which the District would be entitled if it were a State, but in no event more than the least populous State; they shall be in addition to those appointed by the States, but they shall be considered, for the purposes of the election of President and Vice President, to be electors appointed by a State; and they shall meet in the District and perform such duties as provided by the twelfth article of amendment.

Section 2. The Congress shall have power to enforce this article by appropriate legislation.

Amendment XXIV
Ratified January 23, 1964

Section 1. The right of citizens of the United States to vote in any primary or other election for President or Vice President, for electors for President or Vice President, or for Senator or Representative in Congress, shall not be denied or abridged by the United States or any State by reason of failure to pay any poll tax or other tax.

Section 2. The Congress shall have the power to enforce this article by appropriate legislation.

Amendment XXV

Ratified February 10, 1967

Section 1. In case of the removal of the President from office or of his death or resignation, the Vice President shall become President.

Section 2. Whenever there is a vacancy in the office of the Vice President, the President shall nominate a Vice President who shall take office upon confirmation by a majority vote of both Houses of Congress.

Section 3. Whenever the President transmits to the President pro tempore of the Senate and the Speaker of the House of Representatives his written declaration that he is unable to discharge the powers and duties of his office, and until he transmits to them a written declaration to the contrary, such powers and duties shall be discharged by the Vice President as Acting President.

Section 4. Whenever the Vice President and a majority of either the principal officers of the executive departments or of such other body as Congress may by law provide, transmit to the President pro tempore of the Senate and the Speaker of the House of Representatives their written declaration that the President is unable to discharge the powers and duties of his office, the Vice President shall immediately assume the powers and duties of the office as Acting President.

Thereafter, when the President transmits to the President pro tempore of the Senate and the Speaker of the House of Representatives his written declaration that no inability exists, he shall resume the powers and duties of his office unless the Vice President and a majority of either the principal officers of the executive department or of such other body as Congress may by law provide, transmit within four days to the President pro tempore of the Senate and the Speaker of the House of Representatives their written declaration that the President is unable to discharge the powers and duties of his office. Thereupon Congress shall decide the issue, assembling within forty-eight hours for that purpose if not in session. If the Congress, within twenty-one days after receipt of the latter written declaration, or, if Congress is not in session, within twenty-one days after Congress is required to assemble, determines by two-thirds vote of both Houses that the President is unable to discharge the powers and duties of his office, the Vice President shall continue to discharge the same as Acting President; otherwise, the President shall resume the powers and duties of his office.

Amendment XXVI
Ratified July 1, 1971

Section 1. The right of citizens of the United States, who are eighteen years of age or older, to vote shall not be denied or abridged by the United States or by any State on account of age.

Section 2. The Congress shall have power to enforce this article by appropriate legislation.

Amendment XXVII
Ratified May 7, 1992

No law varying the compensation for the services of the Senators and Representatives shall take effect, until an election of Representatives shall have intervened.

Appendix D
Lessons from the
Confederate Constitution

ALTHOUGH THIS BOOK is concerned primarily with the constitutional documents and debates from the early 1770s to drafting and ratifying of the Bill of Rights in the late 1780s and early 1790s, it would be incomplete without some discussion of the Confederate Constitution of 1861. The Confederate Framers sought to revive the Constitution of 1787 by adding, deleting, and modifying various parts to (1) comport with the interpretation promised by the Federalists in the state ratification debates, and (2) correct perceived deficiencies revealed through time and practice. To truly study this document, we must push aside the present clamor averring that nothing can be gained from remembrance or study of the Confederate States of America ("CSA").

As of this writing, there is an effort to erase from the historical narrative any person or entity that does not share twenty-first century sensibilities about slavery or race relations. Across the South, city councils are voting to remove Confederate monuments. At Princeton University, progressive icon Woodrow Wilson (once the school's president) has fallen from favor because he held views supportive of government-enforced segregation. Students have demanded that his name be removed from all buildings throughout campus. In Iowa, the Democratic Party voted to rename its Jefferson-Jackson dinner because both Thomas Jefferson and Andrew Jackson were slave owners.

If Americans insist on applying modern sensibilities to people and institutions of the seventeenth and eighteenth centuries, then they will be compelled to abandon a collection of rich characters, debate, and experience. We risk missing important historical lessons and cannot learn from history when

262 | *Appendix D*

we approach the past with uncritical adherence to present-day values and concepts. With that admonishment about the dangers of presentism, let us turn to the Confederate Constitution, comparing certain relevant provisions to the U.S. Constitution, and see what it teaches us about checks on power and the disputes between the Federalists and Anti-Federalists.[1]

Preamble

U.S.: We, the people of the United States, in order to form a more perfect Union, establish justice, insure domestic tranquility, provide for the common defense, promote the general welfare, and secure the blessings of liberty to ourselves and our posterity, do ordain and establish this Constitution for the United States of America.

C.S.: We, the people of the Confederate States, each State acting in its sovereign and independent character, in order to form a permanent federal government, establish justice, insure domestic tranquillity, and secure the blessings of liberty to ourselves and our posterity invoking the favor and guidance of Almighty God do ordain and establish this Constitution for the Confederate States of America.

A preamble to a constitution or ordinary legislation should not be read as granting authority or limiting power; it is declaratory. Nonetheless, it expresses the underlying concepts of the drafter. A preamble in a constitution informs us about such matters as the objects of the government and the source of power.

In the Virginia ratifying convention, Patrick Henry questioned the Philadelphia Convention speaking in the name of "We the people." "My political curiosity, exclusive of my anxious solicitude for the public welfare, leads me to ask, Who authorized them to speak the language of, *We, the people*, instead of, *We, the states?*"[2] Henry went on to explain that states "are the characteristics and the soul of a confederation. If the states be not the agents of this compact, it must be one great, consolidated, national government, of the people of all the states."[3] (The Anti-Federalist concern about consolidation is fully discussed in Chapter 6).

In response to Henry, Madison admitted the new government was con-solidated in some areas, but stressed that in others it was strictly federal. He disagreed that the people of the nation were parties to the Constitution. He said that true parties were the people of "thirteen sovereignties."[4] Despite Madison's elucidation, nationalists would later point to the preamble as evidence that the Constitution was formed by one great national act.[5] The nationalists then argued from the preamble for various expansive agendas to "promote the general welfare" of the American people.

The Confederate Framers agreed with Henry that the states are the soul of a confederation. They also learned from experience that loose language can give rise to mischievous interpretations. Accordingly, they made clear that sovereignty remained in the several states. Thomas R.R. Cobb, a member of the committee that drafted the Confederate Constitution, observed that "[t]he Preamble of the Confederate Constitution holds unmistakably the sovereignty of the States and declares the Constitution to be a compact between them."[6] Sovereign states joined together to further mutual interests, but ultimate power rested in the states individually. The states were not forming a more perfect union, but a federal government. Not surprisingly, the Confederate Framers deleted any reference to the general welfare in their state-centered preamble.

Impeachment: Article I, Section 2, Clause 5

U.S.: The House of Representatives shall choose their Speaker and other offi-cers; and shall have the sole power of impeachment.

C.S.: The House of Representatives shall choose their Speaker and other officers; and shall have the sole power of impeachment; except that any judicial or other Federal officer, resident and acting solely within the limits of any State, may be impeached by a vote of two-thirds of both branches of the Legislature thereof.

Impeachment is a formal accusation of wrongdoing against a public official. A body that brings the charges is analogous to a grand jury. It is a way for the community to defend itself against the malfeasance of public servants. Under the U.S. Constitution, the House of Representatives issues the indictment against the offending federal official and the Senate adjudicates the case. The impeachment procedure is modeled on the British Constitution whereby the House of Commons levels an accusation and the House of Lords tries the alleged wrongdoer.

The Framers of the Confederate Constitution followed the U.S. model, but empowered a state legislature to bring charges against a Confederate official residing and acting within the state's boundaries. For example, if a Confederate district judge began making policy decisions under the guise of law, the state legislature, by a two-thirds vote in both houses, could level formal charges that would be adjudicated by the Confederate Senate. By granting state legislatures this power, the Confederacy sought to make its federal officers more accountable to the states.

Line Item Veto: Article I, Section 7, Clause 2

U.S.: Every bill which shall have passed the House of Representatives and the Senate, shall, before it become a law, be presented to the president of the United States; if he approve, he shall sign it, but if not, he shall return it, with his objections, to that house in which it shall have originated, who shall enter the objections at large on their journal, and proceed to reconsider it. If after such reconsideration, two thirds of that house shall agree to pass the bill, it shall be sent, together with the objections, to the other house, by which it shall likewise be reconsidered, and if approved by two-thirds of that house, it shall become a law. . . .

C.S.: Every bill which shall have passed both Houses, shall, before it becomes a law, be presented to the President of the Confederate States; if he approve, he shall sign it; but if not, he shall return it, with his objections, to that House in which it shall have originated, who shall enter the objections at large on their journal, and proceed to reconsider it. If, after such reconsideration, two-thirds of that House shall agree to pass the bill, it shall be sent, together with the objections, to the other House, by which it shall likewise be reconsidered, and if approved by two-thirds of that House, it shall become a law. . . . The President may approve any appropriation and disapprove any other appropriation in the same bill. In such case he shall, in signing the bill, designate the appropriations disapproved; and shall return a copy of such appropriations, with his objections, to the House in which the bill shall have originated; and the same proceedings shall then be had as in case of other bills disapproved by the President.

Under the U.S. Constitution, every bill passed by both houses of Congress must be presented to the president, who must sign the bill into law or return it to Congress. Understanding that the president's options are limited, Congress often attaches special interest riders to gigantic funding bills. Members of Congress engage in logrolling. They vote for wasteful projects furthering local interests offered on a *quid pro quo* basis. The president cannot reject the riders and amendments without vetoing the entire bill. Logrolling was not a concern for the Anti-Federalists because no one envisioned the massive bills passed today dealing with diverse subject matter and loaded with pork barrel. The only appropriations bill passed by the First Congress in 1789 contained fewer than 200 words. Not so anymore.

The Confederate Framers believed that the U.S. Congress had abandoned the splendid simplicity of the First Congress and embarked on a course of abusive spending practices. They lamented that the president's hands had been tied by the all-or-nothing veto found in the U.S. Constitution. A Confederate president could veto individual line items that he deemed improvident spending and this would impose a check on congressional fiscal misbehavior. Robert H. Smith, an Alabama lawyer and delegate to Provisional Confederate States Congress, predicted that the line-item veto would allow the president to "arrest corrupt or illegitimate expenditures" and to protect the fiscal integrity of the Confederacy.[7]

In 1996 the U.S. Congress attempted to give the president a line item veto by statute, but the Supreme Court struck the law as violating the express language of the Constitution.[8]

Spending: Article I, Section 8, Clause 1

U.S.: The Congress shall have the power

1. To lay and collect taxes, duties, imposts and excises, to pay the debts and provide for the common defence and general welfare of the United States;

but all duties, imposts and excises shall be uniform throughout the United States: . . . .

C.S.: The Congress shall have power

(1) To lay and collect taxes, duties, imposts, and excises for revenue, necessary to pay the debts, provide for the common defense, and carry on the Government of the Confederate States; but no bounties shall be granted from the Treasury; nor shall any duties or taxes on importations from foreign nations be laid to promote or foster any branch of industry; and all duties, imposts, and excises shall be uniform throughout the Confederate States.

As discussed in Chapter 7, the Anti-Federalists correctly expressed concern about the national government claiming the power to spend money for purposes not specifically enumerated in the Constitution. In 1936, the Supreme Court endorsed Congress's claim that money could be spent for anything conducive to the national welfare. Today, Congress bribes and threatens the states with money (or the loss thereof) to implement policies that otherwise would be beyond federal authority.

The Confederate Framers did away with the general welfare language. They did not want the Confederate Congress abusing this clause as had the U.S. Congress. Much sectional conflict had been caused by the American System of Henry Clay and others who favored congressional appropriation of funds for building roads, dredging rivers, and digging canals to promote commerce and industry for the general welfare. The monies from these projects came from tariff revenue predominantly paid by Southerners. The projects themselves were mostly built in the North. Southerners resented bearing the tax burden for public works projects that did not benefit their states. According to historian William C. Davis: "By and large, Southerners believed that work on Charleston Harbor should be paid for by South Carolina; Louisiana should pay for enhancements to the docks in New Orleans."[9]

In addition to the removal of the general welfare language, the Confederates prohibited Congress from appropriating money for internal improvements other than navigational aids such as beacons and buoys.[10] Such changes were attempts to keep government within the bounds set by the Confederate Constitution.

To address Southern disgust at the protective tariff, the Confederates prohibited their Congress from imposing taxes or duties on imports to encourage any branch of industry. When addressing the Senate before the passage of the Tariff Bill of 1842, John C. Calhoun argued that when tariffs are levied for protective purposes, government descends "from its high and appointed duty, and become[s] the agent of a portion of the community to extort, under the guise of protection, tribute from the rest of the community; and thus defeat[s] the end of its institution, by perverting powers, intended for the protection of all, into the means of oppressing one portion for the benefit of another."[II] Thus, the Confederate Congress could not use the tariff to benefit one part of the community at the expense of the rest.

Appropriations: Article I, Section 9, Clauses 9 & 10

U.S.: No analogous provision.

C.S.: (9) Congress shall appropriate no money from the Treasury except by a vote of two-thirds of both Houses, taken by yeas and nays, unless it be asked and estimated for by some one of the heads of departments and submitted to Congress by the President; or for the purpose of paying its own expenses and contingencies; or for the payment of claims against the Confederate States, the justice of which shall have been judicially declared by a tribunal for the investigation of claims against the Government, which it is hereby made the duty of Congress to establish.

(10) All bills appropriating money shall specify in Federal currency the exact amount of each appropriation and the purposes for which it is made; and Congress shall grant no extra compensation to any public contractor, officer, agent, or servant, after such contract shall have been made or such service rendered.

The U.S. Constitution has no provision analogous to these two clauses. Under the Constitution of 1787, Congress needs only a simple majority to appropriate funds.

In many circumstances, Confederate appropriations required a two-thirds majority rather than a simple majority. Without the President's request, for example, a two-thirds majority of both Houses was necessary for the Confederate Congress to spend any money. The Confederate Framers sought to impose fiscal discipline on the new government and discourage pork-barrel spending. Robert H. Smith, in a speech to the people of Alabama, declared that this change in constitutional structure recognized that "the chief Executive head of the country and his Cabinet should understand the pecuniary wants of the Confederacy" better than the Congress."[12] In elaborating further on this provision, Professor Marshall L. DeRosa observes: "The executive branch was constitutionally responsible for budgeting and accounting, serving as a brake on regionally based legislative coalitions seeking to maximize their influence over budgeting."[13] This one provision, if adopted in the U.S. Constitution, would eliminate much of the spending that goes on today.

Clause 10 took aim at perpetual cost overruns associated with government projects. According to Professor DeRosa: "This provision effectively prohibits cost overruns, thereby enhancing the credibility of the negotiating process for government contracts."[14] Florida State University's Randall G. Holcombe adds that the clause ensures "that there would be no open-ended commitments and no entitlement programs in the Confederate States."[15]

Single Subject: Article I, Section 9, Clause 20

U.S.: No analogous provision.

C.S.: Every law, or resolution having the force of law, shall relate to but one subject, and that shall be expressed in the title.

The single-subject rule found in the Confederate Constitution was designed to restrain lawmakers and to protect against the unsavory practice of logrolling (discussed in the line item veto section above). Many states and localities have adopted the single-subject rule to bring transparency to the legislative process. Attorney Brett Joshpe predicts that "[a] federal single subject rule would also end the practice of Congress passing bills, like the Affordable Care Act, that few people have read, that are far too complicated for anyone to understand, and that are filled with special interest concessions on varying topics."[16] The Confederate Framers were far ahead of their time with this provision targeting logrolling and massive bills bulging with special interest legislation unrelated to the general subject or purpose behind the original legislation.

Presidential Term Limit: Article II, Section 1

U.S.: The Executive power shall be vested in a President of the United States of America. He shall hold office during the term of four years. . . .

C.S.: The executive power shall be vested in a President of the Confederate States of America. He and the Vice President shall hold their offices for the term of six years; but the President shall not be reeligible.

Under the Constitution of 1787, the president was eligible for reelection after serving a four-year term. Federalists believed that a term of at least four years would provide stability to an administration without making the president too dependent on public approval. Men supporting re-eligibility argued that the possibility of reelection would encourage a president to be a dutiful magistrate so he could earn an additional term from his countrymen. Others believed that a term limit could unnecessarily remove from office a man that the people believed best suited for the job. Thomas Jefferson and the Anti-Federalists objected that re-eligibility violated the basic principles of rotation in office. (Anti-Federalist arguments for term limits for federal officials are discussed in Chapter 19).

The Confederate Framers understood the need for a substantial term to provide stability, but rejected the re-eligibility of the president. According to DeRosa, "[w]ith the limitation to one six-year term, the hope was to elevate the statesmanship of the CSA president, while limiting the opportunities for patronage."[17] Of course, the United States eventually recognized the benefit of a presidential term limit and ratified the Twenty-Second Amendment in 1951.

Amendment Process: Article V, Section 1, Clause 1

U.S.: The Congress, whenever two-thirds of both houses shall deem it necessary, shall propose amendments to this constitution, or on the application of the legislatures of two-thirds of the several states, shall call a convention for proposing amendments, which, in either case, shall be valid to all intents and purposes, as part of this constitution, when ratified by the legislatures of three-fourths of the several states, or by conventions in three-fourths thereof, as the one or the other mode of ratification may be proposed by the Congress: Provided, that no amendment which may be made prior to the year 1808, shall in any manner affect the first and fourth clauses in the ninth section of the first article; and that no state, without its consent, shall be deprived of its equal suffrage in the Senate.

C.S.: Upon the demand of any three States, legally assembled in their several conventions, the Congress shall summon a convention of all the States, to take into consideration such amendments to the Constitution as the said States shall concur in suggesting at the time when the said demand is made; and should any of the proposed amendments to the Constitution be agreed on by the said convention, voting by States, and the same be ratified by the Legislatures of two- thirds of the several States, or by conventions in two-thirds thereof, as the one or the other mode of ratification may be proposed by the general convention, they shall thenceforward form a part of this Constitution. But no State shall, without its consent, be deprived of its equal representation in the Senate.

As discussed in Chapter 14, Congress controls the procedure for amending the U.S. Constitution. Congress alone proposes amendments to the Constitution and it reviews state requests for a convention before calling one. The convention method of amending the Constitution has never been tried because of fears about a runaway convention and other hurdles. Accordingly, the states and the people must look to national legislature for amendments.

The Confederate Framers declined to give their Congress a role in suggesting amendments. Because the Confederates viewed their charter as a compact between sovereign states, a mere three states meeting in convention could summon a constitutional convention for amending the Confederate Constitution. The Confederate Framers also made it easier to ratify amendments by reducing the number of concurring states to two-thirds from three-fourths. By choosing the constitutional convention method for amendments, the Confederate Framers apparently did not fret about a runaway convention.

A number of differences exist between the constitutions of the Confederate States and the United States. Only a few of the differences, germane to the Articles of Confederation and the dispute between the Federalists and Anti-Federalists, have been discussed here. Certainly not all the editing done by the Confederate Framers would have pleased the Anti-Federalists. Brutus and his compatriots would have questioned the augmentation of executive power through the line-item veto and executive control over budgeting. They likely would not have anticipated practices leading the Southerners to include a single-subject provision in the Confederate Constitution. But they certainly would have endorsed the deletions, changes, and additions concerning the preamble, impeachment, the General Welfare Clause, and term limits.

If Americans desire to place limits on our omnipotent national government, the Confederate Constitution should be studied along with the various amendments suggested by Anti-Federalists in the state ratifying conventions. If we will listen, the Confederate Framers have much to teach us.

Notes

Introduction

1. Paul Greenberg, Return of the anti-federalists, January 24, 2006, www.washingtontimes.com.
2. Cecelia M. Kenyon, *Men of Little Faith: The Anti-Federalists on the Nature of Representative Government,* 12 Wm. & Mary Q. 3 (1955).
3. *Federalist* No. 1, p. 3 (Alexander Hamilton) (Bantam Books ed., 1982).
4. Greenberg, *supra* note 1.
5. Jon E. Semonche, The Debate over the Constitution: Federalists vs. Antifederalists, www.dlt.ncssm.edu.
6. *Id.*
7. The Federal Farmer, Letter VI (1787), *TAF* 188.

Chapter 1

1. Letter from the New York Committee of Fifty-One to the Boston Committee of Correspondence (1774), reprinted in *A Need of a History of New York* 8 (1915).
2. Thomas Jefferson, A Summary View of the Rights of British America (1774), reprinted in *Paine and Jefferson on Liberty* 3 (Lloyd S. Kramer, ed., 1988).
3. *Id.* at 5.
4. *Id.* at 14.
5. *Id.* at 20–21.

6. *Id.* at 23.
7. James Wilson, Considerations on the Nature and Extent of the Legislative Authority of the British Parliament (1774), reprinted in 1 *Collected Works of James Wilson* 3 (Kermit L. Hall & Mark David Hall, eds., 2007).
8. *Id.* at 4.
9. *Id.* at 18.
10. *Id.* at 28.
11. John Adams to Abigail Adams, September 18, 1774, *LDC* 1:80.
12. *Id.*
13. Extracts from Votes of the Assembly (1774), *JCC* 1:20.
14. Joseph Galloway to William Franklin, September 5, 1774, *LDC* 1:27.
15. Caesar Rodney to Thomas Rodney, September 9, 1774, *LDC* 1:58.
16. *DJA* 2:123.
17. *Id.* at 124–25.
18. *Id.* at 125.
19. Samuel Ward to Samuel Ward, Jr., September 9, 1774, *LDC* 1:59.
20. *DJA* 2:128.
21. *Id.* at 129.
22. *Id.* at 130.
23. *Id.* at 130.
24. The Suffolk Resolves (1774), *JCC* 1:33.
25. *Id.*
26. *Id.* at 35.
27. *Id.* at 36.
28. *JCC* 1:39.

29. *DJA* 2:134–35.
30. Samuel Adams to Charles Chauncy, September 19, 1774, *LDC* 1:83.
31. *Id.* at 138.
32. *Id.*
33. Robert Treat Paine's Notes for a Speech in Congress (1774), *LDC* 1:146.
34. Galloway's Plan (1774), *JCC* 1:44.
35. *Id.* at 49.
36. *Id.* at 50.
37. *Id.* at 49.
38. *DJA* 2:142.
39. *Id.* at 143.
40. The Association (1774), *JCC* 1:76.
41. Address to the People of Great Britain (1774), *JCC* 1:82.
42. *Id.*
43. *Id.*
44. *Id.*
45. *Id.* at 83.
46. *Id.* at 89.
47. Declaration and Resolves (1774), *JCC* 1:66.
48. *Id.* at 68
49. *Id.* at 68–69.
50. Richard Henry Lee to William Lee, September 20, 1774, *LDC* 1:87.
51. *Id.* at 88.

Chapter 2

1. Edmund Burke, Speech on Conciliation with the Colonies (1775), *TFC* 1:6.
2. Burgoyne quoted in Stanley Weintraub, *Iron Tears* 6 (2005).
3. Resolutions Passed in a Committee of the Whole House (1775), *American Archives,* 4th Series, 2:451.
4. Thomas Johnson, Jr. to Horatio Gates, May 3, 1775, *LDC* 1:334.
5. Benjamin Franklin to David Hartley, May 8, 1775, *LDC* 1:335.
6. Richard Caswell to William Caswell, May 11, 1775, *LDC* 1:339.
7. Joseph Hewes to Samuel Johnston, May 11, 1775, *LDC* 1:342.

8. John Adams to Isaac Smith, Sr., June 7, 1775, *LDC* 1:452.
9. Letter from the Massachusetts Provincial Congress (1775), *JCC* 2:25.
10. *JCC* 2:44.
11. Silas Deane's Diary, May 15, 1775, *LDC* 1:351.
12. *Id.* at 352.
13. John Dickinson's Notes for a Speech in Congress, [May 23–25], 1775, *LDC* 1:372.
14. *Id.* at 376.
15. *Id.*
16. *Id.* at 378.
17. John Adams to Moses Gill, June 10, 1775, *LDC* 1:466.
18. *Id.*
19. John Adams to James Warren, July 6, 1775, *WAL* 75.
20. Petition to the King (1775), *JCC* 2:159.
21. Gordon S. Wood, *Radicalism of the American Revolution* 171 (1992); *see also* Bernard Bailyn, *The Ideological Origins of the American Revolution* 301–19 (1967).
22. Gouverneur Morris to Mr. Penn, May 20, 1774, *American Archives,* 4th Series, 1:343.
23. A Proclamation, by the King, for suppressing Rebellion and Sedition, August 23, 1775, *American Archives,* 4th Series, 3:240–41.
24. Samuel Adams to James Warren, October 3, 1775, *WAL* 125.
25. Merrill Jensen, *The Articles of Confederation* 90 (1940).
26. Thomas Paine, Common Sense (1776), reprinted in *Paine and Jefferson on Liberty* 39 (Lloyd S. Kramer, ed., 1988).
27. *Id.* at 60.
28. M.E. Bradford, *A Better Guide Than Reason* 85 (1994).
29. *JCC* 5:425. *See also* John Ferling, *Whirlwind* 57 (2015).
30. *JCC* 6:1,088.
31. *Id.* at 1,089.

32. *Id.*
33. *Id.*
34. *Id.* at 1,090.
35. The Declaration of Independence (1776), reprinted in *From Magna Carta to the Constitution* 58 (David L. Brooks, ed., 1993).
36. *Id.* at 59.
37. *Id.* at 60.

Chapter 3

1. John Adams to Patrick Henry, June 3, 1776, reprinted in 1 *Letters of Members of the Continental Congress* 471 (Edmund C. Burnett, ed., 1921).
2. Dickinson Draft (1776), *JCC* 5:546–47.
3. *Id.* at 547.
4. *Id.* at 548.
5. *Id.*
6. *Id.*
7. *JCC* 6:1,100.
8. *Id.* at 1,080.
9. Merrill Jensen, *The Articles of Confederation* 146 (1940).
10. *JCC* 6:1,102.
11. *Id.*
12. *Id.* at 1,103.
13. *Id.*
14. *Id.* at 1,104.
15. *Id.*
16. *Id.*
17. *Id.* at 1,105.
18. *Id.* at 1,082–83.
19. *Id.* at 1,083.
20. Thomas Burke, Abstract of Debates in Congress (1777), *FTC* 1:445.
21. *Id.*
22. *Id.*
23. Thomas Burke to Richard Caswell, April 29, 1777, reprinted in *States' Rights and American Federalism: A Documentary History* 36 (Frederick D. Drake & Lynn R. Nelson, eds., 1999).

24. *Id.*
25. *Id. See also* Murray N. Rothbard, *Conceived in Liberty* 1,367 (2011).
26. Art. of Conf. art II.
27. Art. of Conf. art IV.
28. Art. of Conf. art V.
29. *Id.*
30. Art. of Conf. art VIII.
31. Art. of Conf. art IX.
32. *Id.*
33. *Id.*
34. There were, of course, "executive departments" functioning during the Confederation period: Postal, Foreign Affairs, Treasury, and War.
35. Art. of Conf. art XII.
36. Art of Conf. art XIII.
37. Robert W. Hoffert, *A Politics of Tensions* 92 (1992); *see also* Ralph Clark Chandler, *Public Administration under the Articles of Confederation*, 13 Pub. Admin. Q. 433, 434 (1990).
38. *See* Keith L. Dougherty, *Collective Action Under the Articles of Confederation* 25–33 (2001).
39. Art. of Conf. art IX.
40. Samuel Elliot Morrison, *The Oxford History of the American People* 277 (1965). *But see* Rothbard, *supra* note 25, at 1,368 (arguing that "the Articles were still a momentous step from the loose but effective unity of the original Continental Congress to the creation of a powerful new central government").

Chapter 4

1. For a laundry list of alleged defects compiled from the writings of those who attended the Philadelphia Convention, see Max Farrand, *The Federal Constitution and the Defects of the Confederation*, 2 Amer. Pol. Sci. Rev. 532, 535–37 (1908).

2. Keith L. Dougherty, *Collective Action Under the Articles of Confederation* 53 (2001).

3. JM to TJ, March 27 & 28, 1780, *TRL* 1:136.

4. James M. Varnum to Governor Greene, March 16, 1781, *LDC* 6:41.

5. *See* Grant of a Power to Collect Import Duties (1781), *JDH* 1:140.

6. Grant of Temporary Power to Collect Import Duties. . . (1783), *JDH* 1:146.

7. Treaty of Peace between the United States and Great Britain (1783), reprinted in *Confederation and Constitution 1781–1789*, at 30 (Forrest McDonald, ed., 1968).

8. Proceedings and Report of the Commissioners at Annapolis, Maryland (1786), *JDH* 1:184.

9. Confederation Congress Calls the Constitutional Convention (1787), *JDH* 1:187.

10. Resolutions Proposed by Mr. Randolph in Convention (1787), reprinted in *The Anti-Federalist Papers and the Constitutional Convention Debates* 37 (Ralph Ketcham, ed., 1986). Later in life, Madison contended that he always expected an enumeration of powers and that the broad language of the Virginia Plan was not opposed to such an enumeration. *See* Lance Banning, *The Sacred Fire of Liberty* 159 (1995).

11. The New Jersey Plan (1787), reprinted in Ketcham, *supra* note 10, at 65.

12. Donald Lutz has correctly pointed out that "from one-half to two-thirds of what is in the Articles showed up in the Federalist Constitution of 1787." Donald S. Lutz, *The Articles of Confederation as the Background to the Federal Republic*, 20 Publius 55, 66 (1990).

13. U.S. Const. art. VI.

14. *Federalist* No. 32, p. 152 (Alexander Hamilton) (Bantam Books, ed., 1982); *Federalist* No. 40, p. 195 (James Madison) (Bantam Books, ed., 1982).

15. *Federalist* No. 46, p. 237 (James Madison) (Bantam Books, ed., 1982).

16. *Federalist* No. 45, p. 236 (James Madison) (Bantam Books, ed., 1982).

17. *Id. See also* Fisher Ames, Speech (1788), *Friends* 199 ("But the business of the federal government will be very different. The objects of their power are few and national.").

18. Peletiah Webster, The Weakness of Brutus Exposed (1787), *Friends* 185.

19. *Federalist* No. 31, p. 152 (Alexander Hamilton) (Bantam Books, ed., 1982).

20. James Wilson, Speech (1787), *Friends* 241.

21. The Federal Farmer, Letter V (1787), *TAF* 180.

22. An Old Whig, Essay IV (1787), *TAF* 335.

Chapter 5

1. Charles Louis de Secondat, Baron de la Brède et de Montesquieu, *The Spirit of the Laws* bk VIII, ch. 16 (David Wallace Carrithers, ed., 1977).

2. *Id.* bk II, ch. 1 at 107.

3. Aristotle, *Politics* 136–7 (2000).

4. *Id.* at 239.

5. *Id.* at 240.

6. John Adams, 1 *A Defence of the Constitutions of Government*. . . xix & xxii (1794).

7. *Federalist* No. 39, p. 190 (James Madison) (Bantam Books, ed., 1982).

8. Patrick Henry, Speech in the Virginia Convention (1788), *Elliot's Debates* 3:396.

9. *Id.*

10. TJ to Monsieur Du Pont de Nemours, April 24, 1816, http://etext.virginia.edu.
11. TJ to Samuel Kercheval, July 12, 1816, reprinted in *The Complete Jefferson* 287 (Saul L. Padover, ed., 1943).
12. Address of the Minority of the Pennsylvania Convention (1787), *TAF* 533. For a good discussion of the question of scale, see Donald Livingston, American Republicanism and the Forgotten Question of Size, in *Rethinking the American Union for the Twenty-First Century* 125 (Donald Livingston, ed., 2012).
13. An Old Whig, Essay IV (1787), *TAF* 335.
14. *Id.*
15. Cato, Letter III (1787), *TAF* 10.
16. George Mason, Speech in the Virginia Convention (1788), *Elliot's Debates* 3:30.
17. Montesquieu, *supra* note 1, bk VIII, ch. 16 at 176.
18. *Id.*
19. *Id.* at bk IX, ch 1, at 183.
20. Johannes Althusius, *Politica* 69 (Frederick S. Carney, ed., 1995).
21. George Mason, Speech in the Virginia Convention (1788), *Elliot's Debates* 3:32. *See also Elliot's Debates* 2:13 (remarks of William Heath in the Massachusetts ratifying convention).
22. Brutus, Essay I (1787), *TAF* 380.
23. *Id.*
24. Federal Farmer, Letter XVII (1788), *TAF* 296.
25. Federal Farmer, Letter III (1787), *TAF* 167.
26. Cato, Letter V (1787), *TAF* 21.
27. Centinel, Letter I (1787), *TAF* 42.
28. Federal Farmer, Letter XI (1788), *TAF* 235.
29. Brutus, Essay I (1787), *TAF* 382.
30. *Id.* at 383.
31. Address of the Minority of the Pennsylvania Convention (1787), *TAF* 546–47.
32. *Federalist* No. 10, p. 43 (James Madison) (Bantam Books, ed., 1982). Faction was seen as a great danger to republican government. Fisher Ames, at the Massachusetts ratifying convention echoed Madison and described "[f]action and enthusiasm" as "the instruments by which popular governments are destroyed." *Elliot's Debates* 2:10.
33. *JM Notes* 76.
34. *Federalist* No. 10, p. 45 (James Madison) (Bantam Books, ed., 1982).
35. *Id.* at 47. For a discussion on the likelihood of Madison collaborating with Hamilton on *Federalist* No. 10 and how this essay builds on the previous number written by Hamilton, see Kevin R.C. Gutzman, *James Madison and the Making of America* 144–46 (2012).
36. *Federalist* No. 10, p. 46–47 (James Madison) (Bantam Books, ed., 1982).
37. *Id.* at 47.
38. *Id.* at 48. *See also Federalist* No. 51, p. 264 (James Madison) (Bantam Books, ed., 1982) (arguing that "by comprehending in society so many separate descriptions of citizens, as will render an unjust combination of a majority of the whole, very improbable" faction is controlled).
39. *Federalist* No. 10, p. 43 (James Madison) (Bantam Books, ed., 1982).
40. Cato, Letter III (1787), *TAF* 11.
41. *Id.*
42. TJ to Samuel Kercheval, July 12, 1816, reprinted in *The Complete Jefferson* 287 (Saul L. Padover, ed., 1943).
43. *Id.*
44. *Id.*

Chapter 6

1. Letter from the Hon. Robert Yates and the Hon. John Lansing, jun., Esquires, *Elliot's Debates* 1:480.
2. *Elliot's Debates* 3:22. An almost identical point was made by Samuel Nason in the Massachusetts ratifying convention. *See Elliot's Debates* 2:134.
3. *Elliot's Debates* 3:350.
4. Address of the Minority of the Pennsylvania Convention (1787), *TAF* 534.
5. *See* James McClellan, *Liberty, Order, and Justice* 255–56 (2000).
6. Forrest McDonald, *States' Rights and the Union* 7–9 (2000).
7. *Elliot's Debates* 3:44.
8. *JM Notes* 15.
9. *Federalist* No. 39 p. 195 (James Madison), (Bantam Books, ed., 1992).
10. *Id.* at 193.
11. *Id.* at 194.
12. *Id.* at 195.
13. *See* Gordon Wood, *Creation of the American Republic* 351–54 (1969).
14. Response of the Worcester Committee of Correspondence (1778), reprinted in *The Popular Sources of Political Authority* 371 (Oscar and Mary F. Handlin, eds., 1966).
15. Samuel Adams, A State of the Rights of the Colonists, reprinted in *Tracts of the American Revolution* 236 (Merrill Jensen, ed., 1967).
16. Centinel, Letter V (1787), *TAF* 81.
17. *Id.*
18. Brutus, Essay VI (1787), *TAF* 416.
19. *Elliot's Debates* 2:403.
20. *Id.*
21. Federal Farmer, Letter V (1787), *TAF* 180.
22. Federal Farmer, Letter III (1787), *TAF* 164.
23. *Elliot's Debates* 3:53.
24. *Id.*
25. Bob Williams, How states should prepare for federal budget cuts, September 1, 2011, www.statebudget solutions.org.

Chapter 7

1. U.S. Const. art I, § 8.
2. Federal Farmer, Letter III, *TAF* 163.
3. *Id.*
4. *Id.* at 163–64.
5. *Id.* at 165.
6. An Old Whig, Essay VI (1787), *TAF* 349.
7. *Elliot's Debates* 2:132.
8. Patrick Henry, Speech (1788), *TAF* 689.
9. *Elliot's Debates* 2:217. A similar proposal was offered by Samuel Spencer in the North Carolina ratifying convention. *See Elliot's Debates* 4:81.
10. *Federalist* No. 15 (Alexander Hamilton) 70 (Bantam Books, ed., 1992).
11. *Id.* at 74.
12. *Federalist* No. 22, p. 105 (Alexander Hamilton) (Bantam Books, ed., 1992).
13. *Federalist* No. 30, p. 145 (Alexander Hamilton) (Bantam Books, ed., 1992).
14. *Federalist* No. 12, p. 57 (Alexander Hamilton) (Bantam Books, ed., 1992). *See also Elliot's Debates* 2:64 ("An impost will probably be a principal source of revenue."); 2:42 ("it was not to be supposed that they would levy such [direct taxes], unless the impost and excise should be found insufficient in case of war").
15. *See Federalist* No. 45, p. 236 (James Madison) (Bantam Books, ed., 1992).
16. *See* Brenda Yelvington, Excise Taxes in Historical Perspective, in *Taxing Choice: The Predatory Politics of Fiscal Discrimination* (William F. Shughart II, ed., 1997).
17. 132 S. Ct. 2566 (2012).
18. 26 U.S.C. § 5000A(a).

19. 26 U.S.C. § 5000A(b).
20. *Sebelius*, 132 S. Ct. at 2594.
21. Centinel, Letter I (1787), *TAF* 39.
22. Richard Henry Lee to Governor Edmund Randolph, December 22, 1787, *TAF* 365.
23. Brutus, Essay VI (1787), *TAF* 419.
24. *Federalist* No. 41 (James Madison) 209 (Bantam Books, ed., 1992).
25. *Id.* at 210.
26. A Citizen of America, An Examination into the Leading Principles of the Federal Constitution (1787), *Friends* 392.
27. *Id.* at 390.
28. Alexander Hamilton, Report on the Subject of Manufactures (1791), reprinted in *Liberty and Order* 101 (Lance Banning, ed., 2004).
29. James Madison, The Report of 1800, reprinted in Banning, *supra,* note 28, at 246.
30. *Id.* at 247.
31. 297 U.S. 1 (1936).
32. *Id.* at 65.
33. *Id.* at 66.
34. 483 U.S. 203 (1987).
35. *Id.* at 207 (internal quotation marks omitted).
36. *See* Amici Curae Brief of the American Civil Rights Union, et al., 2012 WL 195307 at *2 (January 17, 2012).
37. *Id.* at *4–5.
38. *Id.* at *3.
39. *Id.* at *5.
40. *Sebelius*, 132 S. Ct. at 2606.
41. *Id.* at 2604.

Chapter 8

1. Centinel, Letter III (1787), *TAF* 62.
2. The Impartial Examiner, Essay V (1788), *TAF* 675.
3. Address of the Minority of the Pennsylvania Convention (1787), *TAF* 524.
4. *Federalist* No. 22, p. 103 (Alexander Hamilton) (Bantam Books, ed., 1982).
5. U.S. Const. art. I, § 8, cl. 3.
6. Samuel Johnson, *Dictionary of the English Language* 361 (3rd ed., 1765).
7. *Elliot's Debates* 4:18.
8. *Id.*
9. *Elliot's Debates* 4:253.
10. *Elliot's Debates* 2:83.
11. *Elliot's Debates* 2:58.
12. *Id.*
13. *Federalist* No. 22, p. 103 (Alexander Hamilton) (Bantam Books, ed., 1982).
14. *Id.* at 103–04.
15. Hugh Williamson, Remarks on the New Plan of Government (1788), *Friends* 278.
16. Philodemos, Essay (1788), *Friends* 34.
17. *Federalist* No. 41, p. 214 (James Madison) (Bantam Books, ed., 1982).
18. *Elliot's Debates* 2:189.
19. *Id.*
20. *Id.*
21. *Federalist* No. 7, p. 30 (Alexander Hamilton) (Bantam Books, ed., 1982).
22. *Federalist* No. 11, p. 53 (Alexander Hamilton) (Bantam Books, ed., 1982).
23. St. George Tucker, Of the Unwritten, or Common Law of England, reprinted in *View of the Constitution of the United States* 346 (Clyde N. Wilson, ed., 1999).
24. A Freeman, Essay I, *Friends* 92.
25. Art. of Conf. art XI.
26. *JM Notes* 549–50.
27. George Mason, Objection to this Constitution of Government (1787), www.constitution.org.
28. Richard Henry Lee to Governor Edmund Randolph (1787), *TAF* 367.
29. *Elliot's Debates* 4:245.
30. Randy E. Barnett, *Restoring the Lost Constitution* 277 (2004).
31. 301 U.S. 1 (1937).
32. *Id.* at 37.

33. *Wickard v. Filburn*, 317 U.S. 111, 125 (1942).
34. *Id.* at 127–28.
35. *Federalist* No. 17, p. 80 (Alexander Hamilton) (Bantam Books, ed., 1982) (emphasis added).
36. 545 U.S. 1 (2005).
37. *Id.* at 19.
38. *Id.*
39. *Id.* at 24.
40. *Id.* at 58 (Thomas, J., dissenting).

Chapter 9

1. Art. I, 2, cl. 18.
2. An Old Whig, Essay II (1787), *TAF* 324.
3. *Id.* at 325.
4. Federal Farmer, Letter IV, *TAF* 174.
5. Centinel, Letter V (1787), *TAF* 80.
6. Brutus, Essay I (1787), *TAF* 377.
7. James Wilson, Speech (1787), *Friends* 246.
8. *Federalist* No. 33, p. 156 (Alexander Hamilton) (Bantam Books, ed., 1982).
9. *Id.*
10. *Federalist* No. 44, p. 229–30 (James Madison) (Bantam Books, ed., 1982).
11. Alexander Hamilton, Plan for a National Bank (1791), reprinted in *Legislative and Documentary History of the Bank of the United States* 15 (M. St. Clair Clarke & D.A. Hall, eds. 1832).
12. *Id.*
13. *Id.* at 16.
14. *Id.*
15. *Id.*
16. *Id.*
17. *Id.* at 17.
18. *Id.*
19. *Id.* at 18.
20. *Id.* at 47 (Fisher Ames).
21. *Id.* at 51 (Theodore Sedgwick).
22. *Id.* at 53 (John Lawrence).

23. *Id.* at 53.
24. *Id.* at 42.
25. *Id.*
26. U.S. Const. amend. X.
27. Thomas Jefferson, Opinion on the Bank (1791), reprinted in Clarke & Hall, *supra* note 11, at 91.
28. *Id.* at 93.
29. Alexander Hamilton, Opinion on the Bank (1791), reprinted in Clarke & Hall, *supra* note 11, at 95.
30. *Id.* at 99.
31. 17 U.S. 316 (1819).
32. *Id.* at 401.
33. *Id.* at 409–10 & 413.
34. *Id.* at 421.
35. 130 S.Ct. 1949 (2010).
36. *Id.* at 1956.

Chapter 10

1. Art. of Conf. art. V.
2. U.S. Const. art. I, § 2.
3. *Id.*
4. *JM Notes* 401.
5. *Id.*
6. U.S. Const. art. I, § 4.
7. *Id.*
8. *JM Notes* 424.
9. *Id.*
10. *Federalist* No. 59, p. 299 (Alexander Hamilton) (Bantam Books, ed. 1982) (emphasis omitted).
11. *Id.* at 300.
12. *Elliot's Debates* 2:310.
13. Cato, Letter VII (1788), *TAF* 30.
14. Brutus, Essay IV (1787), *TAF* 404.
15. Centinel, Letter I (1787), *TAF* at 41.
16. *Elliot's Debates* 4:71.
17. *See Elliot's Debates* 2:50–51; 3:202–03.
18. *Elliot's Debates* 3:661.
19. Slip Op. No. 12-71.
20. *Id.* at 3.
21. *Black's Law Dictionary* 815 (6th ed. 1991).

22. 42 U.S.C.A. § 1973gg-4(a) (1).
23. *Inter Tribal Council*, Slip Op. No. 12-71, at 12.
24. *Id.* at 5 (citing *Smiley v. Holm*, 285 U.S. 355, 366 (1932)). *Smiley*, however, had nothing to do with the scope of the Times, Places, and Manner Clause. Instead, the issue presented was whether the state legislature, in crafting congressional districts, had to submit the bill or measure to the governor for his approval. The Supreme Court held that nothing in the federal Constitution allowed "the legislature of Minnesota to create congressional districts independently of the Governor as required by the state Constitution with respect to the enactment of laws." *Smiley*, 285 U.S. at 373.
25. *Id.* at 5–6 (internal quotation marks omitted).
26. *Id.* at 5 (Thomas, J., dissenting).

Chapter 11

1. John Trenchard & Thomas Gordon, Further Reasonings against Standing Armies (1722), reprinted in *The English Libertarian Heritage* 226–27 (David L. Jacobson, ed., 1994).
2. James Burgh, Political Disquisitions (1774), *TFC* 3:23.
3. William Blackstone 1 *Commentaries* *401.
4. *Id.*
5. *Id.* at *401–02.
6. Virginia Declaration of Rights, § 13 (1776), *TFC* 3:173.
7. Brutus, Essay VIII (1788), *TAF* 434.
8. Addresss of the Minority of the Pennsylvania Convention (1787), *TAF* 547.
9. *Id.*
10. *Elliot's Debates* 2:136.
11. *Elliot's Debates* 3:380.

12. *Id.* at 378.
13. Saul Cornell, *A Well-Regulated Militia* 13 (2006).
14. *Elliot's Debates* 2:521.
15. *Federalist* No. 22, p. 105 (Alexander Hamilton) (Bantam Books, ed., 1982).
16. *Id.* at 107.
17. *Elliot's Debates* 3:381.
18. *Id.*
19. *Id.* at 383.
20. *Federalist* No. 25, p. 123 (Alexander Hamilton) (Bantam Books, ed., 1982).
21. *Id.* at 124.
22. 1 Stat. 271 (1792).
23. Murray Rothbard on War, www.antiwar.com.
24. Randall G. Holcombe, Federal Government Growth Before the New Deal, September 1, 1997, www.independent.org.
25. *See generally*, Robert Higgs, *Crisis and Leviathan* 158 (1987).
26. Katrina vanden Heuvel, Around the Globe, US Military Bases Generate Resentment, Not Security, June 13, 2011, www.thenation.com.
27. Hugh Gusterson, Empire of bases, March 10, 2009, www.thebulletin.org.
28. Active Duty Military Personnel Strengths by Regional Area and by Country (2011).
29. Nicholas D. Kristof, The (Big) Military Taboo, December 25, 2010, www.nytimes.com.
30. Katrina vanden Heuvel, *supra* note 26.
31. William Graham Sumner, The Conquest of the United States by Spain (1899), reprinted in *On Liberty, Society, and Politics* 272 (Robert C. Bannister, ed., 1992).
32. *Id.* at 277.
33. *Id.*
34. *Id.* at 291.
35. Dwight D. Eisenhower, Farewell Address (1961), reprinted in 2 *Reading*

the *American Past* 248 (Michael P. Johnson, ed., 2012).

36. *Id.*

37. Andrew J. Bacevich, *The Tyranny of Defense Inc.* (January/February 2011), www.theatlantic.com.

38. Andrew J. Bacevich, *The New American Militarism* 26 (2005).

39. *Id.* at 27.

40. Thomas E. Ricks, The Widening Gap Between Military and Society (July 1997), www.theatlantic.com.

Chapter 12

1. *See* Jackson Turner Main, *The Anti-Federalists* 140 (1961).

2. Federal Farmer, Letter XIV (1788), *TAF* 261.

3. *Id.* at 260.

4. Cato, Letter IV (1787), *TAF* 17.

5. *Id.* at 18.

6. William Blackstone, 1 *Commentaries* *254.

7. *Elliot's Debates* 4:107.

8. *Elliot's Debates* 4:287.

9. *Federalist* No. 24, p. 116 (Alexander Hamilton) (Bantam Books, ed., 1982).

10. *Id.* at 117.

11. *Elliot's Debates* 2:528.

12. *Id.*

13. JM to TJ, April 2, 1798, *TRL* 2:1032.

14. *Id.*

15. James Madison, Helvidius Number IV (1793), reprinted in *The Pacificus-Helvidius Debates* 87 (Morton J. Frisch, ed., 2007).

16. *Id.*

17. *Id.*

18. *Id.*

19. 6 U.S. (2 Cranch) 170 (804).

20. Raoul Berger, *War-Making by the President,* 121 U. Pa. L. Rev. 29, 80 (1972); *see also Bas v. Tingy,* 4 U.S. (4 Dall.) 37 (1800) (holding that the Constitution delegates to Congress the power

of declaring a general state of war or a limited, partial war).

21. Thomas Jefferson, Special Message to Congress on Foreign Policy (1805), reprinted in 2 *American State Papers* 613 (William Lowrie & Matthew St. Clair Clarke, eds., 1832).

22. *Id.*

23. *Id.*

24. Quoted in William Michael Treanor, *Fame, the Founding, and the Power to Declare War,* 82 Cornell L. Rev. 695, 725 (1997).

25. President Truman's executive order is reprinted as an appendix to Mr. Justice Black's opinion in *Youngstown Sheet & Tube Co. v. Sawyer,* 343 U.S. 579, 589 (1952).

26. *Youngstown,* 343 U.S. at 587.

27. 69 Stat. 7.

28. Pub. Law 88-408.

29. 115 Stat. 224 (emphasis added).

30. National Security Strategy Statement, NSS-002 at 1(2002).

31. *Id.* at 2.

32. 87 Stat. 555, § 3.

33. *Id.* at §(5)(C).

34. Bruce Ackerman & Oona Hathaway, *Limited War and the Constitution: Iraq and the Crisis of Presidential Legality,* 10 Mich. L. Rev. 447, 458 (2011).

35. *Id.* at 481.

36. *Id.* at 477.

Chapter 13

1. Art. of Conf. art. IX.

2. *Id.*

3. Anonymous, Letter IV (1776), reprinted in *The Origins of the American Constitution* 6 (Michael Kammen, ed., 1986).

4. *Id.*

5. Thomas Jefferson, *Notes on the State of Virginia* 120 (William Peden, ed., 1982).

6. Massachusetts Constitution (1780), *TFC* 1:13–14.
7. Brutus, Essay XV (1788), *TAF* 477.
8. The Declaration of Independence (1776), reprinted in *From Magna Carta to the Constitution* 59 (David L. Brooks, ed., 1993).
9. William Blackstone, 1 *Commentaries* 156.
10. Brutus, Essay XV (1788), TAF 478.
11. *Id.*
12. James I, Speech to the judges in Star Chamber (1616), reprinted in *The Stuart Constitution 1603–1688* at 85 (J.P. Kenyon, ed., 1986).
13. Brutus, Essay XV (1788), *TAF* 478.
14. *Id.* at 478–79.
15. *Id.* at 479.
16. *Federalist* No. 78, p. 393 (Alexander Hamilton) (Bantam Books, ed., 1982).
17. *Id.*
18. *Id.*
19. *Id.* at 394.
20. Brutus, Essay XV (1788), *TAF* 480.
21. *Id.*
22. U.S. Const. art. III, § 2.
23. *Black's Law Dictionary* 593 (6th ed. 1991).
24. Brutus, Essay XV (1788), *TAF* 480.
25. Brutus, Essay XII (1788), *TAF* 456.
26. *Id.*
27. Brutus, Essay XVI (1788), *TAF* 483.
28. Brutus, Essay XV (1788), *TAF* 478.
29. Brutus, Essay XII (1788), *TAF* 457.
30. Brutus, Essay XV (1788), *TAF* 477.
31. Brutus, Essay XI (1788), *TAF* 453.
32. *Id.*
33. *Federalist* No. 78, p. 394 (Alexander Hamilton) (Bantam Books, ed., 1982).
34. *Id.*
35. *Id.*
36. *Id.* at 395.
37. *Id.*
38. *Id.*
39. *Federalist* No. 81, at 411 (Alexander Hamilton) (Bantam Books, ed., 1982).
40. *Id.*
41. *Id.*
42. *Id.*
43. U.S. Const. art. II, § 4.
44. Raoul Berger, *Impeachment* 75–76 (1973).
45. Quoted in *id.* at 93.
46. Gordon S. Wood, *Empire of Liberty* 423 (2009).
47. Berger, *supra* note 44, at 234.
48. TJ to Charles Hammond, August 18, 1821, reprinted in 15 *The Writings of Thomas Jefferson* 331 (Andrew A. Lipscomb & Alebert Ellery Bergh, eds., 1904).
49. U.S. Const. art. III, § 2.
50. Centinel, Letter I (1787), *TAF* 43–44.
51. Federal Farmer, Letter XV (1788), *TAF* 277.
52. U.S. Const. art. III, § 2.
53. An Old Whig, Essay III (1787), *TAF* 330.
54. A Maryland Farmer, Essay III (1788), *TAF* 590 (emphasis omitted).
55. *Elliot's Debates* 2:109–110.
56. *Elliot's Debates* 4:154.
57. *Id.*
58. William E. Nelson, *Americanization of the Common Law* 28–29 (1975).
59. William E. Nelson, *The Province of the Judiciary*, 37 J. Marshall L. Rev. 325, 326 (2004).
60. TJ to Edmund Pendleton, August 26, 1776, http://avalon.law.yale.edu.
61. *See* Jackson Turner Main, *The Sovereign States, 1775–1783*, pp. 171–72 (1973).
62. *Federalist* No. 83, p. 432 (Alexander Hamilton) (Bantam Books, ed., 1982).
63. *Baker v. Carr*, 369 U.S. 186, 211 (1962).
64. *Cooper v. Aaron*, 358 U.S. 1, 18 (1958).
65. Sandra Day O'Connor, *Judicial Accountability Must Safeguard, not Threaten Judicial Independence: An Introduction*, 86 Denv. U. L. Rev. 1, 1 (2008).
66. JM to TJ October 15, 1788, *TRL* 1:562.

67. *Id.* (emphasis added).
68. Thomas Jefferson, Draft of a Constitution for Virginia (1783), reprinted in *The Complete Jefferson* 119 (Saul K. Padover, ed., 1943).

Chapter 14

1. Art. of Conf. art. IX.
2. U.S. Const. art. II, § 2.
3. U.S. Const. art. VI.
4. *TFC* 4:589.
5. Hampden, A Note Protesting the Treaty-Making Provisions of the Constitution (1788), http://www.utulsa.edu.
6. *Id.*
7. Federal Farmer, Letter IV (1787), *TAF* 173.
8. *Id.* at 174.
9. Brutus, Essay II (1787), *TAF* 391.
10. *Elliot's Debates* 3:508.
11. *Id.* at 509.
12. An Old Whig, Essay III (1787), *TAF* 328.
13. *Id.*
14. *Elliot's Debates* 4:246.
15. *Elliot's Debates* 3:514.
16. *Id.* at 507.
17. *Elliot's Debates* 4:132.
18. *Federalist* No. 64, p. 326 (John Jay) (Bantam Books, ed., 1982).
19. 3 U.S. (3 Dall.) 199 (1801).
20. Treaty of Paris art. 4.
21. 252 U.S. 416 (1920).
22. *Id.* at 433.
23. *Id.* at 432.
24. 354 U.S. 1 (1957).
25. *Id.* at 16.
26. *Id.* at 17.
27. 552 U.S. 491 (2008).
28. *Id.* at 504.
29. *Id.* at 527.
30. *Id.* at 506.
31. *Oyama v. California*, 332 U.S. 633 (1948) (Black, J., concurring) (internal quotation marks omitted).

32. Frank E. Holman, *The Story of the "Bricker Amendment"* 8 (1954).
33. *Id.* at 15.
34. *Id.*
35. *Id.* at 22.
36. S. Rep. No. 412, at 1 (1953).
37. Holman, *supra* note 32 at 24.
38. Curtis A. Bradley, *The Treaty Power and American Federalism*, 97 Mich. L. Rev. 390, 396 (1998).
39. *Id.* at 397.
40. International Convention on the Elimination of All Forms of Racial Discrimination, art. I, §4.
41. U.N. convention ties U.S. to affirmative action (October 17, 1997), http://natcath.org.
42. *Elliot's Debates* 3:513.

Chapter 15

1. Charles Pinckney, Observations on the Plan of Government, *TFC* 4:578.
2. *JM Notes* 33.
3. *Id.* at 104.
4. *Id.*
5. *Id.* at 69.
6. *Id.* at 609.
7. *Id.*
8. *Id.*
9. *Id.* at 649.
10. *Id.*
11. U.S. Const. art V.
12. An Old Whig, Essay I (1787), *TAF* 318.
13. Federal Farmer, Letter IV (1787), *TAF* 179.
14. *Id.*
15. *Elliot's Debates* 3:49.
16. *Id.* at 101.
17. *Elliot's Debates* 4:178.
18. *Elliot's Debates* 3:37.
19. *Id.*
20. St George Tucker, View of the Constitution of the United States, reprinted in *View of the Constitution of the United States* 306 (Clyde N. Wilson, ed. 1999).

21. *See* James Kenneth Rogers, *The Other Way to Amend the Constitution: The Article V Constitutional Convention Amendment Process*, 30 Harv. J.L. & Pub. Pol'y 1005, 1021 (2007).
22. U.S. Const. art. V.
23. William J. Quirk & Robert Wilcox, *A 28th Amendment: Democracy and Constitutional Change*, *Chronicles*, July 1996, at 19.
24. U.S. Const. amend. 27.
25. *See Coleman v. Miller*, 307 U.S. 433 (1939).
26. Quirk & Wilcox, *supra* note 23, at 20.
27. *Federalist* No. 43, p. 223 (James Madison) (Bantam Books, ed., 1982).
28. *Legislative and Documentary History of the Bank of the United States* 15 (M. St. Clair Clarke & D.A. Hall, eds. 1832).

Chapter 16

1. *JM Notes* 630.
2. *Id.*
3. Federal Farmer, Letter IV (1787), *TAF* 173.
4. *Id.* at 174.
5. A Maryland Farmer, Essay I (1788), *TAF* 560.
6. Brutus, Essay II (1787), *TAF* 385.
7. *Id.* at 387.
8. *Id.*
9. *Id.*
10. *Id.*
11. James Wilson, State House Yard Speech (1787), reprinted in 1 *Collected Works of James Wilson* 171 (Kemit L. Hall & Mark David Hall, eds., 2007).
12. *Id.* at 172.
13. *Id.*
14. *Id.*
15. *Id.*
16. *Federalist* No. 84, p. 436 (Alexander Hamilton) (Bantam Books, ed., 1982).
17. *Id.*
18. *Id.* at 437.
19. *Id.*
20. *Id.* at 438.
21. *Id.* at 439.
22. Brutus, Essay II (1787), *TAF* 389.
23. *Id.*
24. Federal Farmer, Letter IV (1787), *TAF* 176.
25. Federal Farmer, Letter XIV (1788), *TAF* 284.
26. JM to TJ, April 22, 1788, *TRL* 1:534.
27. *Elliot's Debates* 2:122–23.
28. *Id.* at 123.
29. *Id.* at 124.
30. *Id.* at 177.
31. *Id.*
32. *Id.* at 178.
33. *Id.* at 177.
34. *Id.* at 131.
35. *Id.*
36. *Id.* at 177.
37. *Id.* at 131.
38. *Id.* at 177.
39. *Id.*
40. *Elliot's Debates* 3:587 (emphasis in original).
41. *Elliot's Debates* 1:327.
42. *Id.*
43. *Elliot's Debates* 3:657.
44. *Id.* at 658.
45. *Id.*
46. *Id.*
47. *Id.*
48. *Id.*
49. *Id.*
50. *Id.*
51. *Id.* at 658–59.
52. *Id.* at 659.
53. *Id.*
54. *Id.*
55. *Id.*
56. *Id.*
57. *Id.*
58. *Id.*
59. *Id.*
60. *Id.* at 660.

61. *Id.*
62. U.S. Const. art. I, § 8.
63. *Elliot's Debates* 3:660.
64. *Id.*
65. U.S. Const. art III, § 2.
66. *Elliot's Debates* 3:661.
67. *Id.*
68. Pauline Maier, *Ratification* 341 (2010).
69. Melancton Smith, Address by a Plebian to the People of the State of New York (1788), reprinted in *The Anti-Federalist Writings of the Melancton Smith Circle* 267 (Michael P. Zuckert & Derek A. Webb, eds. 2009).
70. *Id.*
71. *Id.* at 269.
72. *Id.* at 280.
73. *Id.* at 270.
74. *Elliot's Debates* 2:322.
75. *Id.*
76. *Id.* at 324.
77. *Id.* at 325.
78. *Id.*
79. *Id.*
80. *Elliot's Debates* 1:329.
81. *Id.*
82. *Id.*
83. *Id.* at 330.
84. *Id.*
85. *Id.*
86. *Id.*
87. U.S. Const. art I, §3.
88. *Elliot's Debates* 1:331.
89. *Id.*
90. *Id.*
91. *Elliot's Debates* 2:413–14.
92. *Id.*
93. *Id.*
94. *Id.*
95. *Elliot's Debates* 4:4.
96. *Id.*
97. *Id.* at 5.
98. *Id.* at 6.
99. *Id.* at 217.
100. *Id.* at 225.
101. *Id.* at 226.

102. *Id.* at 235.
103. *Id.*
104. *Id.* at 239.
105. TJ to JM, February 19, 1788, *TRL* 1:531.
106. *Id.* at 242.
107. *Id.* at 245.
108. *Id.* at 246.
109. U.S. Const. art I, § 9.
110. *Elliot's Debates* 4:246–47.
111. *Id.* at 247.

Chapter 17

1. Proceedings of the Meetings at Harrisburg (1788), *Elliot's Debates* 2:543.
2. *Id.*
3. *Id.*
4. Virginia's Application for a Second Convention (1788), *Creating* 236.
5. *Id.*
6. *Id.* at 237.
7. New York's Application for a Second Convention (1789), *Creating* 237–38.
8. *Id.* at 238.
9. JM to TJ, August 23, 1788, *TRL* 1:550.
10. JM to TJ, September 21, 1788, *TRL* 1:552.
11. Pauline Maier, *Ratification* 434 (2010).
12. JM to TJ, October 17, 1788, *TRL* 1:564.
13. *Id.*
14. TJ to JM, July 31, 1788, *TRL* 1:546.
15. JM to TJ, October 17, 1788, *TRL* 1:564.
16. *Id.*
17. *Id.*
18. *Id.* at 565.
19. TJ to JM, March 15, 1789, *TRL* 1:587.
20. *Id.*
21. *Id.*
22. *Id.*
23. JM to TJ, December 8, 1788, *TRL* 1:579.
24. George Washington, Inaugural Address (1789), *Creating* 233.
25. *Id.* at 234.
26. *Gazette of the United States*, June 10, 1789, *Creating* 65.

27. *Daily Advertiser*, June 9, 1789, *Creating* 64.
28. *Gazette of the United States*, June 10, 1789, *Creating* 65.
29. *Gazette of the United States*, June 10, 1789, *Creating* 64.
30. *Gazette of the United States*, June 10, 1789, *Creating* 68.
31. *Congressional Register*, June 8, 1789, *Creating* 76.
32. *Gazette of the United States*, June 10, 1789, *Creating* 68.
33. *Congressional Register*, June 8, 1789, *Creating* 72.
34. Madison Resolution, June 8, 1789, *Creating* 12.
35. *Id.* at 13.
36. *Id.* at 14.
37. *Congressional Register*, August 18, 1789, *Creating* 175.
38. *Id.*
39. *Daily Advertiser*, August 14, 1789, *Creating* 105.
40. Akhil Reed Amar, *The Bill of Rights* xi (1998).
41. Gordon S. Wood, *Empire of Liberty* 72 (2009).
42. JM to Edmund Randolph, June 15, 1789, *Creating* 250.
43. George Clymer to Tench Coxe, June 28, 1789, *Creating* 255.
44. Samuel Johnston to James Madison, July 8, 1789, *Creating* 260.
45. Roger Sherman to Henry Gibbs, August 4, 1789, *Creating* 271.
46. William Grayson to Patrick Henry, September 29, 1789, *Creating* 300.
47. Theodorick Bland Randolph to St. George Tucker, September 9, 1789, *Creating* 293.
48. Thomas Tudor Tucker to St. George Tucker, October 2, 1789, *Creating* 300.
49. *Congressional Register*, August 15, 1789, *Creating* 175.
50. Richard Henry Lee to Patrick Henry, September 15, 1789, *Creating* 295.
51. *Id.*
52. Alexander Hamilton, Address to the Electors of the State of New York (1801), reprinted in 7 *The Works of Alexander Hamilton* 733 (John C. Hamilton, ed., 1851).
53. *Id.*
54. TJ to JM, March 15, 1789, *TRL* 1:587.
55. 19 How. (60 U.S.) 393 (1857).
56. Amendments to the Constitution, September 28, 1789, *Creating* 3.
57. 32 U.S. (7 Pet.) 243, 250 (1833).
58. *Id.*
59. 381 U.S. 479, 484 (1965).
60. 410 U.S. 113 (1973).

Chapter 18

1. Answers to Questions Propounded by M. De Meusnier, January 24, 1786, reprinted in 4 *The Writings of Thomas Jefferson* 141 (Paul Leicester Ford, ed., 1894).
2. TJ to Edward Carrington, August 4, 1787, reprinted in Ford, *supra* note 1, at 424.
3. TJ to Joseph Jones, August 14, 1787, reprinted in Ford, *supra* note 1, at 438.
4. TJ to George Washington, August 14, 1787, reprinted in 2 *The Diplomatic Correspondence of the United States of America* 79 (1837).
5. TJ to John Adams, November 13, 1787, reprinted in *The Adams-Jefferson Letters* 212 (Lester J. Cappon, ed., 1959).
6. TJ to William Stephens Smith, November 13, 1787, reprinted in Ford, *supra* note 1, at 467.
7. *See* David N. Mayer, *The Constitutional Thought of Thomas Jefferson* 91 (1997).
8. *See* James Morton Smith, "The Dark Side of Our Commercial Affairs": The Minister to France and the Virginia Legislator, 1784–1785, *TRL* 1:326.

9. TJ to Edward Carrington, August 4, 1787, reprinted in Ford, *supra* note 1, at 424.

10. *Id.* at 424–25.

11. *Id.* at 425.

12. *Id.* at 424.

13. Answers to Questions Propounded by M. De Meusnier, January 24, 1786, reprinted in Ford *supra* note 1, at 147.

14. TJ to George Washington, August 14, 1787, reprinted in 2 *The Diplomatic Correspondence of the United States of America* 78 (1837).

15. Centinel, Letter IV (1787), *TAF* 70.

16. Centinel, Letter III (1787), *TAF* 62.

17. The Federal Farmer, Letter I (1787), *TAF* 144 & 146.

18. *Id.* at 143.

19. The Impartial Examiner, Essay V (1788), *TAF* 675.

20. An Old Whig, Essay VI (1787), *TAF* 346.

21. The Federal Farmer, Essay VI (1787), *TAF* 192.

22. TJ to Francis Hopkinson, March 13, 1789, reprinted in *Letters and Addresses of Thomas Jefferson* 77 (William B. Parker & Jonas Viles, eds., 1907).

23. *Id.*

24. Thomas Jefferson, *Notes on the State of Virginia* 210 (William Peden, ed., 1954).

25. *Id.* at 210.

26. *Id.*

27. *Id.* at 119.

28. Charles Louis de Secondat, Baron de la Brède et de Montesquieu, *The Sprit of the Laws* bk XI, ch. 6 (David Wallace Carrithers, ed., 1977).

29. Jefferson, *supra* note 24, at 120.

30. For a good discussion of how bicameralism is analogous to requiring a supermajority in a unicameral legislature, see James M. Buchanan & Gordon Tullock, *The Calculus of Consent* (1962).

31. Jefferson, *supra* note 24, at 214.

32. *Id.*

33. *Id.* at 217.

34. *Id.* at 120.

35. Art. of Conf. art V.

36. JM to TJ, March 19, 1787, *TRL* 1:470.

37. JM to TJ, October 24 & November 1, 1787, *TRL* 1:498.

38. TJ to JM, June 20, 1787, *TRL* 1: 480.

39. *Id.*

40. *Id.*

41. *Id.* at 480–81.

42. *Id.* at 481.

43. Merrill Jensen, *The Articles of Confederation* 241 (1940).

44. *Id.* at 239.

45. Thomas A. Bailey, *The American Pageant* 132 (1966).

Chapter 19

1. Ecclesiastes 1:9.

2. U.S. Const. amd. X.

3. William C. Davis, *"A Government of Our Own"* 83 (1994).

4. Clyde N. Wilson, Secession: The Last, Best Bulwark of Our Liberties, in *Secession, State & Liberty* 95 (David Gordon, ed., 1998).

5. *Id.*

6. *See* John Joseph Wallis & Wallace E. Oates, The Impact of the New Deal on American Federalism, in *The Defining Moment* 155 (Michael D. Bordo, et al., eds., 1998) ("A cursory look at the course of federal fiscal structure in the United States might suggest that the Great Depression and the New Deal merely accelerated already existing tendencies toward centralization of the public sector.")

7. Robert P. Sutton, *Federalism* 194 (2002).

8. 297 U.S. 1, 68 (1936). *See also* William F. Shughart II, *Bending before*

the Storm: The U.S. Supreme Court in Economic Crisis, 1935–1937, 9, The Independent Review 55 (2004).

9. *Id.* at 75.

10. The Republican Party Platform (1936) reprinted in Sutton, *supra* note 7, at 203.

11. *Butler*, 297 U.S. at 204.

12. *See, e.g.*, Rosalie Berger Levinson, *Will the New Federalism Be the Legacy of the Rehnquist Court?*, 40 Val. U. L. Rev. 589 (2006).

13. 426 U.S. 833 (1976).

14. 514 U.S. 549 (1995).

15. *Id.* at 563.

16. Robert E. Moffit, Obamacare and the Individual Mandate: Violating Personal Liberty and Federalism, January 18, 2011, www.hertiage.org.

17. *McCulloch v. Maryland*, 17 U.S. 316, 405 (1819).

18. Craig Eyermann, Does the U.S. Risk a Fiscal Tipping Point, March 21, 2013, www.MyGovCost.org.

19. David C. John, Social Security Finances Significantly Worse, Says 2012 Trustees Report, April 23, 2012, www.heritage.org. Of course, there is no trust fund. Social Security operates much like any other Ponzi scheme. The government neither invests nor banks the funds paid into the system. The money received by retirees comes straight from the paychecks of working Americans or from government printing presses.

20. *Id.*

21. Phillip Moeller, The Future of Social Security, http://money.usnews.com.

22. Medicare Adding to Federal Deficits Faster than Other Government Spending Programs, September 2, 2012, www.heritage.org.

23. Medicare Shortfall Is Driving Federal Deficit Spending, May 22, 2012, www.heritage.org.

24. *Id.* at 330.

25. U.S. Const. art I, § 2.

26. *JM Notes* 655.

27. *Federalist* No. 56, p. 285 (James Madison) (Bantam Books, ed. 1982).

28. *Federalist* No. 55, p. 282 (James Madison) (Bantam Books, ed. 1982).

29. Brutus, Essay I (1787), *TAF* 174.

30. *See* Mark P. Petracca, Rotation in Office: The History of an Idea, in *Limiting Legislative Terms* 20 (Gerald Benjamin & Michael J. Malbin, eds., 1992).

31. Aristotle, *Politics* 49 (Benjamin Jowett, ed. 2000).

32. Art. of Confed. art. V.

33. *See* Gordon S. Wood, *The Creation of the American Republic 1776–1787*, at 87 (1969).

34. *JM Notes* 41.

35. An Officer of the Late Continental Army, Reply to Wilson's Speech (1787), *DC* 1:99–100.

36. *Elliot's Debates* 2:310.

37. *Id.*

38. TJ to JM, December 20, 1787, *TRL* 1:512.

39. Congressional Research Service, Congressional Careers: Service Tenure and Patterns of Member Service 1789–2011, at 1 (2011).

40. *Id.* at 5.

41. *Id.*

42. 2012 House Incumbent Reelection Rates, November 8, 2012, http://informationknoll.wordpress.com.

43. *Id.*

44. Patrick Basham, Term Limits: A Reform that Works at 3, June 9, 2011, http://ourgeneration.org.

45. *See* Doug Bandow, The Political Revolution that Wasn't: Why Term Limits Are Needed Now More Than Ever, September 5, 1996, www.cato.org.

46. Petition for a Writ of Certiorari at 8, *U.S. Term Limits, Inc. v. Thornton*,

514 U.S. 779 (1995), 1994 WL 16011957 (1994).

47. *U.S. Term Limits, Inc. v. Thornton*, 514 U.S. 779 (1995).

48. 2012 Election Results: Americans Speak with One Voice on Term Limits, November 27, 2012, http://termlimits.org.

49. Rachel Werner, Joe Lieberman Backs Term Limits, December 17, 2012, www.washingtonpost.com.

50. Rudman quoted in Bandow, *supra* note 45, at 2.

51. Vitter Reintroduces His Bill to Establish Term Limits for Congress, January 23, 2013, www.vitter.senate.gov.

Appendix D

1. *See* Marshall L. DeRosa, *The Confederate Constitution of 1861* (1991); Randall G. Holcombe, *The Distributive Model of Government: Evidence from the Confederate Constitution*, 3 S. Econ. J. 762 (1992). I am greatly indebted to both these authors for their work on the Confederate Constitution.

2. *Elliot's Debates* 3:22.

3. *Id.*

4. *Elliot's Debates* 3:94.

5. *See, e.g.*, Daniel Webster, Speech of Mr. Webster of Massachusetts (1830), reprinted in *The Webster-Hayne Debate on the Nature of the Union* 126 (Herman Belz, ed., 2000). For a good discussion of Webster's views, see Kent Masterson Brown, Secession: A Constitutional Remedy that Protects Fundamental Liberties, in *Rethinking the*

American Union for the Twenty-First Century 53–54 (Donald Livingston, ed. 2012). *See also Hawke v. Smith*, 253 U.S. 221, 226 (1920) ("The Constitution of the United States was ordained by the people, and, when duly ratified, it became the Constitution of the people of the United States."); *U.S. Term Limits, Inc. v. Thornton*, 514 U.S. 779, 838 (1995) (Kennedy, J. concurring) ("In my view, however, it is well settled that the whole people of the United States asserted their political identity and unity of purpose when they created the federal system.").

6. Cobbs notes are reprinted in A.L. Hull, *The Making of the Confederate Constitution*, 9 S. Hist. Soc. Papers 272, 291 (1900).

7. Robert H. Smith, An Address to the Citizens of Alabama (1861), reprinted in *Southern Pamphlets on Secession* 99 (Jon L. Wakelyn, ed. 2009).

8. *Clinton v. City of New York*, 524 U.S. 417 (1998).

9. Davis, supra note 1, at 245.

10. C.S. Const. art I, § 8, cl. 3.

11. John C. Calhoun, Speech before the Passage of the Tariff Bill (1842) reprinted in *The Essential Calhoun* 198 (Clyde N. Wilson, ed., 1992).

12. Wakelyn, *supra* note 7, at 200.

13. Marshall L. DeRosa, *Redeeming American Democracy* 35 (2007).

14. *Id.* at 36.

15. Holcombe, *supra* note 1, at 768.

16. Bent Joshpe, How about a federal single subject rule?, October 24, 2014, www.washingtonexaminer.com.

17. DeRosa, *supra* note 13, at 37.

Selected Bibliography

Ackerman, Bruce and Neal Katyal. "Our Unconventional Founding." *University of Chicago Law Review* 62 (1995): 475.

Adams, Willi Paul. *The First American Constitutions: Republican Ideology and the Making of State Constitutions in the Revolutionary Era* (New York: Rowman & Littlefield Publishers, Inc., 2001).

Adams, William Howard. *Gouverneur Morris: An Independent Life* (New Haven, Conn.: Yale University Press, 2003).

Amar, Akhil Reed. "The Central Meaning of Republican Government: Popular Sovereignty, Majority Rule, and the Denomination Problem." *University of Colorado Law Review* 65 (1994): 749.

————. *The Bill of Rights: Creation and Reconstruction* (New Haven, Conn.: Yale University Press, 1998).

Banning, Lance. *The Sacred Fire of Liberty: James Madison & the Founding of the Federal Republic* (Ithaca, N.Y.: Cornell University Press, 1995).

Barnett, Randy E. *Restoring the Lost Constitution: The Presumption of Liberty* (Princeton, N.J.: Princeton University Press, 2004).

Bartrum, Ian. "Constructing the Constitutional Canon: The Metonymic Evolution of Federalist 10." *Constitutional Commentary* 27 (2010): 9.

Beiter, Benjamin. "Beyond Medellín: Reconsidering Federalism Limits on the Treaty Power." *Notre Dame Law Review* 85 (2010): 1163.

Berger, Raoul. *Impeachment: The Constitutional Problems* (New York: Bantam Books, 1974).

————. "War-Making by the President." *University of Pennsylvania Law Review* 121 (1972): 29.

Blumrosen, Alfred W. & Steven M. Blumrosen. "Restoring the Congressional Duty to Declare War." *Rutgers Law Review* 63 (2011): 407.

Boyd, Steven R. *The Politics of Opposition: Antifederalists and the Acceptance of the Constitution* (Millwood, N.Y.: KTO Press, 1979).

Bradley, Curtis A. "The Treaty Power and American Federalism." *Michigan Law Review* 97 (1998): 390.

Burnett, Edmund Cody. *The Continental Congress: A Definitive History of the Continental Congress from Its Inception in 1774 to March, 1789* (New York: W. W. Norton & Company, 1964).

Carey, George W. *In Defense of the Constitution* (Indianapolis, Ind.: Liberty Fund, 1995).

Chandler, Ralph Clark. "Public Administration under the Articles of Confederation." *Public Administration Quarterly* 13 (1990): 433.

Charles Rappleye. *Robert Morris: Financier of the American Revolution* (New York: Simon & Schuster, 2010).

Clinton, Robert N. "A Brief History of the Adoption of the United States Constitution." *Iowa Law Review* 75 (1990): 891.

Colbourn, Trevor. *The Lamp of Experience: Whig History and the Intellectual Origins of the American Revolution* (Indianapolis, Ind.: Liberty Fund, 1998).

Cornell, Saul. *The Other Founders: Anti-Federalism & the Dissenting Tradition in America, 1788–1828* (Chapel Hill, N.C.: The University of North Carolina Press, 1999).

Denning, Brannon P. and Glenn Harlan Reynolds. "It Takes a Militia: A Communitarian Case for Compulsory Arms Bearing." *William and Mary Bill of Rights Journal* 5 (1996): 185.

Dougherty, Keith L. *Collective Action Under the Articles of Confederation* (New York: Cambridge University Press, 2001).

Duncan, Christopher M. "Men of a Different Faith: The Anti-Federalist Ideal in Early American Political Thought." *Polity* 26 (1994): 387.

Farrand, Max. "The Federal Constitution and the Defects of the Confederation." *The American Political Science Review* 2 (1908): 532.

Freedman, Eric M. "Why Constitutional Lawyers and Historians Should Take a Fresh Look at the Emergence of the Constitution from the Articles of Confederation Period: The Case of the Drafting of the Articles of Confederation." *Tennessee Law Review* 60 (1993): 783.

Garver, Frank Harmon. "The Transition from the Continental Congress to the Congress of the Confederation." *Pacific History Review* 1 (1932): 221.

Gerson, Noel B. *Free and Independent: The Confederation of the United States 1781–1789* (New York: Thomas Nelson, Inc., 1970).

Geslison, Ben. "Treaties, Execution, and Originalism in *Medellín v. Texas*, 128 S. Ct. 1346 (2008)." *Harvard Journal of Law and Public Policy* 32 (2009): 767.

Goebel, Julius, Jr. "Melancton Smith's Minutes of Debates on the New Constitution." *Columbia Law Review* 64 (1964): 26.

Gutzman, Kevin R.C. *James Madison and the Making of America* (New York: St. Martin's Press, 2012).

Henderson, James H. *Party Politics in the Continental Congress* (New York: McGraw-Hill Book Company, 1974).

Herzog, Simcha. "States' Rights and the Scope of the Treaty Power: Could the Patriot Act Be Constitutional as a Treaty?" *Pierce Law Review* 3 (2005): 161.

Higgs, Robert. *Crisis and Leviathan: Critical Episodes in the Growth of American Government* ([New York: Oxford University Press, 1987] Oakland, Calif.: Independent Institute, 2013).

Hoffert, Robert W. *A Politics of Tension: The Articles of Confederation and American Political Ideas* (Niwot, Colo.: The University Press of Colorado, 1992).

Holman, Frank E. *The Story of the "Bricker" Amendment* (New York: Committee for Constitutional Government, Inc., 1954).

Hutson, James H. "Country, Court, and Constitution: Antifederalism and the Historians." *William and Mary Quarterly* 38 (1981): 337.

Jacobson, David L. "John Dickinson's Fight Against Royal Government, 1764." *William and Mary Quarterly* 19 (1962): 64.

Jensen, Merrill. *The Articles of Confederation: An Interpretation of the Social-Constitutional History of the American Revolution, 1774–1781* (Madison, Wisc.: The University of Wisconsin Press, 1940).

———. *The New Nation: A History of the United States during the Confederation, 1781–1789* (New York: Vintage Books, 1950).

Johnson, Calvin H. "The Panda's Thumb: The Modest and Mercantilist Original Meaning of the Commerce Clause." *William and Mary Bill of Rights Journal* 13 (2004): 1.

———. "Homage to CLIO: The Historical Continuity from the Articles of Confederation into the Constitution." *Constitutional Commentary* 20 (2004): 463.

Kistler, Cameron O. "The Anti-Federalists and Presidential War Powers." *Yale Law Journal* 121 (2011): 459.

Knollenberg, Bernhard. "John Dickinson vs. John Adams: 1774–1776." *Proceedings of the American Philosophical Society* 107 (1963): 138.

Kramer, Larry D. "Madison's Audience." *Harvard Law Review* 112 (1999): 611.

Labunski, Richard. *James Madison and the Struggle for the Bill of Rights* (New York: Oxford University Press, 2006).

Lash, Kurt T. "Rejecting Conventional Wisdom: Federalist Ambivalence in the Framing and Implementation of Article V." *American Journal of Legal History* 38 (1994): 197.

Livingston, Donald, ed. *Rethinking the American Union for the Twenty-First Century* (Gretna, La.: Pelican Publishing Co., 2012).

Lutz, Donald S. "The Articles of Confederation as the Background to the Federal Republic." *Publius* 20 (1990): 55.

Lynch, Timothy. "Amending Article V to Make the Constitutional Amendment Process Itself Less Onerous." *Tennessee Law Review* 78 (2011): 823.

Main, Jackson Turner. *The Anti-Federalists: Critics of the Constitution, 1781–1788* (Chicago, Ill.: Quadrangle Books, 1961).

————. *The Sovereign States, 1775–1783* (New York: New Viewpoints, 1973).

Manne, Neal S. "Good Intentions, New Inventions, and Article V Constitutional Conventions." *Texas Law Review* 58 (1979): 131.

Marks, Frederick W, III. *Independence on Trial: Foreign Affairs and the Making of the Constitution* (Wilmington, Del.: Scholarly Resources, Inc., 1986).

Mayer, David N. *The Constitutional Thought of Thomas Jefferson* (Charlottesville, Va.: University of Virginia Press, 1994).

McClellan, James. *Liberty, Order and Justice: An Introduction to the Constitutional Principles of American Government* (Indianapolis, Ind.: Liberty Fund, 2000).

McCormick, Richard P. "Ambiguous Authority: The Ordinances of the Confederation Congress 1781–1789." *American Journal of Legal History* 41 (1997): 411.

McCullough, David. *John Adams* (New York: Simon & Schuster, 2001).

McDonald, Forrest. *E Pluribus Unum: The Formation of the American Republic, 1776–1790* (Indianapolis, Ind.: Liberty Fund, 1979).

————. *States' Rights and the Union: Imperium in Imperio* (Lawrence, Kan.: University of Kansas Press, 2000).

————. *Novus Ordo Seclorum: The Intellectual Origins of the Constitution* (Lawrence, Kan.: University Press of Kansas, 1985).

McDowell, Gary L. "'High Crimes and Misdemeanors': Recovering the Intentions of the Founders." *George Washington Law Review* 67 (1999): 626.

McGaughy, J. Kent. *Richard Henry Lee of Virginia* (New York: Rowman & Littlefield Publishers, Inc., 2004).

McWilliams, Wilson Carey. "The Anti-Federalists, Representation, and Party." *Northwestern University Law Review* 84 (1989): 12.

Monaghan, Henry Paul. "We the People[s], Original Understanding, and Constitutional Amendment." *Columbia Law Review* 96 (1996): 121.

Morris, Richard B. *The Forging of the Union, 1781–1789* (New York: Harper & Row, 1987).

Natelson, Robert G. "The Constitutional Contributions of John Dickinson." *Penn State Law Review* 108 (2003): 415.

————. "A Republic, not a Democracy? Initiative, Referendum, and the Constitution's Guarantee Clause." *Texas Law Review* 80 (2002): 807.

————. "The Legal Meaning of "Commerce" in the Commerce Clause." *St. John's Law Review* 80 (2006): 789.

―――. "The Original Understanding of the Indian Commerce Clause." *Denver University Law Review* 85 (2007): 201.

Nelson, William E. "The Province of the Judiciary." *John Marshall Law Review* 37 (2004): 325.

O'Connor, Sandra Day. "Judicial Accountability Must Safeguard, not Threaten, Judicial Independence: An Introduction." *Denver University Law Review* 86 (2008): 1.

Paulsen, Michael Stokes. "A General Theory of Article V: The Constitutional Lessons of the Twenty-Seventh Amendment." *Yale Law Journal* 103 (1993): 677.

Perlin, Adam A. "The Impeachment of Samuel Chase: Redefining Judicial Independence." *Rutgers Law Review* 62 (2010): 725.

Philbin, James P. "The Political Economy of the Antifederalists." *Journal of Libertarian Studies* 11 (1994): 79.

Pryor, William H., Jr. "Not-So-Serious Threats to Judicial Independence." *Virginia Law Review* 93 (2007): 1759.

Rahe, Paul A. *Republics Ancient and Modern: Classical Republicanism and the American Revolution* (Chapel Hill, N.C.: The University of North Carolina Press, 1992).

Rakove, Jack N. *The Beginnings of National Politics: An Interpretative History of the Continental Congress* (New York: Alfred A. Knopf, 1979).

Rappaport, Michael B. "Reforming Article V: The Problems Created by the National Convention Amendment Method and How to Fix Them." *Virginia Law Review.* 96 (2010): 1509.

Richards, Nelson. "The Bricker Amendment and Congress's Failure to Check the Inflation of the Executive's Foreign Affairs Powers, 1951–1954." *California Law Review* 94 (2006): 175.

Roes, Carol M. "The Ancient Constitution vs. The Federalist Empire: Anti-Federalism from the Attack on 'Monarchism' to Modern Localism." *Northwestern University Law Review* 84 (1989): 74.

Rogers, James Kenneth. "The Other Way to Amend the Constitution: The Article V Constitutional Convention Amendment Process." *Harvard Journal of Law and Public Policy* 30 (2007): 1005.

Rossiter, Clinton. *1787: The Grand Convention* (New York: W. W. Norton & Company, 1966).

Rothbard, Murray N. *Conceived in Liberty* (Auburn, Ala.: Ludwig von Mises Institute, 2011).

Rubin, Edward L. "Getting Past Democracy." *University of Pennsylvania Law Review* 149 (2001): 711.

Rutland, Robert Alan. *The Ordeal of the Constitution: The Anti-Federalists and the Ratification Struggle of 1787–1788* (Boston, Mass.: Northeastern University Press, 1983).

Sevi, Michael. "Original Intent, Timetables, and Iraq: The Founders' Views on War Powers." *Texas Review of Law and Politics* 13 (2008): 73.

Sinopoli, Richard C. "Liberalism and Political Allegiance in Anti-Federalist Political Thought." *Publius* 22 (1992): 123.

Skinner, Stephen. "Blackstone's Support for the Militia." *American Journal of Legal History* 44 (2000): 1.

Slonim, Shlomo. "Federalist No. 78 and Brutus's Neglected Thesis on Judicial Supremacy." *Constitutional Commentary* 23 (2006): 7.

Smith, Douglas G. "An Analysis of Two Federal Structures: The Articles of Confederation and the Constitution." *San Diego Law Review* 34 (1997): 249.

Sobel, Russell S. "In Defense of the Articles of Confederation and the Contribution Mechanism." *Public Choice* 99 (1999): 347.

Storing, Herbert J. *What the Anti-Federalists Were For: The Political Thought of the Opponents of the Constitution* (Chicago, Ill.: University of Chicago Press, 1981).

Szatmary, David P. *Shays' Rebellion: The Making of an Agrarian Insurrection* (Amherst, Mass.: The University of Massachusetts Press, 1980).

Tarr, Alan G. "Contesting the Judicial Power in the States." *Harvard Journal of Law and Public Policy* 35 (2012): 643.

Treanor, William Michael. "Fame, the Founding, and the Power to Declare War." *Cornell Law Review* 82 (1997): 695.

Van Alstyne, William. "What Do You Think about the Twenty-Seventh Amendment?" *Constitutional Commentary* 10 (1993): 9.

Wiener, Frederick Bernays. "The Militia Clause of the Constitution." *Harvard Law Review* 54 (1940): 181.

Wood, Gordon S. *The Radicalism of the American Revolution* (New York: Alfred A. Knopf, 1992).

———. *Empire of Liberty: A History of the Early Republic, 1789–1815* (New York: Oxford University Press, 2009).

Woods, Thomas E. and Kevin R. C. Gutzman. *Who Killed the Constitution? The Federal Government vs. American Liberty from World War I to Barack Obama* (New York: Random House, Inc., 2008).

York, Neil L. "The First Continental Congress and the Problem of American Rights." *Pennsylvania Magazine of History and Biography* 122 (1998): 353.

Index

Note: "The Articles" refers to the Articles of Confederation.

About the Author

WILLIAM J. WATKINS, JR. is a Research Fellow at the Independent Institute. He received his B.A. in history and German summa cum laude from Clemson University and his J.D. cum laude from the University of South Carolina School of Law. He is a former law clerk to Judge William B. Traxler, Jr. of the U.S. Court of Appeals for the Fourth Circuit. He has served as a prosecutor and defense lawyer, and has practiced in various state and federal courts.

His books include *Judicial Monarchs: The Case for Restoring Popular Sovereignty in the United States* and the Independent Institute book, *Reclaiming the American Revolution: The Kentucky and Virginia Resolutions and Their Legacy* (Palgrave/Macmillan). His scholarly articles have appeared in the *South Carolina Law Review*, *The Independent Review*, *Duke Journal of Constitutional Law and Public Policy*, *Exploring American History Encyclopedia*, and *America in World History Encyclopedia*.

Mr. Watkins has been a Humane Studies Fellow at the Institute for Humane Studies at George Mason University. He is the recipient of the R. Glen Ayers Award for Historical Writing from Clemson University. His popular articles have appeared in the *Christian Science Monitor, Forbes, Daily Caller, USA Today, Washington Times, Austin American-Statesman, Providence Journal, San Jose Mercury News, Washington Examiner, Denver Post, Fort Worth Star-Telegram, Bellingham Herald, Lexington Herald-Leader, Sacramento Bee, Duluth News Tribune, Janesville Gazette, Walworth County Today, Wapakoneta Daily News, Dispatch, La Crosse Tribune, Lewiston Sun Journal, and Newport Daily News, San Francisco Examiner, Human Events, Chronicles,* and *Silicon Valley/San Jose Business Journal.*

Independent Institute Studies in Political Economy

For further information:

510-632-1366 • orders@independent.org • http://www.independent.org/publications/books/